The Military Art of People's War

Selected Writings of General Vo Nguyen Giap

Edited and with an introduction
by Russell Stetler

New York and London

Copyright © 1970 by Monthly Review Press
All Rights Reserved

Library of Congress Catalog Card Number: 75-105317

First Modern Reader Paperback Edition 1971
Third Printing

Monthly Review Press
62 West 14th Street, New York, N.Y. 10011
21 Theobalds Road, London WC1X 8SL

Manufactured in the United States of America

*To the memory of Dr. Pham Ngoc Thach,
Minister of Health of the Democratic Republic of Vietnam,
who died in November 1968 at the front,
in fulfillment of the highest duties of an internationalist
and a revolutionary.*

Acknowledgments

Many friends throughout the world helped in the preparation of this volume. While no one else bears any responsibility for the book's shortcomings, many should share the credit for making it a more comprehensive volume. I am grateful to Mark Cook, Claude Henaff, Bruce Kuklick, Leonard Liggio, and Ray Ryan for helping to locate texts which could not be found in London. The staff of the Bertrand Russell Peace Foundation and the British Library of Political and Economic Science were efficient in providing texts and documents from their files and stacks. The most valuable cooperation and assistance came from the three London representatives of *Vietnam Courier* (*Cuu Quoc*), an information weekly of the Democratic Republic of Vietnam. These three friends, Nguyen Van Sao, Nguyen Linh Qui, and Phan Duc Thanh, gave generously of their time and repeatedly interrupted their busy schedules to see me to discuss the book. They furnished official translations of new texts very promptly, provided several photographs which we have reproduced here, and were an invaluable source of information for my introduction and footnotes. Another friend from the DRV, Colonel Ha Van Lau, took time out from his work in the Paris talks to discuss the early military history of the Vietnamese resistance and the genesis of General Giap's thought, and I wish to express my full appreciation of his help.

I also wish to thank Wilfred Burchett, Madeleine Riffaud, and Roger Pic for permitting me to include their interviews with General Giap in this volume. Pic kindly provided photographs as well, and I am very pleased that we were able to use them in the book. My discussions with Pic and Burchett over a period of several years have helped to clarify many of my ideas about Vietnamese military strategy and have given me a more vivid understanding of its application.

All the translations used in this volume are official, with the exception of the three interviews, which were conducted originally in French rather than in Vietnamese. In these three cases, my own translations, from authoritative French texts, appear. In the case of official translations, the reader will find some variation in style and quality. Some were carefully prepared for publication in English-language journals originating in Hanoi; others were produced more hastily for limited mimeograph distribution and were not originally intended for publication in book format. With these latter texts, we have therefore made occasional alterations, so that the particular article or essay will be more readable and the book as a whole more uniform.

Finally, I must thank Lesley Churchill, Sarah Poulikakou, and Terri Raymond for helping to type portions of the manuscript.

Contents

Introduction	11
The War Against the French	
Origins of the People's Army	39
The War of Liberation, 1945–1954	79
People's War, People's Army	101
Dien Bien Phu	117
The War in the South	
The Political and Military Line of Our Party	163
The South Vietnamese People Will Win	185
The Liberation War in South Vietnam	226
Once Again We Will Win	257
The War of Escalation	
The War of Escalation: An Interview	277
American Defeats: An Interview	282
Great Victory, Great Task	285
The Final Phase of Battle	308
The United States Has Lost the War: An Interview	319
Their Dien Bien Phu Will Come: An Interview	328
Map of Vietnam	pp. 44-45

Introduction

"In real life," Mao Tse-tung once remarked wryly, "we cannot ask for 'ever victorious' generals."[1] This characteristic realism derives from decades of hard struggle, in which progress is measured not according to customary battle statistics or in terrain gained and held but in the persistence of the revolutionary forces, in their sheer capacity to survive over time. As in China, so, too, in Vietnam: the revolutionary forces have emerged the victors by showing their ability to endure protracted conflict. Vietnam has experienced nearly uninterrupted war since the mid-1940's, and the insurgents have had an ever widening impact. Set in deeper perspective, Vietnam has fought for its independence for two thousand years. Her statesmen frequently refer to this long history of resistance warfare, and they do so for more than rhetorical effect. Out of this long history a distinctive military science has evolved, with direct relevance to the present situation.

In all their wars, the Vietnamese have confronted a more powerful enemy, whether numerically, as in the case of the ancient Chinese, or technologically, as in the case of their contemporary opponents. A strategy of passive defense, in which one relies on fortresses and treats material resources and terrain as ends in themselves, has never worked. The Vietnamese suffered their own Dien Bien Phu five and a half centuries before the French, when the impregnable stronghold of Da Bang in the interior of Thanh Hoa fell under siege by the Chinese. The common features of the successful resistance wars stand out clearly. All relied on tactical, and often strategic, flexibility. (This conception was elaborated in the first Vietnamese handbook of the military profession—in the thirteenth century!) All have utilized the natural advantages of terrain and environment to permit a mobile defense. All have utilized the expanse of time to the advantage of the resistance, building up strong forces in a war of long duration so as to be in a decisive position at the critical time. All have had a popular character, based on the support of the peasantry through a general mobilization. (A system of conscription affecting every village has existed in Vietnam from the tenth century.) Every victorious leader understood politics as the key to success.[2]

The inventiveness of the Vietnamese is well known. We are familiar with the use of thousands of bicycles to carry ammunition and supplies to Dien Bien Phu and with the tunnel warfare of the National Liberation Front. All this has a precedent in the Vietnamese past. In the 1780's, Quang Trung surprised an army of two hundred thousand Chinese by raising a massive army and bringing it five hundred miles in a month and ten days. He grouped his men in threes: in the long, swift march, two men carried the third between them in hammocks. Few in the West have comprehended the significance of this tradition. From a sociological and historical point of view, the Vietnamese are uniquely equipped to understand military dynamics and to fight the present war.

The contrast with American strategists and popular thinking is stunning. As secretary of defense in 1962, Robert S. McNamara stated: "Every quantitative measurement we have shows we're winning this war."[3] It is fruitless to speculate on the extent to which successive administrations fell victim to their own propaganda: the Pentagon appears to be incapable of understanding the dynamics of people's war. It is not so much that McNamara's statistics were exaggerated or even false. His military algebra is itself barren. America has been unable to endure the Vietnam war; yet this moral incapacity has never shown on the IBM punchcards. It was well understood in Hanoi long before the first GI's mutinied at Da Nang, for the Vietnamese understanding of war goes deeper than balance sheets and kill ratios. More than this, their senior strategist approaches, in real life, the status of an ever victorious general.

The life of Vo Nguyen Giap, taken as a whole, evinces remarkable energy and determination. Although he is less than sixty years old at the time of writing, he has helped to shape the decisive events of his nation's history in the twentieth century. Giap was born in 1912 in An Xa village of Quang Binh province, one of the country's poorest regions in the days of French rule. His peasant family was strongly nationalistic. Giap's father was respected among the peasants not only for his learning but also for his participation in the last resistance to French dominion in the late 1880's. He remained an active nationalist and sent young Giap, in 1924, to the Quoc Hoc, or Lycée National, at Hue. With its emphasis on integrating traditional (Vietnamese) and modern (Western) learning, the school was to serve as the training ground for nearly all the important figures in national politics after independence, including Ho Chi Minh and Ngo Dinh Diem. At school, Giap became acquainted with diverse currents of nationalist opinion. Records left behind by the French Sûreté indicate that even as a schoolboy his idealism was noted as subversive. His dynamism was equally impressive from an early age.[4]

As a teen-ager, Giap was dismissed from school because of his role in the growing student movement. His involvement with the underground nationalist organization, Tan Viet (Revolutionary Party for a Great Vietnam), drew the attention of the police soon thereafter. In 1930, the entire Indochinese colony was shaken by an eruption of nationalist revolts. These events stirred young Giap, who had been recalled to Hue by the Tan Viet. The Vietnam Quoc Dan Dang (VNQDD), a nationalist party styled after the Chinese Kuomintang, began an abortive revolt with an uprising at the Vietnamese garrison at Yen Bai, along the Chinese border, on February 9. It was crushed ruthlessly, and the VNQDD virtually ceased to exist for the next fifteen years. The fledgling Communist Party attempted to maintain the revolutionary mood. When railwaymen struck at Vinh and other workers followed suit in the Ben Thuy match factories, the communists organized solidarity actions among the peasants in the provinces of Ha Tinh and Nghe An in Annam, who had themselves felt acutely the effects of the worldwide depression on Vietnamese agriculture. Facing the swift French repression, peasant groups established rudimentary "soviets" to sustain the revolt. As six thousand peasants marched in Nghe An, young Giap in turn organized and led a student demonstration of solidarity in Hue, for which he was arrested by the French authorities for the first time. He was sentenced to three years' imprisonment, but as the revolutionary mood seemed to wane, he was released after serving a few months.[5]

The Communist Party's first years were difficult. It was founded officially in Canton in 1930, with a membership of 211, as a result of Ho Chi Minh's negotiations with various communist groups which had come into existence from 1925 onward. Ho's time was soon given over to other activities, and in the period which followed, the Party was directed by Tran Phu and Le Hong Phong, both of whom had been trained by the Comintern. Throughout the first decade of the Party's existence, the influence of the Comintern (especially through the intermediary of the French Communist Party) was preponderant. In the mid-1930's, the Party created a legal organization known as the Indochinese Democratic Front. Giap was active in the Front and probably joined the Party as a result of this association.[6]

In 1936 the situation was eased by the establishment of the Popular Front in France. Important cadres, such as Pham Van Dong and Tran Van Giau, were liberated from prison, and numerous restrictions on political activity were removed. The Communist Party functioned semilegally for the first time. By this time, Giap had reached Hanoi, after passing the exacting *baccalauréat* in Hue. He studied for one year at the Lycée Albert Sarraut before enrolling as an undergraduate in law at the university. For a time he boarded at the home of a distinguished Vietnamese writer, Professor Dang Thai Mai, whose daughter he was later to marry. He received his law degree in 1937 and pursued postgraduate studies in political economy the following year. Financial hardships obliged him to work as a history teacher during this period, and he also devoted an increasing portion of his time to political journalism. Writing in Vietnamese for *Tin Tuc* (The News) and *Thoi The* (Current Situation) and in French for *Le Travail* and *Notre Voix,* Giap soon emerged as a leading Party intellectual.[7] He completed his first major work at this time, a two-volume analysis entitled *The Peasant Problem,* on which Truong Chinh collaborated. This work was signed under the pseudonyms Van Dinh and Qua Ninh. When the Popular Front government fell, an order was issued to confiscate and burn all copies of the book. Those which were preserved gave the guidelines for subsequent communist policy in peasant regions.[8]

On September 26, 1939, the Communist parties were banned in France and in the colonies. In the repression which followed, more than a thousand Party members were arrested in Vietnam alone. Many, including the secretary general, Tran Phu, were summarily shot. Giap and his young bride, Nguyen Thi Minh Giang, were in jeopardy. She and her sister, Minh Khai, were also Party members; Minh Khai had, in fact, studied in the Soviet Union and was a member of the Central Committee. The sisters fled to Vinh with Giap's small infant. In May 1941 they were captured by the French and taken to Hanoi for trial by court martial. Both were found guilty on conspiracy charges. Minh Khai was guillotined. Minh Giang was sentenced to fifteen years at forced labor in the Maison Centrale. Her infant died, and she herself perished in prison in 1943.[9]

Giap himself was more fortunate, escaping to China in May 1940. The difficulty and danger of the escape, however, should not be underestimated. The Japanese had penetrated deeply into southern China in November 1939, capturing Nanning, a city only 147 miles from the Vietnamese border. Only internal political developments in Tokyo inhibited the Japanese from moving toward Indochina at that time. A Japanese strike in the six months from November to May might have sealed the border or at least increased the difficulty of exit. As it was, the train on which Giap and Pham Van Dong traveled to Kunming[10] was searched several times by the French police.

Giap was soon to meet the legendary Nguyen Ai Quoc, alias Ho Chi Minh. Ho had been teaching political courses in a Kuomintang military training school during the uneasy truce between the Chinese Communists and Chiang Kai-shek. He assembled a formidable group of émigrés in Kunming, and they were to be particularly important in the organization of the Vietminh's first military units. They lived for much of the time in the Sino-Vietnamese border regions, inhabited by the same ethnic minorities on both sides of the arbitrary demarcation. When the alliance between Mao and Chiang foundered, the Vietnamese communists were harassed by the Kuomintang and often crossed back into Indochina—only to return when the French conducted a sweep on their side of the border.[11]

The bulk of the Central Committee exposed itself to great danger by remaining in Vietnam throughout World War II. Truong Chinh, who replaced the executed Tran Phu as secretary general, risked his life daily by staying on in the vicinity of Hanoi. France fell in Europe in 1940, and the Vichy government soon capitulated to Japanese demands on the strategically important Indochinese colony. When the French garrison at Lang Son was relieved by the Japanese, the local *montagnards* of Bac Son revolted spontaneously in September 1940.[12] Other nationalist uprisings of a spontaneous character followed in Do Luong and My Tho. In October, a high-level meeting was held in Kweilin to discuss the new situation in Vietnam, indicated by the arrival of some thirty-five thousand Japanese troops and by the nationalist reaction. Across the border in Bac Ninh, the Seventh Meeting of the Central Committee agreed that the Party should support the Bac Son maquis. Tran Dang Ninh, who later organized logistics at Dien Bien Phu, was sent there for this purpose. The Kuomintang, moreover, were vaguely contemplating some intervention in Indochina. Under the leadership of two Kuomintang officers, Truong Boi Cong and Ho Ngoc Lam, a small Vietnamese military force was already being organized in the town of Tsingsi, twenty miles from the Vietnamese border. The Vietnamese communists in China made contact with this group, which already included newer communist refugees in its ranks. Giap, Pham Van Dong, and other top-level cadres organized a course for some forty of the new arrivals who were working with Truong Boi Cong, in anticipation of the imminent need to return to Vietnam. To effect closer coordination between the exiles and their comrades in Vietnam, Ho returned to Vietnam for the first time in decades to preside at the Eighth Enlarged Meeting of the Central Committee, held in Pac Bo in May 1941.[13]

This meeting marked the re-emergence of Ho Chi Minh's influence in the Party and of national liberation as the dominant theme in Party policy.[14] It was agreed that the Party should organize a broad patriotic front, called the League for the Independence of Vietnam (or Vietminh), whose purpose would be to unite "all patriots, without distinction of wealth, age, sex, religion or political outlook, so that they may work together for the liberation of our people and the salvation of our nation."[15] The Party then decisively moved toward armed struggle. Since its formation, it had accepted armed struggle as the necessary means of liberation. This perspective was outlined as early as May 1930 in the Party's first constitutive documents, but the first military activities awaited the decisions of 1941. Phung Chi Kien, a veteran cadre who had been trained in the Whampoa military academy and who served as head of a unit of the Chinese Red Army in Kwangsi from 1927 to 1934, was assigned the task of reorganizing the guerrillas of Bac Son into an Army of National Salvation. Half of this group was soon decimated; the remainder held on for some eight months before being obliged to disperse.[16] A more successful start was made in Cao Bang, a mountainous province along the border, where the armed bands of the ethnic minorities traditionally defended local rights and autonomy. The head of an important Nung band, Chu Van Tan, traveled to Kwangsi in 1942 for discussion with the Vietminh representatives. He agreed to collaborate with the Vietminh, and Giap worked with him in Cao Bang. Both were barely thirty, but were men of exceptional ability. They worked painstakingly and with great success across a large area of northern Tonkin.[17]

As the Vietminh moved cautiously toward insurrection in Tonkin, many forces were at work abroad which would shape Vietnam's destiny for more than two decades. America was already arrogating to herself the prerogative of determining Vietnam's future. Beside her stood lesser powers who were also concerned to safeguard their interests in Indochina. Thus, political developments relating to Vietnam during the middle years of World War II were extremely complex. Allied policy-makers all attached importance to Indochina, at least in a negative sense. They saw the value of its raw materials and regarded its location as strategic, but their primary objective in the early stages of the war was to *deny* the Japanese access to these bases and resources rather than to attempt to seize them for Allied purposes. This was accomplished by the successes of the U.S. Navy in the Pacific.[18]

Political objectives were necessarily more intricate. Roosevelt was angry at the Vichy French for yielding Indochina to the Axis and at the time was unsympathetic toward de Gaulle. American policy in Asia clashed with that of the British, and de Gaulle's close association with England caused United States policy-makers often to regard him as little more than an instrument of long-term British objectives in the Far East. Roosevelt voiced his now well-known declarations on the desirability of ending French rule in Indochina in this context.[19] Reports of such declarations certainly reached the Vietminh during the war, and they were often transmitted by unsophisticated Western sympathizers of the Vietminh who embellished them or placed their own optimistic interpretations upon ambiguous phrases. Giap, Ho, and others in the leadership who understood something of the ambivalent heritage of the Western democracies, in which the ideals of liberty coexisted with racism and social injustice, studied these developments with great interest,

Introduction 19

especially in the light of the collaboration of the Anglo-American powers and the Soviets.[20]

The cornerstone of America's Asian policy was Nationalist China. Washington policy-makers vainly hoped to establish Chiang's China as a great and entirely loyal Pacific power after the war. Hence, Roosevelt's first concrete move in regard to Indochina was his proposal at the Teheran Conference that Chiang Kai-shek should look after it following the war. Only after the generalissimo had declined such responsibility did Roosevelt put forward the idea of a trusteeship, leading to independence in thirty years, which received the endorsement of Chiang and Stalin.[21] Throughout the war Chiang continued to have his own, slightly different, policy. Ironically, it was characterized by a higher degree of realism than Roosevelt's. While he paid lip-service to all the American proposals, he pursued his own interests and objectives without hesitation. In 1942, he ordered the arrest of Ho Chi Minh, whose final release in late 1944 is generally attributed to Allied pressure. Some have argued that Chiang's arrest of Ho resulted from his resentment of the Vietminh-OSS collaboration in the recovery of American pilots downed in Japanese-held areas. But the political motivation was surely deeper. Chiang knew of the Vietminh's potential and was seeking to revive a Vietnamese nationalist party styled after his own. In fact, Ho's release was made conditional on his undertaking to collaborate with the new nationalist group. All this intrigue had little effect on Vietnam's internal development in the middle years of the war. It was not until 1945–1946 that the Chinese intervention was of substantial importance.[22]

The intrigues worried the French, however. The Gaullists were naturally alarmed at their exclusion from Big Power discussions on the fate of their lucrative colony. From the autumn of 1944 onward, they responded with a rash of propaganda in *Foreign Affairs*[23] and in other scholarly journals widely read in State Department circles. There were two essential messages. The first was a catalogue of the benefits French colonialism had brought to the natives of Vietnam, in the manner of classic racist apologetics. The second was to show that Gaullist intentions for the colony's future conformed to America's now explicit interests and inclinations. The French were undertaking, in these unofficial policy indicators, to open the territory to broader economic penetration and to guarantee independence after a suitable period of adjustment. Unhappily for the French, a third message was often gratuitously inserted. Sensitive to the accusation that the French apparatus had willingly collaborated with the Axis, the Gaullists began to claim that this collaboration was purely tactical, dictated by the futility of resistance without American and British support in 1940. They argued that the French *colons* were in their hearts disposed to the Allied cause and would rise up against the Japanese at a more opportune moment in the progress of the war. If the Americans were largely unmoved by the two main points of the argument, the Japanese were profoundly impressed by the last. In consequence, they staged a lightning coup d'état on March 9, 1945, and incarcerated the main elements of the French apparatus in Vietnam.

The Japanese putsch was of singular importance: it was to provide the *thoi co,* or critical moment, of the Vietnamese revolution. Vietnamese strategists have always attached great importance to timing, stressing the need both to develop a long-term perspective and to recognize the crucial moment when decisive action is required. Giap's work in the border regions had developed steadily, and by the summer of 1944 the Party was moving toward a decision to launch a general insurrection. The Central Committee met in December 1944 and outlined such a perspective. On Ho's return from China immediately thereafter, he insisted on a more cautious approach, mainly in terms of timing. He ordered the creation of *Tuyen truyen Giai phong quan* (Armed Propaganda and Liberation Detachments) under Giap's command. These detachments lay somewhere between military and political organizations. Their objectives were of both kinds: to make known the objectives of the

Vietminh and to establish a secure line of communication between the highlands and the delta. The first official military unit dates from December 22, 1944. This platoon, in the Dinh Ca Valley, consisted of only thirty-four men, but it succeeded in liquidating two French garrisons along the Chinese border two days later. Ho continued to stress that the general insurrection must await that moment when conditions are ripe both nationally and internationally. The Japanese putsch produced such a conjuncture.[24]

The entire Indochinese situation was transformed overnight. The Japanese set out to dismantle the French administration and security structure and to establish a more reliable replacement for the duration of the war. Psychologically, the Japanese crumbled the myth of French omnipotence and invulnerability. At a more practical level, the Japanese were obliged to encourage Vietnamese participation on every level of administration and even to establish local militia forces. Japanese propaganda (under the general rubric "Asia for the Asians") openly encouraged nationalism, and the unprecedented responsibilities delegated to the Vietnamese gave the local people confidence in their own capabilities. At the same time, Japan's failure to accord a full measure of independence to the colony only strengthened the position of the political forces which had opposed the Axis from the start: the Vietminh.[25]

Outside the cities, the impact of the Japanese coup came in the rapid disintegration of the French intelligence network and the imprisonment of their security forces. These forces had been built up over many decades, and their efficiency in crushing insurrections has already been noted. When they were removed from the scene, the Japanese had no comparable network to replace them. The result was an altogether new opportunity for political and military organizing and recruitment among the Vietnamese peasantry. Vo Nguyen Giap and his comrades took full advantage of this opportunity: they were able to build an army of ten thousand men by the middle of 1945. The Japanese could not afford to send troops to attack Giap's base areas in Tonkin. By May 1945 the seven northernmost provinces—Cao Bang, Lang Son, Ha Giang, Bac Can, Tuyen Quang, Thai Nguyen, and Bac Giang—had been liberated.[26]

Throughout the spring and summer, the guerrilla campaign against the Japanese mounted. In early summer, a military conference was held at Hiep Hoa. As a result of the deliberations at this conference, the Armed Propaganda Detachments merged with the National Salvation troops (born in the Bac Son guerrilla area) to form the Liberation Army. The units at its disposal were substantial. On July 17, for example, they were able to deploy a force of five hundred men against the Japanese garrison in the mountain resort of Tam Dao. Politically, the Vietminh consolidated its position throughout the country. Japanese-sponsored organizations, including militias and youth brigades, were heavily infiltrated. The Vietminh anticipated another *thoi co* at the moment of Japan's surrender to the Allies and moved to be in a position to receive the Japanese surrender and fill the power vacuum. Revolutionary committees were set up everywhere to provide a de facto provisional government.[27]

In August the revolution was unleashed. On the fifteenth, General Giap and his troops marched into Hanoi, greeted by massive demonstrations. Between August 19 and August 25, the Vietminh moved to power from the Red River to the Mekong. On August 26, Bao Dai, descendant of the ancient emperors, head of the Japanese-approved government in Hue, abdicated in favor of the revolutionary government. At this point, the complicated positions of the Allied powers came to bear on Vietnam. No one felt the conflicting pressures so acutely as Giap. At the head of a people's army, he knew the dynamism of the revolutionary forces. As minister of the interior in the provisional government, he had daily contact with Western diplomats and officials of every stripe, ready to impose by force what the Vietnamese would refuse to negotiate. In these crucial months, Giap's political understanding matured swiftly.[28]

On August 27, the French made their awkward return to Tonkin: the new French commissioner, Jean Sainteny, arrived hastily in

Hanoi by parachute. Giap led the delegation of the Liberation Committee which went to meet him. Significantly perhaps, the head of the American OSS mission, Maj. Archimedes Patti, presented Sainteny to Giap. Major Patti was regarded as sympathetic to the Vietminh, and Sainteny appears to have resented Patti's matchmaking efforts. In this chaotic situation, the Vietminh declared their nation's independence on September 2. Ho Chi Minh's famous declaration began with a long quotation from the American Declaration of Independence and carried on with references to the ideals of the French Revolution of 1789. As a whole, it was calculated to appeal to the victorious Allies.[29]

When Ho finished, Giap spoke. Even more than Ho, in his speech Giap took account of all the conflicting forces at work and noted the latent dangers in the immediate situation. He spoke passionately of the felt desire for independence, but his words were heavy with admonitions. Giap knew that the revolution had arrived swiftly and that its organizational strength had not been adequately tested. He understood the divisions, both political and social, which might reach the surface and render the struggle more difficult in the coming period. Hence, his speech stressed unity again and again. He also emphasized the need to curtail excesses in order to foster the progress of peaceful bargaining. Turning to international questions, he stated:

> As regards foreign relations, our public opinion pays very much attention to the Allied missions . . . at Hanoi, because everyone is anxious to know the result of the foreign negotiations of the government.

He gave no evidence of hope concerning the French. His meetings with Sainteny must have only confirmed his expectations regarding French intentions. His speech continued:

> They [the French] are making preparations to land their forces in Indochina. In a word, and according to latest intelligence, France is preparing herself to reconquer our country. . . . The Vietnamese

people will fight for independence, liberty and equality of status. If our negotiations are unsuccessful, we shall resort to arms.[30]

The position of the United States government was less ambiguous than the unofficial conversations of the Americans in Hanoi at that time. The senior United States official in Tonkin, Brig. Gen. Philip Gallagher, informed Washington on September 20 that Ho Chi Minh "is an old revolutionist . . . a product of Moscow, a communist."[31] The Allies never had the intention of permitting the Vietminh to take the Japanese surrender and receive their arms. As early as the Potsdam Conference, it was agreed that Kuomintang troops would enter the northern half of the country and British forces from the Burmese theater would supervise the surrender in the South. This arbitrary Allied demarcation at the sixteenth parallel served to reinforce the tendencies of power concentration already established by the Vietminh in the last months of Japanese rule.[32]

The most secure Vietminh strongholds in northern Tonkin were scarcely affected. At an official level, the Kuomintang had been effectively neutralized in Ho's ongoing negotiations with the Vietnamese nationalists who enjoyed their backing. The Vietminh had respected the commitments entered into by Ho at the time of his release from prison and had allotted the VNQDD's representatives more posts in the new government than their strength within the country would have commanded. At the practical level, the Kuomintang were in no position to intervene significantly with effective troops. (Although some three hundred Chinese divisions existed on paper at the end of the war, Gen. Albert Wedemeyer estimated that only five were militarily effective units—and three of these were in India under American command!) Some 185,000 Kuomintang troops are reported to have reached Vietnam, but many merely paused at the border to sell their arms to the Vietminh. Large numbers of those who entered Vietnam were actively engaged in looting; they were certainly not concerned about restoring the French presence. Those disciplined units on hand carried out their official instructions literally and saw to the rapid repatriation of the Japanese troops.³³

In the South, the situation was radically different. The British had long been on record as supporting the French return to Indochina. Their command in southern Vietnam saw this as their major task and even resorted to the use of Japanese troops forcibly to depose the provisional Vietminh government. To be sure, there was resistance to the French restoration in the South, and there was vigorous fighting. But the rapid re-establishment of the French security network and the early landing of French troops made the over-all tasks of military organizing difficult. Giap continued to build his army in the North. The resulting situation prefigured the political division of the country which was to persist two decades later. French power was restored in Cochin China in a short time, and the Vietminh were left to wage a political struggle, against impossible odds, to avert a quick reconquest of the entire colony.³⁴

While serving as interior minister, Giap carried on informal discussions throughout the autumn of 1945 with the French commissioner in Tonkin. Although Chu Van Tan held the post of defense minister, Giap retained effective control of the army, and his heavy burden of responsibility in this tense atmosphere can hardly be exaggerated. Simultaneously, he had to build an army and to keep the peace, to prepare his people for an inevitable war, and to restrain their hatred as an earnest of the new government's capacity to govern. In January 1946 nationwide elections were organized, in which the Vietminh candidates fared well. Ho emerged as undisputed leader of the new nation. Only he received a higher percentage of the votes than Giap, who took 97 percent of the count in his home province of Nghe An. Diplomacy continued within the government, as the Vietminh maintained lingering hopes of convincing the Western powers and the coalition government in France of their capacity to govern responsibly and with moderation.³⁵

Giap was removed as minister of the interior and was replaced by a noncommunist.³⁶ He understood the acute crisis which was developing. On February 27, 1946, Jean Lacouture interviewed him for

Paris-Saigon, and he commented thus on the progress of the talks between the Vietminh and the French:

> If the conditions on which we do not compromise and which can be summarized in these two words, independence and alliance, are not accepted, if France is so shortsighted as to unleash a conflict, let it be known that we shall struggle until death, without permitting ourselves to stop for any consideration of persons, or any destruction.[37]

On March 2, he was named head of the Committee of National Resistance, in consideration of the increasing danger of the outbreak of war.[38]

The negotiations were difficult. The Vietminh were in an unfavorable position. The dikes in the Red River delta had been in disrepair for some months, and floods brought famine to Tonkin. United States bombing of the Japanese had disrupted communications between North and South, making it difficult to transport needed rice to Tonkin; over a million people were to die as a result. The famine could not be relieved without a restoration of normal relations between North and South, since Cochin China traditionally supplied its rice surplus to Tonkin. The Chinese were by then using Indochina as a pawn in a larger chess game, yielding to French demands there in return for important concessions with respect to their own territory. The Americans and the United Nations had turned a deaf ear toward Vietminh appeals for assistance and support. The Communists' political opponents of both Left and Right accused the Vietminh of treason for consenting to talks with the French. Racial incidents erupted in Hanoi and Haiphong, the legacy of a century of racial oppression; and bitter fighting continued in the South.[39]

Agreement was finally reached on March 6. In a dramatic meeting in Hanoi the following afternoon, Ho and the other leaders came forward to explain why they had signed the accord. A hundred thousand people assembled. Giap spoke first, and his speech distills all the tensions then confronting Vietnam. It is remarkable for its candor:

First of all, there is the disorder of the international situation, characterized by the struggle of two world forces. One force has pushed us toward stopping the hostilities. Whether we want to or not, we must move toward the cessation of hostilities. The United States has taken the part of France, the same as England. But because we have resisted valiantly, everywhere and implacably, we have been able to conclude this preliminary agreement.

In this agreement, there are arrangements which satisfy us and others which don't satisfy us. What satisfies us, without making us overjoyed, is that France has recognized the Democratic Republic of Vietnam as a free country. Freedom is not autonomy. It is more than autonomy, but it is not yet independence. Once freedom is attained, we shall go on until independence, until complete independence.

Free Vietnam has a government, a Parliament, finances—which amounts to saying that all the interior powers are entirely in our hands. Moreover, we have troops under us, which means that we preserve our forces and can augment them.

On the question of the unification of the three *Ky*, the discussions between the government and the representatives of France have been heated enough. France wants to retain Cochin China, but the government has firmly declared: if Cochin China, Annam and Tonkin are separated, we are resolved to resist to the end. In the final reckoning, the representatives of France had to yield to recognize the unification of the three *Ky* after a referendum of all the people of Vietnam. The result of this referendum we know in advance. Is there anyone in Vietnam who doesn't want Annam, Cochin China and Tonkin to be a single country?

We now turn to the arrangements which do not satisfy us. First, the return of the French troops. We had to accept this provision, although it was against our hearts. We have done it nevertheless, knowing that we bore responsibility for it before our country. Why has the Government permitted the French troops to come? Above all, because if we hadn't signed it they would have come anyway. China has signed a treaty with France permitting French troops to come to replace the Chinese troops. Moreover, France has already made numerous concessions to us. That is why we have accepted the advent of French troops. If not, there would have been no accord. . . .

The people who are not satisfied understand independence only as a catch-word, a slogan, on paper or on one's lips. They do not see that the country's independence results from objective conditions and that in our struggle, to obtain it, there are moments when we must be firm and others when we must be mellow.

In the present circumstances, there were three solutions: resistance of long duration; resistance, but not of long duration; and negotiation, when the time has come to negotiate.

We have not chosen resistance of long duration because the international situation is not favorable to us. France has signed a treaty with China, America has joined the French clan. England has been with France for many months. Therefore, we are nearly isolated. If we had resisted, we would have had all the powers against us.

Then, in some places where the revolutionary movement has not penetrated deeply, many people have not taken it seriously, and if we had prolonged the resistance, there would have been a collapse of certain sectors or even loss of combative spirit. By continuing the military struggle we would have lost our forces and, little by little, our soil. We would have been able to hold only some regions. To resist in this fashion would have been very heroic, but our people would have endured terrible sufferings, for which we cannot foresee whether they would be recompensed.

From the economic point of view, from the fact that a resistance of long duration is accompanied by scorched-earth tactics, wherever we would have drawn back, it would have been necessary to destroy everything. Provisions and houses would have been turned into ashes. The whole population would have to be evacuated. Life would have become impossible. As we don't yet have solid economic bases, a resistance of long duration would present economic dangers which would grow a little graver every day. So the Government has not chosen this way, so that the people may avoid grievous sacrifices.

If we had wished to make a resistance of some months, we would equally have succumbed, for France has every modern arm at her disposal. . . . So we have chosen the third way, that of negotiations.

We have elected to negotiate in order to create favorable conditions for the struggle for complete independence, to be able to await the occasion of total independence.

Negotiations have already led to the cessation of hostilities and have avoided a bloodbath. But we have above all negotiated to protect and reinforce our political, military and economic position. Our country is a free country, and all our freedoms are in our hands. We have all the power and all the time (we need) to organize our interior administration, to reinforce our military means, to develop our economy and to raise the standard of living of our people. Soon the three *Ky* will be reunited. The rice of Cochin China will be able to come up to Tonkin, the specter of famine will disappear.

When we consider world history, we see that numerous peoples in a bad position have been able to surmount difficulties by knowing how to wait for an occasion more favorable to their progress. Russia, for example, signed Brest-Litovsk in 1918 to stop the German invasion, in order to be able, by means of the truce, to strengthen its army and its political power. Hasn't Russia become very strong thanks to this treaty?

The guiding idea, the goal of government is peace for progress. The way opened by the agreement is that of independence, near at hand and total, and it remains our goal.[40]

The French strategy is clear in retrospect. First they sought to hold on to Cochin China, where most of their investments in Indochina were concentrated in rice plantations, rubber estates, and the vast commercial network. Their promise of a referendum to determine the future status of this region was patently unenforceable. Likewise, the undertaking given in the military annex signed by Giap, Sainteny, and Gen. Raoul Salan to withdraw French troops within five years rested solely on the honor of the French. The crucial point is that the French were permitted to introduce troops into Tonkin. The Vietminh had promised to maintain order as this occurred; that is, to insure that popular resentment against the French would be restrained. On the over-all question of military forces, the agreement specified: "The whole of these forces will be placed under superior French command, assisted by Vietnamese delegates."[41]

The French commander treated the delegated Vietnamese with

contempt. When Giap left the first delegation to meet with Leclerc in Haiphong on March 6, the French general saw them for only five minutes and explained simply, "I would have come with or without your assent." When Giap returned to meet Leclerc the following day, he was more than diplomatic. He introduced himself as the "first partisan of Vietnam" and called Leclerc the "first partisan of France." He went on to speak of Paris as a capital of culture and liberty and stressed the impact of its liberation on his forces in Tonkin. Leclerc was unmoved. He emphasized that he was happy to have the cooperation of the Vietminh, that they should think of him as a friend but one who regarded himself as French before all else. When Giap left Leclerc and headed back to Hanoi by road, he was stunned by the sight of the tanks and armored cars pouring out of the LST's onto the beaches surrounding Haiphong.[42]

In the days that followed Giap struggled with determination to exact as much as possible from the guarantees of the March 6 accord and its Military Annex. He asserted his right to be consulted about all French troop movements. But the Vietminh could do little more than stall for time. The French took over the functions of the Kuomintang forces in Tonkin. All the Frenchmen imprisoned by the Japanese were liberated and rearmed. The Vietminh worked hard to prevent provocative incidents which would be exploited by the French. At the same time, they prepared for the inevitable flight back to the old guerrilla bases in the hills.[43]

At a rally on March 22, Leclerc and Giap lay wreaths on the graves of French and Vietnamese dead and reviewed their troops together. Diplomacy and negotiation had not yet ended. On April 3, Giap and Salan signed the *Convention d'État-Major,* dealing with the application of the Military Annex of the March 6 accord. Points won and lost in these agreements were to matter little in the future. The political future of South Vietnam remained the crux of the issue, as it has ever since. The penultimate attempt at a negotiated settlement came at Da Lat, where Giap emerged as a brilliant politician.[44]

The conference opened on April 17. The French delegation was unimpressive and asserted immediately that it had no authority to discuss the question of the South. When the French denied that hostilities continued in Cochin China (claiming that there were only occasional "police operations"), Giap intervened forcefully:

> To say that there are no longer hostilities in Cochin China is a defiance of truth. In fact, attacks continue everywhere in Nambo. It can certainly be said that they were launched against lawbreakers and that distinctions are difficult to make.
>
> Thus, our elements would be assimilated into bands of lawbreakers for the sole reason that they fight in the *maquis*, that they possess fearless souls and shoeless feet. On this score, your FFI would also be irregulars. Radio Saigon speaks only of Vietminh troops. Our elements are Vietnamese soldiers of the Vietnamese Army. . . . We shall never give up our arms. . . . We want peace, yes, but peace in liberty and fairness, a peace which conforms to the spirit of the March 6 convention, and not peace in resignation, dishonor and servitude. . . .
>
> Our position is clear. A month and a half after the March 6 convention, we demand that hostilities cease against our troops in Nambo, with preservation on both sides of their respective positions. We demand that an armistice commission be established in Saigon, for this tragic ignominy must cease. . . .

The talks soon deadlocked on the precise nature of the federal assembly to be established for the new Indochinese Federation. On the key question of the future of Cochin China, the French would only equivocate. Giap argued tirelessly, and on June 25 *Le Monde* described him as "a political man in every sense of the word." When the conference ended, Giap wept. He knew that there would be no peace.[45]

In late May, President Ho departed for Fontainebleau for further talks with the French. These negotiations dragged on through the summer, and the stratum from which the French delegation was drawn made clear that they attached little importance to the conference. In Vietnam, Giap was a de facto head of state. As chairman of the Supreme Council for National Defense, he worked to strengthen and consolidate the Vietminh position. A modus vivendi was reached at Fontainebleau in September, but by then no one seriously regarded it as functional. It was only a matter of weeks before the first Indochinese war had officially begun.[46]

Henceforth, Vo Nguyen Giap was to be known to the world not as a diplomat, but as commander in chief of the Vietnam People's Army. As such, his day-to-day life is much less a matter of public record. Few foreign journalists have had an opportunity to see him, and there are few personal accounts of the historic moments in which he has participated directly. Even the history of the Indochinese war has not been recorded in detail from the Vietminh side. The early period is especially obscure. These were the difficult months in which the Vietminh had to build its bases in Tonkin and begin to send organized units southward. Giap's own work was not merely practical; building an army also entailed developing an understanding of the war and an analysis of the struggle to be waged. In 1947 he published, in a limited Vietnamese edition, a work entitled *Liberation Army,* which was to serve as a key text for military cadres.[47] The People's Army built up regular units gradually. Its structure was a pyramid. The base was the peasant masses, who created their own local defense forces. From these, guerrilla and mobile forces could be organized. The process of selection carried on to the point of recruitment of regular forces from the most seasoned units. An army structured in this way could not be destroyed. The regular units were constantly replenished from below with combat veterans. In 1950 the Vietminh had built up its forces to the point of organizing its first regular divisions. By 1951—in two years—the People's Army had increased the strength of its regular forces fourfold.[48]

The broad contours of the war are indicated by General Giap in the writings that follow. These articles, interviews, and speeches represent the most complete body of analytical writings on the two Indochinese wars written from the point of view of the insurgent forces. The lessons of failed negotiations and broken promises which we have narrated in this introduction are reflected in the principles expounded in these writings. When the Vietnamese entered their second round of negotiations with the French in 1954, they did so from a position of incomparably greater strength, dramatically highlighted by the Dien Bien Phu victory. Yet in many ways, the Geneva settlement was flawed in similar ways to the 1946 accords. The concessions made by the West were again unenforceable. As commander of the People's Army, General Giap was to appeal repeatedly to the International Control Commission established at Geneva to demand the enforcement of the agreement's provisions and to protest at violations of the agreement by the Diem regime. When conditions grew worse in the South and the revolt against Diem brought into existence a new organ of struggle—the National Liberation Front, in December 1960—the task fell to Giap to explain the new circumstances to the ICC. In a historic letter of January 26, 1961, to Ambassador M. Gopala Menon, chairman of the ICC, Giap wrote that "violence and oppression have led them [the southern people] into a situation wherein they have no way out other than to take in to their own hands the defense of their lives, property and living conditions." [49]

The second Indochinese war was set in a new global context, in the wake of successful revolutions in Cuba and Algeria and at a time of ferment throughout the Third World. Giap's later writings take full account of these developments and are imbued with a deep internationalism. Eighteen months before Che Guevara called for "many Vietnams," Giap considered how "many Santo Domingos" would sharpen the contradictions in which imperialism is fixed.[50] But internationalism has never blurred Giap's respect for the sovereignty and independence of nations in the struggle for socialism.[51] His determination is strong, and he knows that his country cannot be independent until the last foreign soldier is gone. We hope that the writings presented here will help the reader understand this determination and gain some insight into the strategy which has led

Vietnam to its victory over the United States. We also hope that these writings will constitute the final chapter in Vietnam's two-thousand-year saga of war and injustice, and we trust that the 1970's will begin a new period of liberation.

Russell Stetler

London
November 1969

Notes

1. Quoted in J. S. Girling, *People's War: The Conditions and the Consequences in China and in South-East Asia* (London, 1969), p. 58.
2. The best analysis of the impact of Vietnamese military history on present-day strategy is that of Georges Boudarel, "Essai sur la pensée militaire vietnamienne" in *L'Homme et la Société*, n. 7 (January-February-March, 1968). Though marred by small inaccuracies, this article is a first-rate contribution.
3. Quoted in Arthur M. Schlesinger, Jr., *A Thousand Days: John F. Kennedy in the White House* (Boston, 1965), p. 549.
4. Source material on the life of Vo Nguyen Giap is scant, and most of the Western accounts are unreliable. We have, therefore, relied wherever possible on conversations and interviews with Vietnamese friends who are personally acquainted with General Giap. He has contributed two brief memoirs himself, but these deal only with a limited period of his life. One is included as the first chapter of this volume, and the other appears in two slightly different versions as "Stemming from the People" in *A Heroic People* (Hanoi, Foreign Languages Publishing House, n.d.) and as "Naissance d'une armée" in *Récits de la résistance vietnamienne* (Paris, Maspero, 1966). We shall cite below the standard Western texts which we have consulted. For a discussion of Giap's family and early life, for example, see Bernard Fall, "Vo Nguyen Giap: Man and Myth" in *People's War, People's Army* (New York, Praeger, 1962), pp. xxix–xxx; Philippe Devillers, *L'Histoire du Vietnam de 1940 à 1952* (Paris, 1952), p. 70; and Robert J. O'Neill, *General Giap, Politician and Strategist* (Melbourne, 1969), pp. 1–4.

Introduction 35

5. See Fall, *op. cit.*, p. xxx; O'Neill, *op. cit.*, pp. 5–10; and Jean Chesneaux, "The Historical Background of Vietnamese Communism" in *Government and Opposition*, v. 4, n. 1 (winter 1969), p. 121.
6. Chesneaux, *op. cit.*, p. 119, and *The Vietnamese Nation: Contribution to a History* (Sydney, 1966), p. 144; Devillers, *loc. cit.*; and Fall, *op. cit.*, p. xxxi.
7. Fall, *op. cit.*, pp. xxxi-xxxii, and O'Neill, *op. cit.*, pp. 10–11.
8. Wilfred G. Burchett, *Vietnam Will Win* (New York, 1968), p. 161.
9. Devillers, *op. cit.*, pp. 72–73 and 264.
10. O'Neill, *op. cit.*, pp. 16–17.
11. See Jean Lacouture, *Ho Chi Minh* (London, 1968), pp. 55–56, 60–61.
12. Boudarel, *op. cit.*, p. 188.
13. *Ibid.*; Lacouture, *op. cit.*, pp. 57–58; O'Neill, *op. cit.*, pp. 21–24; Hoang Quoc Viet, "Peuple Héroïque" in Vo Nguyen Giap *et al.*, *Récits*, pp. 162–165; and Ellen J. Hammer, *The Struggle for Indochina, 1940–1955* (Stanford, 1966), pp. 95–96.
14. Chesneaux, "Historical Background," p. 119.
15. Lacouture, *op. cit.*, p. 55.
16. Boudarel, *op. cit.*, p. 188.
17. Devillers, *op. cit.*, pp. 102, 105.
18. See Gabriel Kolko, *The Politics of War: The World and United States Foreign Policy 1943–1945* (New York, 1968), chapters 4, 9, and 24 (especially, pp. 607–610).
19. *Ibid.*
20. French journalists and historians writing during the war (including Devillers, Fall, and Lacouture) shared the view that the OSS was entirely anti-French and, by implication, an agent of the Vietminh. This view is also to be found in standard American works which rely heavily on French sources (e.g., Hammer, *op. cit.*). It is, therefore, hardly surprising that the Vietminh should have been confused about American intentions.
21. Kolko, *loc. cit.*
22. See chapter six of Hammer, *op. cit.*
23. For example, Gaston Rueff, "The Future of French Indochina," *Foreign Affairs*, v. 23, n. 1 (October 1944).
24. Boudarel, *op. cit.*, pp. 188–189; Fall, *op. cit.*, pp. xxxiv–xxxv; Hammer, *op. cit.*, pp. 99–102.
25. Hammer, *op. cit.*, pp. 101–103.
26. *Ibid.*, p. 100.
27. Boudarel, *op. cit.*, pp. 188–189; Fall, *op. cit.*, pp. xxxiv–xxxv; Hammer, *op. cit.*, pp. 102–105.

28. Truong Chinh, *The August Revolution* (Hanoi, 1947); Boudarel, *op. cit.*, pp. 188–189; Devillers, *op. cit.*, p. 151; Hammer, *op. cit.*, 102–105.
29. Hammer, *op. cit.*, pp. 105, 128–131; Devillers, *op. cit.*, p. 182.
30. Devillers, *op. cit.*, p. 182; Hammer, *op. cit.*, p. 131. Giap's remarks are quoted in Hammer, from D.R.V., *Documents*, n. d.
31. Cited by Kolko, *op. cit.*, p. 610.
32. *Ibid.*, pp. 609–610.
33. *Ibid.*, p. 202; Hammer, *op. cit.*, chapter six.
34. Hammer, *op. cit.*, chapter five.
35. Devillers, *op. cit.*, p. 201.
36. Hammer, *op. cit.*, p. 144.
37. Cited in Devillers, *op. cit.*, p. 221.
38. Hammer, *op. cit.*, p. 144; Devillers, *op. cit.*, p. 220.
39. Hammer, *op. cit.*, pp. 144–156; Girling, *op. cit.*, p. 120.
40. Quoted in Devillers, *op. cit.*, pp. 228–230, as translated from the Vietnamese version from *Quyet Chien*, Hue, March 8, 1946.
41. Girling, *op. cit.*, p. 17; Hammer, *op. cit.*, pp. 148–156; Devillers, *op. cit.*, p. 225.
42. Devillers, *op. cit.*, pp. 234–235.
43. *Ibid.*, pp. 236–237.
44. *Ibid.*, p. 250; Hammer, *op. cit.*, p. 159.
45. Hammer, *op. cit.*, pp. 159–165; Devillers, *op. cit.*, pp. 256–257.
46. Hammer, *op. cit.*, pp. 165–174 and chapter seven; Devillers, *op. cit.*, pp. 256–257; Fall, *op. cit.*, p. xxxvi.
47. Burchett, *op. cit.*, p. 163 *et seq.*; Hammer, *op. cit.*, p. 232.
48. George K. Tanham, *Communist Revolutionary Warfare: The Vietminh in Indochina* (New York, 1961), p. 102; Girling, *op. cit.*, pp. 131–135.
49. Vo Nguyen Giap, *We Open the File* (Hanoi, 1961), p. 16.
50. See "The Liberation War in South Vietnam," below.
51. On the occasion of the Prague Army Day celebration in the autumn of 1968, Giap personally cabled his Czech counterpart, General Martin Dzur, urging him to consolidate the national defense and defend the gains of socialist construction of the Czech people by strengthening the army. See Reuters dispatch, Hong Kong, October 5, 1968, quoting Vietnam News Agency.

The War Against the French

Origins of the People's Army

The Second World War broke out. The revolutionary movement in Vietnam was mercilessly repressed; all legal and semilegal organizations of the Party had withdrawn into the underground. In 1938, at the time of the Indochinese Democratic Front there emerged in Vietnam a big mass movement such as was never seen before, while in France the Daladier government surrendered to the fascists and itself became fascist. In Indochina, the Japanese fascists were waiting for a favorable opportunity to invade this country. In 1940, they attacked Lang Son.* The French colonialists on the one hand kowtowed to the Japanese fascists and on the other sought to deal most violently with the popular movement. Arrests and terror increased in ferocity. In the face of such a situation, the Party had to carry on underground revolutionary activities.

On a Party decision, Pham Van Dong and I would cross the border and go to China. We were then in very difficult conditions. Pham Van Dong was ill, and I was teaching at the Thang Long private school; every movement of mine was closely watched by secret agents just as they had done previously when we openly

---

This memoir appeared under the title "President Ho Chi Minh, Father of the Vietnam Revolutionary Army" in the collection *Days with Ho Chi Minh* (Hanoi: Foreign Languages Publishing House, rev. ed., 1962), pp. 179-228. It was not, in the strict sense, written by Giap, but his oral account was recorded and edited by those compiling the original volume.

* Despite the fact that Admiral Decoux, the French governor general in Indochina, had yielded to their ultimatum and signed an agreement granting Japan the right to establish three air bases and garrison six thousand troops in Vietnam, the Japanese launched an attack on the same day, September 22, on the cities of Lang Son and Dong Dang in northern Tonkin. Lang Son surrendered on September 24, and the following day all French resistance to the Japanese crumbled.

carried out journalistic activities for the Party in Hanoi. But, despite all the difficulties, careful preparations for our departure could be made in complete secrecy.

Before we went, I was able to meet Hoang Van Thu once more for the last time in my life. The meeting took place at Quang Thien cemetery on the Hanoi–Ha Dong road. I entered the cemetery in the dusk of twilight. A man clad in a long black robe walked in my direction: it was Thu who was waiting for me.

Thu said, "We should make preparations to start guerrilla warfare. At present the Japanese fascists are about to occupy Indochina, hence there is every possibility that Allied troops will land here. Our revolutionary movement must have armed forces. We must prepare ourselves in every way, so as to be able to start guerrilla war in time."

Before we parted, Thu said, "When you go abroad, you may meet Nguyen Ai Quoc. Try to get information on the activities of the League of Oppressed Peoples of East Asia."

That week, I taught on Friday in order to have Saturday and Sunday free. Then, on Monday morning when it was realized that I was missing, I would already be far from Hanoi. On May 3, 1940, at 5:00 P.M., after school hours, I went directly to the Great Lake, just as if going for a walk or for normal activity. Comrade Thai, with little Hong Anh in her arms,* was waiting for me on the Co Ngu road. In parting we expressed the hope to meet each other again in underground work when she was able to commit her child to someone's care. We had no idea that we were meeting for the last time. I called a rickshaw which was moving slowly in my direction. That rickshaw pulled by Comrade Minh took me to Chem in the city suburbs as had been previously arranged.

The following day, Pham Van Dong and I took the train to Lao Cai at the End-of-the-Bridge Station. During the journey we had to get down twice when the train was searched. It was the rainy season.

---

* Giap's wife and infant, both of whom were to die during World War II.

Rivers were swollen. At Lao Cai, we crossed the Nam Ti River on a bamboo raft to the Chinese territory. From there Pham Van Dong and I took the train for Kunming. This leg of our journey was more difficult still. As soon as we caught sight of railway employees and policemen boarding the train to search at the far end of the train, we surreptitiously moved behind them. We finally reached Kunming.

At Kunming, we were able to contact Phung Chi Kien* and Vu Anh† who were doing revolutionary work there. We were told that we had to wait for Vuong before any decision could be made.

At that time, our comrades in Kunming maintained secret contacts with the local branch of the Chinese Communist Party. Owing to our Chinese comrades' help, we could set up our quarters, have books and papers at our disposal, and organize communication links as well, etc. Of course we had to act very secretly to avoid the watchful eyes of the Kuomintang clique lest they should assassinate us. Life in our quarters was very hard. We had to do the marketing and cooking. When my turn came, I cooked so badly that from that day on I was only entrusted with cleaning the dishes. We learned Chinese eagerly while waiting for Vuong.

I did not ask who Vuong was. Inwardly I vaguely imagined the man as I recalled Thu's words telling me in Hanoi that I might meet Nguyen Ai Quoc.

At that time, for those youths of our age, Nguyen Ai Quoc had become our ideal, the object of our dreams. In the years 1926–1927, while the student movement in Hue was developing due to the great impact of the Russian and Chinese revolutions, we often called on Phan Boi Chau‡ in Hue where he had been brought from Hanoi

---

* A member of the Central Committee, killed in July 1941 in a clash with the French.

† A veteran cadre and soldier; now an officer in the Vietnam People's Army.

‡ Leader of the Dong Du (Go East) movement and of many other movements against the French from 1904 to 1925, when he was arrested in Shanghai. He lived under house arrest in Hue subsequently and died on October 29, 1941.

and kept under forced residence. Often he told us about world events. On the walls of his house were portraits of Sun Yat-sen, Lenin, and Sakyamuni. We were of those youths so eagerly searching for truth. But what made us most excited were the stories whispered among students about the revolutionary Nguyen Ai Quoc. One day Nguyen Khoa Van got from I don't know where, a pamphlet entitled *Colonialism on Trial* written by Nguyen Ai Quoc. We passed it from hand to hand. The pamphlet cover was also printed with Arabic script. To read for the first time a book denouncing colonialism inspired us with so much hatred, and thrilled us. Later, there came to my ears many interesting stories about Nguyen Ai Quoc. Some of my friends told them with as much excitement and enthusiasm as if they themselves had seen Nguyen Ai Quoc publish *Le Paria* in Paris, or traveling throughout the world. Nguyen Khoa Van even showed us a blurred photograph of Nguyen Ai Quoc wearing a fur hat. But, with our active imagination and our veneration for the man, it was for us the clear-cut image of a devoted and noble-minded revolutionary youth.

Following the quit-school movement staged by the students in Hue in 1927, I was dismissed from school and had to go to my native village. At that time, the student movement in Hue also maintained contacts with revolutionary organizations abroad. Many, including myself, had made up our minds to get out of the country, but difficulties prevented us. However, we continued to hope and waited for a favorable occasion. Meanwhile, I went to my native village. One day, Nguyen Chi Dieu, a very intimate friend of mine in Hue, came to my house, talked about the political situation, and admitted me to membership of the Tan Viet Party whose aim was to carry out "first a national revolution and then a world revolution." Dieu handed me a book written in French dealing with communism, a pamphlet printed in Brussels by the World League of Oppressed Peoples, and documents on the Canton meeting including a speech delivered by Nguyen Ai Quoc. I went to the fields with these documents, climbed up a tree, and read them. It might be said that through the pages of the book internationalist ideas became clearer and clearer to me and were gradually instilled in me, and each page of the book was a very powerful inspiring force. Some time later I returned to Hue, not to resume study but to carry out underground activities as a member of the Tan Viet Party. Here Phan Dang Luu,* who had just come from Canton, told us many stories about Nguyen Ai Quoc.

But it was not only in those early days of my revolutionary life that Uncle's name was to be familiar to me. Later, at the time of the democratic movement in Hanoi, when I wrote for *Notre Voix* (Our Voice), the Party's official organ published in French, the editorial board often received articles signed "P. C. Lin" sent from abroad as contributions to the paper. These typed articles were read carefully again and again, for we knew they were written by Comrade Nguyen Ai Quoc. In them, Uncle expressed his opinions about a broad-based democratic front, or his opinions on the international situation, and the experiences provided by the Chinese Revolution. Each of these articles began with sentences which cleverly drew the attention of the readers, such as "If I were a Vietnamese revolutionary I . . ." or, "If the Yenan experience of the Chinese Communist Party is to be introduced, even a thick book would not be enough to expound it all, here I would like to give only a summary . . ."

All these images, ideas, all the tasks I performed at that time, are still fresh in my memory. And till the day when I was to meet Vuong, I hoped and I felt sure that he was Nguyen Ai Quoc himself, especially when I recalled Thu's words as I was leaving the country. All that made me impatient.

It was already June, midsummer in Kunming. One day, Phung Chi Kien asked me to accompany him to Tsuy Hu where Vuong was waiting for us. We walked leisurely on the Tsuy Hu bank and

---

* A member of the Central Committee of the Indochinese Communist Party, executed by the French May 24, 1941.

Provinces in the North

Bac Thai	4			
Cao Bang	2			
Ha Bac	13			

Provinces in the South

Ha Giang	1	An Giang	35	Kontum	6
Hai Duong	16	An Xuyen	43	Lam Dong	19
Ha Tai	14	Ba Xuyen	42	Long An	29
Ha Tinh	24	Bac Lieu	44	Long Khanh	24
Hoa Binh	18	Bien Hoa	23	Ninh Thuan	15
Hung Yen	15	Binh Dinh	7	Phong Dinh	39
Lai Chau	6	Binh Duong	21	Phu Bon	10
Lang Son	5	Binh Long	17	Phuoc Long	18
Lao Cai	9	Binh Thuan	20	Phuoc Thanh	22
Nam Ha	20	Binh Tuy	25	Phuoc Tuy	26
Nghe An	23	Chau Doc	33	Phu Yen	11
Nghia Lo	8	Chuong Thien	41	Pleiku	8
Ninh Binh	19	Dar Lac	9	Quang Duc	13
Phu Tho	11	Dinh Tuong	31	Quang Nam	3
Quang Binh	25	Gia Dinh	28	Quang Ngai	5
Quang Ninh	17	Go Cong	32	Quang Tin	4
Son La	7	Hau Nghia	27	Quang Tri	1
Thai Binh	21	Khanh Hoa	12	Tai Ninh	16
Thanh Hoa	22	Kien Giang	38	Thua Thien	2
Tuyen Quang	3	Kien Hoa	37	Tuyen Duc	14
Vinh Phuc	12	Kien Phong	34	Vinh Binh	40
Yen Bai	10	Kien Tuong	30	Ving Long	36

French	Vietnamese	English
Tonkin	Bac Bo	North Vietnam
Annam	Trung Bo	Central Vietnam
Cochin China	Nam Bo	South Vietnam

came across a thin middle-aged man wearing a European-style suit and a gray fur hat. Kien introduced him to me as "Comrade Vuong." I immediately recognized the man as Nguyen Ai Quoc. Compared with the photograph I had seen, he was much more active, more alert. And compared with what he was twenty years previously, he was as thin as before, the only difference was that at that time he was young and had had no beard. I still remember that, when I met him, I had no particular feeling as I had expected I would, except that I found in him that simplicity of manner, that lucidity of character which later when I worked by his side, had the same impact on me. Right at that first meeting I found him very close to me as if we were old acquaintances. I thought that a great man like him was always simple, so simple that nothing particular could be found in him. One thing which nevertheless struck me was that he used many words peculiar to central Vietnam. I never expected that a man who had been so long abroad would still speak dialects of his native place with their particular accents.

Vuong, Kien, and I talked while walking slowly along the Tsuy Hu bank like the many fresh-air seekers around us. He inquired about our journey, the difficulties we had to face. He asked about the Democratic Front and the movement at home in recent times. About revolutionary work he said, "It is a good thing that you have come; you are badly needed here." I did not forget to ask him, as Thu had suggested, about the League of Oppressed Peoples. He said, "An important question indeed, but conditions are not ripe enough for its organization."

Then we parted. After that, I met him quite often together with Phung Chi Kien, Vu Anh, and Pham Van Dong. He often talked about the world situation, analyzed minutely the situation in China, and the Chinese resistance war against the Japanese. He laid particular stress on the double-faced attitude of the Kuomintang, apparently cooperating with the Chinese Communist Party in the fight against the Japanese but in reality striving to destroy it. The great task of the Chinese Communist Party was to unite all the anti-Japanese forces of the nation. As regards the Kuomintang, it must also unite with it, striving to win over the relatively progressive elements in its rank for the common struggle against the Japanese. But unity must go together with the fight against their wrong ideas and more particularly with vigilance against rightist tendencies among them, vigilance against the pro-Japanese group and those inclined to make concessions and to stop fighting.

As regards our work, he said, "You will go to Yenan. There you'll enter the Party school to study politics. Strive to study military technique as well."

At subsequent meetings before we went to Yenan, Uncle asked us again and again also to study military technique.

Thus, three of us, Pham Van Dong, Cao Hong Lanh, and I left Kunming for Kweiyang. The journey took three days in the hot sun. At Kweiyang we had to wait for a bus for Yenan.

At Kweiyang, we stayed at the office of the Eighth Route Army.* Since my coming to China, I had realized all the more clearly to what extent the Chinese and Vietnamese revolutions were closely related to each other. I was especially aware of the heartfelt care the Chinese Communist Party showed the Vietnamese revolution. Our Chinese comrades were very helpful. Wherever we went we were treated like blood brothers. At the Kweiyang office of the Eighth Route Army, I had the opportunity to read for the first time the paper *Liberation* and to learn about the situation in Yenan. Another thing to which our attention was drawn was the high esteem our Chinese comrades showed Uncle. We didn't know how many times he had come to Kweiyang, but there everybody, from the man in charge of the office to those who did the cooking, knew Ho Quang very well. (Ho Quang was Uncle's pseudonym.) Each of them talked

---

* Following the agreement reached at Nanking by the Chinese Communists and the Kuomintang on September 22, 1937, the Red Army in the Yenan area was renamed the Eighth Route Army.

about Ho Quang in a different way but all loved him. Many wished that Ho Quang would come often to their office to work and teach them Russian and English.

As food supplies in a region situated deep in the country like Kweiyang were very difficult to find and the Party's finances were limited, we had to grow our own vegetables. Meat was very scarce. But the question of transportation was the greatest of our difficulties. We had to wait quite a long time for a bus.

Just when we were about to leave for Yenan, we received a message from Ho Quang telling us to wait for him instead. At that time Paris fell, the German fascists had already occupied France; we thought that, because of this new development, there had been a new decision. Some days later, Phung Chi Kien and Vu Anh also arrived at Kweiyang. They said that in the face of the new situation, they had come on Uncle's instructions to go with us to Kweilin and from there to try to return to Vietnam. As France had surrendered, they added, there must be new developments in the situation in Indochina.

Thus, we didn't go to Yenan, but to Kweilin instead.

In Kweilin, we contacted the office of the Eighth Route Army. As in Kweiyang, our Chinese comrades there did a great deal to help us. They often organized meetings with pressmen to whom we were to give information on the situation in Vietnam and the Vietnam revolutionary movement. As Vietnamese revolutionaries, we made contact with Gen. Ly Tji-shen, director of Chiang Kai-shek's Southwest Headquarters. During the talk, Ly Tji-shen put forward the question of Allied troops entering Indochina and requested our help in elaborating plans for the coming of Chinese troops to Vietnam.

When Uncle came to Kweilin, and after we had told him of this request, he said, "We must have a clear-cut understanding regarding this question. Only the Soviet Red Army and the Chinese Red Army are fraternal to us, are really our allies. We really welcome them. As to Chiang Kai-shek troops, though they are also anti-Japanese to some extent, their nature is reactionary. In the Nationalist-Communist collaboration they talked of fighting the Japanese but actually sought every possible means to destroy the Communists. We must realize their reactionary character; otherwise it will be dangerous."

At that moment if all of us stayed in Kweilin for a long time, we would be discovered by the Kuomintang authorities. Moreover, "the Kiangnan incident" occurred when Chiang Kai-shek troops launched a sudden attack against a unit of the New Fourth Army led by Seng Yang right in Kweilin city. They arrogantly confiscated and banned all books and papers in the local libraries. Terror reigned. The situation was tense. We were in a predicament. At any moment arrest could befall us should the Kuomintang happen to be on our trail.

Uncle suggested that we should move close to the Vietnam border and continue our revolutionary work there. We could thus get out of difficulty. But the main reason justifying the decision was that the situation at home required us to do so.

Chiang Kai-shek's general, Chiang Fa-kwei, had already set up a Frontier Work Group placed under the direction of Truong Boi Cong, who had been entrusted with the task of paving the way for the penetration of Kuomintang troops into Vietnam on Allied powers' orders. We knew that clique perfectly well and were also fully aware that they were capable of no good. Nevertheless, we availed ourselves of our acquaintances to ask for transport means to reach the Vietnam border easily. Arriving in Tsingsi, we set up an office of the Vietnam Liberation League and maintained contacts with the Kuomintang. Later when Nguyen Hai Than,* who also

---

* An old nationalist who had lived in China since before World War I. The Kuomintang placed him at the head of the moderate nationalist coalition organized under their auspices during World War II (known as the Vietnam Cach Menh Dong Minh Hoi).

came to Tsingsi, informed the Kuomintang that we were communists, Kuomintang men in Tsingsi immediately changed their attitude toward us.

When we were in Kweilin, Uncle came and discussed with us preparations for the task ahead when we returned to the country.

Our meetings with him usually took place in the Kweilin outskirts. He used to stay every time he came in a house of the local branch of the Chinese Communist Party. Disguising ourselves as leisurely strollers, we would sit around on the grass, in the shade of a tree. Uncle listened to our report on the work done and gave his opinions and suggestions. Once, when I met him together with Phung Chi Kien and Vu Anh, he said, "In face of the new situation, national unity becomes all the more important, we must think of organizing a broad national united front, with appropriate form and name. Should it be called Vietnam Liberation League? or Vietnam Anti-Imperialist League? or Vietnam Independence League? I think we had better call it Vietnam Independence League. But it is too long for a name, so we will shorten it and call it Vietminh. People will easily keep it in memory."

That exchange of views was later discussed at the Eighth Session of the Party Central Committee held in Pac Bo where it was decided to found the Vietnam Independence League, or Vietminh for short.

Some days after our arrival at Kweilin, papers were full of news on the Nam Ky insurrection in Vietnam. Having no contact with our country as yet, we felt very impatient.

Just then, Uncle came, assembled us, and told us his views on the event as follows: "The general situation in the world and in Indochina has become more and more favorable for us, but the time has not come yet, the uprising should not have broken out. But as it has, the retreat should be made in a clever way so that the movement can be maintained." He wrote a message accordingly, but unfortunately our efforts to get it sent home failed.

Stirred by the news of the movement which was taking place in our country, we tried every possible means to get into contact with the Central Committee at home.

Meanwhile, news reached us that the French imperialists had terrorized revolutionary organizations in Cao Bang. Many youths of various nationalities in Cao Bang had crossed the border for safety and had come to Truong Boi Cong's quarters. Uncle said, "We shall organize a training course for them. When they return to Cao Bang, they will consolidate and develop the movement further and organize communication links with abroad." His suggestion regarding Cao Bang as a revolutionary base opened up bright prospects for the Vietnamese revolution, inasmuch as Cao Bang had long since had its steady revolutionary movement,* and was situated close to the border and therefore favorable for maintaining relations with foreign countries. But it was also necessary to expand the movement from there to Thai Nguyen and still farther south in order to establish connections with the movement throughout the country. Only after achieving this could we start armed struggle and launch the offensive when conditions were favorable, and hold out in case of the reverse.

These suggestions, made prior to our entering Cao Bang, underlined most strikingly the important character of what was later to be the Viet Bac liberated area.

We succeeded in bringing all those comrades from Cao Bang out of Truong Boi Cong's control. They were originally Party cadres and partisans who had been at a loss after they had crossed the border and had had temporarily to rely on Truong Boi Cong on

---

* The revolutionary traditions of Cao Bang go back to 1929, when the Young Comrades Association had many adherents in this region. When the Communist Party was founded the following year, a number of cells were organized in Cao Bang, and many were preserved during the most difficult years of the 1930's. In the Popular Front period, numerous meetings were held there in support of the All Indochina Party Congress. In the repression which followed, the cadres were forced underground, but they maintained their political strength.

being told about his Frontier Work Group. We gathered them together, forty in all, among whom were Le Quang Ba, Hoang Sam, Bang Giang,* and others, and together with them we shifted to Tsingsi. Plans were made to set up a training course in a region of Nung nationality† which had been under the influence of the Chinese Red Army. The Longchow region had once been occupied by Chinese Communist troops, and the local inhabitants of Nung nationality had shown much sympathy toward the Vietnamese revolution. We stayed there, scattered in two villages.

The setting up of a training course brought up two important and difficult problems—food supply and training program—which had to be solved first and foremost. In those border villages, thinly populated and poor, to provide food for fifty at a time and for fifteen days was by no means easy, in spite of the fact that the local inhabitants had both revolutionary spirit and sympathy toward revolutionaries. Comrade Cap was given the job, and every morning we all would carry rice and maize to the quarters, husk rice, grind maize, and gather firewood. Uncle was also very active. He did a great deal of firewood splitting.

Phung Chi Kien, Vu Anh, Pham Van Dong, and I worked out the training program under Uncle's guidance. Each of us had to elaborate a program: propaganda, organization, training, or struggle.

---

* Le Quang Ba is now commander of the air force of the Democratic Republic of Vietnam. Hoang Sam is now a general in the Vietnam People's Army. Bang Giang is now a general in the Vietnam People's Army, responsible for the conduct of military affairs in the Viet Bac zone.

† The Nung, Tho, and Man minorities (see below) are ethnic groupings who live traditionally in the mountainous Sino-Vietnamese border regions. These tribes were usually hostile to the ethnic Vietnamese; autonomous in their cultural, economic, and political life; and neglected by the central authorities. Often these tribesmen (and especially the women) did not speak the Vietnamese language, and Vietminh organizers, including Giap, were obliged to learn local dialects and resort to crude drawings in order to propagate their ideas. Despite these difficulties, the tribes were to play an important role in the early days of the Vietminh.

After tracing out the main points, we met together to adopt the plan and then began to write. When we finished writing, we met again for checking. Uncle worked with much patience and care. He paid great attention to the political content as well as to the lucidity, conciseness, and intelligibility of the material. As regards any work, any writing of ours, he asked questions and cross-questions, and paid particular attention to practical work. "Only through being integrated with practical work could the training become effective," he said. Each item ended with the question: "After study what will you do in your locality?" or "After this first step what should you do next?" If that second step was not clearly defined, it would have to be written out or discussed once again. Since the first time I worked with him, I was deeply impressed by his methods: concrete and cautious to the end. This style of work in that small training course had a great effect on me and guided me in my military work all through the resistance war. It also brought home to me from that training course that only with easily understandable words, only through being in line with the aspirations of the masses, could we rouse the latter's spirit. It was due to that spirit, to the experience I got from my work at that first training course intended for those forty comrades—and for myself as well—that I later could win success in my practical work in the liberated area.

When the training course was over, all the forty comrades felt highly enthusiastic. It was with much emotion that on the closing day, all of us pressed around Uncle and with great animation proceeded with the ceremony of hoisting our flag.

Immediately after that, all the forty comrades returned to Cao Bang, to their former base. As for us, we stayed to enjoy the Lunar New Year Festival and to make further preparations for the work to come. According to the Nung custom, each of us paid New Year visits to a number of families in the village. As they had already sympathy for the Vietnamese revolution, and we correctly observed the rule governing relations with the masses, they esteemed us all the more when we lived close to them.

Also according to custom, New Year's Day visitors had to share large meals with the families they visited. Uncle was also one of the New Year's Day visitors, moving along briskly, stick in hand, clad simply in a blue suit of the Nung people with his trousers rolled up to the knees. I recalled the day when he was in Kunming, wearing European clothes, with a stiff collar, a felt hat on his head, and realized that he easily adapted himself to the local ways of living in a most natural way. At each house he visited he was invited to a meal, and he offered a red paper bearing the traditional "Best wishes for New Year" written by himself.

The festival over, we divided into two groups. The first group, comprising Phung Chi Kien and Vu Anh with Le Quang Ba guiding the way, went to Cao Bang with the mission of contacting revolutionary organizations there and setting up the Party's quarters. Uncle would join them afterward. That was in Pac Bo region,* Ha Quang district. The second group, which comprised Pham Van Dong, Hoang Van Hoan,† and I, remained in Tsingsi to work.

Uncle came to Pac Bo. The Pac Bo region with its high peaks was not only the starting point of the Cao-Bac-Lang revolutionary base but also the meeting place of the Eighth Enlarged Session of the Central Committee of the Indochinese Communist Party. Held in May 1941 under Uncle's chairmanship, the plenum decided on May 19, 1941, on the foundation of the Front called Vietnam Independence League and mapped out new Party policies. It was also decided that national liberation was to be the central and immediate task facing the people as a whole and that preparations for an armed uprising should be made.

The Central Committee decided also at that session that the Bac Son and Vu Nhai guerrilla bases should be maintained and expanded together with the consolidation and expansion of the Cao

---

* Less than a mile from the Chinese border.

† A veteran cadre, now a member of the Political Bureau and deputy chairman of the National Assembly of the D.R.V.

Bang base, and that these two bases should be built into centers for preparation of the armed uprising in Viet Bac.

From China we headed for the Vietnam border and came across a stone landmark after crossing a long stretch of maize and going down a slope. This is the Vietnam-China border, a man-made border, for the people on either side are of the same Nung nationality. Immediately after crossing the border, we set foot in Ha Quang district, Cao Bang province. Pac Bo region bristles with mountains and hills and is thinly inhabited by the Nung people. They were good-natured people, who had for long sympathized with the revolution and been maintaining relations with revolutionaries. That is why we could contact them immediately after we arrived in the region. Though Pac Bo was so remotely situated, it was visited quite often by the French and their troops coming from their posts in Soc Giang village to arrest bootleggers and search for revolutionaries.

We lived in a cave on a mountain. There were a great many such caves on these rocky mountains, the air therein being very cold. These caves were not easily discovered. From the one in which we lived, we could see here and there sheets of limpid water and a stream meandering around the mountain base. Uncle called it the Lenin stream.

Every day he woke very early and stirred up all of us. After physical exercises, he usually bathed in the stream, notwithstanding the cold weather, and then set to work. (This habit of his has not changed a bit, even at present when he is in Hanoi.) He was always very active, always doing something, going to work or holding meetings, studying, gathering firewood, or visiting the old folks as well as his little nephews in the village in the valley. Sometimes he organized a political training course for the old or taught the children to read and write. If he did not get out, he worked all day long at his desk, a flat rock near the stream, and would stop only for meals. At night everybody slept on a bed made of branches put together in a most simple way, a bed which of course was neither soft nor warm! It was very cold by night. We had to make a fire and sit around it to warm ourselves until daybreak. During these hours, uncle would tell us the history of the world's peoples who since their inception had lived through many wars and revolutions. He foretold that within four or five years, the war in our country would enter its decisive phase, and that would be a very favorable time for our revolution. This he told us again and again, like folk tales while we sat around the fire in our cave by night.

The border areas were often searched by imperialist troops. Whenever we found ourselves no longer secure, we shifted to another place, sometimes even to a place situated in the middle of a waterfall to which access was very difficult. We had to ford the stream and climb rocks and finally reach the top of a steep rock by means of a rope ladder. There our quarters were set up. They were dark and humid, hidden under a canopy of broad-leaved rattan plants. Sometimes feeling that the enemy was on our trail and as our lodgings were not yet laid out, we had to work and live separately in different caves. Once I returned there from work in another region, and as rain had been pouring heavily, I saw snakes and insects creeping into our cave. Uncle seemed to bother little about all this and carried on as if nothing had happened. He used to say, "The struggle between the enemy and us is one of life and death; we must courageously endure all hardships, overcome all difficulties and carry on the fight to the end."

However difficult the situation might be, his simple way of life never changed. His meals were frugal; he ate rice with a slice of salted meat or a fish that had just been caught in the stream. For him, revolutionary work must be above everything else. He never cared a bit about where he had to live or the meals he was served with.

After his arrival in Cao Bang, what he did first and foremost was to publish the paper *Viet Lap*, the abbreviated form of *Vietnam Doc Lap* (Independent Vietnam), a task of prime importance closely connected with that of consolidating Cao Bang as a base. Just a flat piece of stone, a bottle of ink, and some paper constituted all the printing materials. Though it was of small size, its effect was very great. The *Viet Lap* was like a cadre who most effectively and rapidly carried out propaganda and organizational work, who fought for, and enhanced the revolution's influence. After I had been back from Tsingsi and during the time I stayed at the office, I was entrusted with writing news for the paper or treatises on self-defense work, women's work, or writing on the crimes committed by the French and Japanese. Uncle gave me the limit for each of these articles: fifty words, a hundred words, and no more. Of course, it was not easy to achieve this. More than once I was at a loss. During the time we were in Tsingsi, we also published a lithographed paper. The print was small but the paper was large. When I returned to Cao Bang for work, he smiled and said, "We have received your articles but I didn't read them, nor did the other comrades. Usually they were long and unintelligible. The *Viet Lap*, though written in simple terms, was legible and could be understood easily." Later when I came to various localities for work I saw myself that the *Viet Lap* was welcomed by the broad masses. Uncle decided that the paper should be sold instead of being distributed free. "He who pays for it will love it," he said. Gradually, the *Viet Lap* became a very effective propagandist, agitator, and organizer. It was regularly read in every village, in every national salvation group.

The growth of the *Viet Lap* meant also the growth of the revolution. The Vietminh movement had already spread to many districts in the mountain region as well as the delta. Associations for national salvation sprang up in every village. Party cells were organized where the movement developed. There existed whole villages, whole cantons, and whole districts in the mountain region where every person was a member of an organization for national salvation. A duality of power came into being in nearly all the localities where the Party had its branches. Village authorities sided with the revolution, became members of organizations for national salvation and in whatever they did, Vietminh committees were consulted beforehand. In reality our own administration already dealt with nearly all the people's affairs. The inhabitants came to us for marriage registration, for settling their land disputes. Orders were given by French provincial and district military authorities to set up guard posts in every village as defense measures against revolutionary activities. But unfortunately for them, there existed right in the village revolutionaries for whom both militiamen and villagers had sympathy. As a result, the majority of these guard posts did not yield their authors the expected results. In many localities they were turned into our own communication links or guard posts.

Together with the expansion of our organization for national salvation, we organized self-defense units, and sought to give them arms. At the end of 1941, within little more than half a year following the Eighth Session of the Central Committee, and the setting up of the Vietminh Front, there were in Cao Bang province many bases for self-defense armed units. The first one set up in Cao Bang was of the size of a section.

Many pamphlets such as *Guerrilla Tactics, Experience in Guerrilla Warfare in Russia, Experience in Guerrilla Warfare in China* were written by Uncle and lithographed with the aim of propagating military knowledge among the people. They were much appreciated and avidly read by members of self-defense units and associations for national salvation.

The movement spread. Our headquarters gradually shifted toward the delta together with the southward expansion of the movement, according to the decision of the Eighth Session of the Central Committee.

We moved to Lam Son.

Lam Son is a region covered by laterite mountains. It was in this red-blockhouse region, as we called it, that our first Party Inter-Provincial Committee set up its headquarters. The provinces of Cao Bang, Lang Son, and Bac Can had had their leading organ for which we became an advisory committee appointed by the Central

Committee with the task of helping the Party Inter-Provincial Committee. We were located in a dense forest on the border between the Hoa An and Nguyen Binh districts. Uncle was also with us. We first stayed in a house built on poles on a mountain slope. This was for us an improvement, much better than Pac Bo.

But the more the movement grew, the more the imperialists stepped up their terror, especially when we had come close to their top provincial organ. Their patrols came quite close to our place and arrested many people. Many times, we had to shift to the region of the Man Trang people, in a vast and thick forest until then untrodden by man, where now and then centuries-old trees fell from old age and decay. We drank water from the streams. Food supply was very difficult. We ate maize or maize gruel. Once we could spare some rice and decided to give it to Uncle, but he refused. He never thought that he was old and weak and gladly shared hardship with us. Sometimes maize and wild banana trunks were our only food for a whole month.

The more the enemy intensified their terror, the more Uncle paid minute attention to the movement. This could be seen not only in every idea of his on revolutionary work but also in the special care he gave it. When the cadres came from various regions, he inquired in detail about their work, their living conditions, the difficulties they had to face and together with them discussed ways of solving them, be they more or less important.

When the movement surged up, all of us were happy, sharing the people's enthusiasm. He also was gay, but he remained calm, as was his habit, and often at such times, he foresaw the difficulties lying ahead.

He constantly reminded us: a revolutionary must always be patient, calm, and vigilant.

I recall once when we were in Kwangsi, we had an appointment in Tsingsi with a liaison man from the Central Committee at home. The meeting took place at Lu Sung market, on a market day. We were dressed like the Nung people. Uncle was 100 percent like an old Nung with his blue clothes, his trousers rolled up above the knees, and a stick in his hand. Hardly had the liaison man seen Uncle than he hurriedly announced, "Comrade T. has been arrested." But Uncle calmly took us to an inn nearby for a little rest just as the local people usually did. After taking vermicelli soup we leisurely drank tea; then he said, "Now, tell us all that happened at home. Don't be in a hurry."

On another occasion, when we had returned to Cao Bang, after the Eighth Session of the Central Committee, Phung Chi Kien and a number of other comrades were sent by the Central Committee to Bac Son to help consolidate and expand the guerrilla base there. He set up a military training course which had just ended when the imperialists launched a fierce mopping-up operation in the locality. Part of the Bac Son platoon of the National Salvation Army, while fighting their retreat to Cao Bang, was attacked by the enemy at Bac Can, and Phung Chi Kien fell in an enemy ambush in Lung Sao, Ngan Son district. The heartrending news of his death came to us when we were on our way to a conference. Uncle stopped suddenly, and tears streamed down his cheeks. Only after a while could he resume his way.

Every time we returned to our headquarters and saw him, we felt as if we returned to our own home, a home where revolutionaries lived together like brothers of a family, keeping in mind that they must endure hardships and that revolutionary work must be long. He often said, "In everything we must be prompted by the Party's interests. The Party is like our own family." We learned a great deal from his patience, his calmness. The warm feeling of solidarity when we were together gave us confidence in the outcome of the revolution and permeated all our thinking, our words, our deeds.

We came to Lam Son just when the popular movement was developing strongly. Each monthly military training course organized by the Inter-Provincial Committee drew in from fifty to sixty persons. The third course, held first in Kim Ma district, had to be shifted to another place before it was destroyed by the enemy. The latter, when coming to the place, could not conceal their surprise on seeing that, though deep in the forest, there was everything: lecturing hall, dining rooms, dormitory, and a training ground large enough for hundreds of persons.

As the movement was mounting, its consolidation was a task of prime importance. First, we organized training courses only at the district or provincial headquarters, grouping students from various localities. Later, Uncle deemed it necessary to organize mobile training groups moving from one locality to another, short-term training courses of a few days for even two or three persons. These were regrouped for the purpose or could come in between their daily work. In this way, members of national salvation organizations and village self-defense units could, one after another, be trained. As we came from other parts of the country, Uncle always insisted on our paying particular attention to the question of national unity. Such a great question was described by him under the form of concrete, effective, and easy tasks. For instance he said, "Be practical in work, be in harmony with the masses in your way of living and social contacts." As for myself, I strove to learn the Tho, the Man Trang, and the Man Tien languages during the training courses from the students themselves and could speak a little of each of these languages. Thus, under Uncle's direct leadership, the cadres and masses of various nationalities of Cao Bang province upheld the spirit of unity in the struggle.

When the movement was expanding, he paid particular attention to organization work and closely followed the activists and cadres. "The movement is like the rising tide," he often said, "the activists are like piles driven into the earth, only with these piles can silt be retained when the tide ebbs." As a rule, almost every time he heard a report on the movement, he asked, "How many cadres have been trained? How many activists have come to the fore? How many people have been selected for admission to the Party?" Then he reminded us to keep secrecy, and the way to do it. This enabled us to realize the important role played by the activists of the Party cells.

Every query or piece of advice of his brought new tasks with new solutions, for he did not abide by the old routine and took into consideration the new situation.

All the tasks set by the Eighth Session of the Central Committee were carried out one after another along with the development of the movement. The question of the Southward March was put in the forefront. Besides maintaining contacts through usual secret liaison links, we deemed it urgent to organize southward liaison from Cao Bang through the broad masses.

We set out to work. Uncle went abroad. Time passed rapidly as we threw all our energies into our work.

One day, when we had fought our way to Ngan Son district and were organizing a training course for local cadres, we received an urgent letter from Pham Van Dong asking us to return immediately to Cao Bang. Upon arrival we learned that Uncle had been arrested in China by Chiang Kai-shek troops and had died in prison. I fainted. We suffered greatly and were at a loss. We decided to report the news to the Central Committee and planned to hold memorial services for him. Pham Van Dong was entrusted with writing the funeral oration. We opened his rattan portmanteau to see what he had left which could be kept as a remembrance. Nevertheless, we wanted to send someone to China to get confirmation of the news and also to know the place of his tomb. All this is still fresh in my memory. After days of worry, I went again to Ngan Son district, accompanied by a comrade of the Southward March group. We walked at night along the flanks of deserted tiger-grass-covered mountains, through biting cold under a serene sky. Sadness seized me. Tears crept down my cheeks. Some time later, we received most unexpectedly a paper from China. On its cover were written these words which we recognized immediately as written by Uncle, "Wish all brothers at home good health. Hope you are striving in work. I am quite well." There followed a poem by him:

> The clouds embrace the peaks, the peaks embrace the clouds,
> The river below shines like a mirror, spotless and clean.

Origins of the People's Army

On the crest of the Western Mountains, my heart stirs as I wander
Looking toward the Southern sky and dreaming of old friends.

We were overjoyed, but extremely astonished. We looked at one another and asked, "Why is that? What does it mean?" We gathered around Cap, the man who had brought us the news of Uncle's death in China, and asked him for explanations. Cap said, "I don't know myself what happened. It was a Kuomintang officer who told me that."

We asked him to repeat exactly what the Kuomintang officer had said. He did. Perhaps, we thought, he had mistaken the word *su lo, su lo*, which means "yes, yes," for *su la, su la*, which means "already dead." As a result, we had been tormented for months by pain and sorrow.

Our Southward March was steadily progressing. It drew in ever greater numbers of cadres and enjoyed an ever mightier response from the youth. Hundreds of boys and girls in Cao Bang province left their families and took part in various armed shock-operative groups. The road had by then been fought through from the Phia Biooc Mountain southward to the limits of Cho Chu. We had arrived at Nghia Ta village, Cho Don district. From Nghia Ta we went straight to the foot of the hill named Lang Coc and entered a burned-out clearing deep in the forest where we met Chu Van Tan and a number of combatants of the National Salvation Army from Bac Son. Thus, two roads had been opened, all along which local organizations had been set up, and armed forces organized. We finally met together, linking up a road surrounding the provinces of Cao Bang, Bac Can, and Lang Son, which had been decided upon at the Central Committee Plenum, namely, to open the way for southward expansion, and for communicating with the Central Committee and the nationwide movement. At that historic junction we had a meeting with the Bac Son cadres working in the region and those of the Southward March group to exchange experiences. After the meeting, a small festival was held. We sang for joy. Nghia Ta was thus dubbed "Victory village."

Later on I returned to Cao Bang. It was Lunar New Year's Day. Cadres belonging to some twenty Southward March groups who had opened up their way southward also came to enjoy their success. The Central Committee of the Vietminh Front and the Cao-Bac-Lang Party branch presented them with a flag on which was written "Successful shock work."

While the movement developed steadily and enthusiastically, the enemy began their terrorist raids.

After we had parted with the combatants for national salvation and as we passed by Ra market, the news came that Duc Xuan, head of a Southward March of the locality had just been killed in an ambush near Phu Thong. At Cao Bang, the Inter-Provincial Committee headquarters was besieged. Once the printing shop of the *Viet Lap* was shelled.

In all localities, proclamations and admonitions were issued by the imperialists warning the population not to sympathize with the Vietminh, to continue to carry on their daily work. Those families whose members had gone with the Vietminh must call them back. But there was no response to this appeal. The imperialists' scheme failed woefully.

Then came terror. Cadres were arrested, whole families whose members had secretly joined the movement were arrested, their houses burned, their property confiscated. Many villages and hamlets were razed to the ground. Those arrested who had revolutionary papers on them, were immediately shot, beheaded, or had their arms cut off and exhibited at market places. Thousands of piasters and tons of salt were promised as rewards to those who could bring in a revolutionary cadre's head. Then just as they had done in Vu Nhai and Bac Son, the imperialists proceeded to concentrate the population into camps to make their control easier.

Under such circumstances, Anti-Terror Volunteer Committees were set up. The people's fighting spirit against terror ran high. Secret groups maintained close contact with them, carrying on propaganda and organizational work, exhorting, consolidating, and strengthening their spirit, enabling professional cadres and youths to join the bases in safety. Owing to that, revolutionary bases in certain regions became smaller but consolidated. In many localities which had been subjected to the enemy's terrorist operation, the movement surged up again and armed struggle began.

Members of secret groups which were the nuclei of the revolutionary movement in every locality took more feverishly to training themselves militarily and to raising their political understanding. Regular armed sections, some of platoon size, were organized in the districts. These local armed platoons carried out propaganda work, annihilated the most reactionary elements, or ambushed enemy patrols. The Southward March group, for their part, re-established the mass road links interrupted by the enemy terrorist operations. Thus the large-scale terrorist campaign launched by the imperialists, though creating difficulties for us, steeled further the fighting spirit of both cadres and people, once we had stood the test. That spirit was the essential condition for our advance toward armed insurrection.

In June 1944 the terrorist campaign still raged.

But the general situation became more and more unfavorable for the fascists. In Europe, the German fascists suffered telling blows at Stalingrad. The Red Army launched repeated offensives. The second front was opened. In the Pacific area, a number of important naval bases around the Japanese territorial waters changed hands. In July 1944, the French reactionary government under Pétain collapsed. General de Gaulle returned to France at the heels of the United States and British troops and set up a new government. This situation sharpened the contradictions between the Japanese fascists and the French colonialists in Indochina. The Party foresaw an inevitable coup d'état staged by the Japanese fascists in order to destroy the French power. Throughout the country the revolutionary movement was spreading, and Vietminh organizations sprang up.

Under these circumstances, the Cao-Bac-Lang Inter-Provincial Committee convened a conference at the end of July 1944, to discuss the question of armed insurrection. Many district groups attended the conference and at the same time carried out guard duty. Boundless was our joy, of all of us, to meet together to discuss a subject which we had so much longed for, after months of arduous struggle against the terrorist campaign. The political report to the conference concluded as follows: "On the basis of the situation in the world and in the country and the revolutionary movement in Cao-Bac-Lang provinces, it can be said that conditions are ripe for starting guerrilla warfare in these provinces." Seething debate at the conference led directly to the decision that the insurrection be launched to keep pace with the general situation which was favorably developing. That explained why the debate was most animated though the solution could not yet be found for many important and concrete tasks such as how to defend those liberated areas against the enemy's counterattack. What measures should be adopted, and tasks done, to carry out a drawn-out fight? Nevertheless, the cadres were most enthusiastic, all burning with the desire to bring back this important decision to their respective localities as soon as possible.

The Cao-Bac-Lang Inter-Provincial Committee planned to hold another conference together with us with a view to finding a solution to these pending questions and to decide when to start guerrilla warfare.

In the meantime, we learned that Uncle had just returned to the country.

I was sent to Pac Bo together with Vu Anh and some other comrades to report to him on the situation and to ask for his instructions.

As usual, he let us know his opinion immediately after we had finished our report. He criticized our decision saying that to start guerrilla warfare in Cao-Bac-Lang provinces was only to act on the basis of the local situation and not on the concrete situation of the whole country.

Under present conditions, he said, if guerrilla warfare is to be waged at once throughout the country on the scale and scope mentioned in the decision, great and numerous will be the difficulties we will have to face. They will be greater still than those we had already undergone during the last terror campaign. For not a single locality outside Cao-Bac-Lang is yet sufficiently prepared for armed struggle to be able to rise up in response to the decision even though the movement is mounting throughout the country. The imperialists will rapidly concentrate their forces to cope with the situation. As for the Cao-Bac-Lang area itself, we could not yet, as far as the military viewpoint was concerned, concentrate our forces, while our cadres and arms were still scattered, and we still lacked the nucleus forces.

His analysis was as follows: "Now, the period of peaceful development of the revolution is over, but that of nationwide uprising has not yet begun. To limit ourselves now solely to carrying out our work under political form is not sufficient to speed up the movement. But if we start armed insurrection right now, our forces will be destroyed by the enemy. The present struggle must necessarily proceed from the political form to the military form. But for the time being more importance must still be given to the political form. We must, therefore, adopt a more appropriate form in order to bring the movement forward."

Also at that meeting, Uncle put forth the question of organizing the National Liberation Army. Turning to me, he said in conclusion, "This you should carry out. Can you do that? We are still weak, the enemy is strong. But we must not let them annihilate us, must we?"

I answered, "Yes, I'll do it."

Thus the Vietnam Liberation Unit came into being. Uncle thought it over and the next day proposed to add the word "propaganda" to its name in view of its present task. The Vietnam Liberation Unit then became the Vietnam Propaganda and Liberation Unit. It had the task of using armed struggle to mobilize and arouse the population, but our guiding principle was to consist in attaching more importance to political activities, to propaganda than to armed attack. From the depth of the forest, he wrote instructions for the formation of regular units, the backbone of the military forces. These instructions became the main line of our army not only during that period but also during the hard and protracted war of resistance waged by our army and people.

We stayed on another day to assess the situation and draw up an all-sided plan for the formation of the future army. We reviewed the situation of the enemy, our own situation, the strength of our cadres, the problem of food supply, the regions in which our guerrilla bases were to be expanded first, and so on. In the cold and lightless hut, we rested our heads on wooden pillows and talked until far into the night. After listening to Uncle we impatiently looked to the forthcoming activities of the units. He insisted again and again, "There must be military activity within a month, the unit must launch a sudden attack and the first battle must be successful. This first military success will provide us with the best content for our propaganda work."

The next day, just before we left, he again said, "Be secret, rapid, active, now in the East now in the West, arriving unexpectedly and leaving unnoticed." On my way back, I thought out and wrote the ten-clause oath for the Propaganda Unit.

When we came to the Cao-Bac-Lang Inter-Provincial Committee to report Uncle's decision, all were overjoyed. The Propaganda Unit immediately came into being. Cadres and arms were called for. The thirty-four comrades who originally composed the first unit were chosen from section leaders, platoon commanders, or from outstanding members of local armed groups. In addition, there were also a number of cadres who had just returned to the country after their military training in China. Thus, in the Cao-Bac-Lang area, there took shape three kinds of armed groups: the Vietnam Propaganda and Liberation Unit which was the main armed force, the district armed groups, and the village self-defense semiarmed units. These three forces closely coordinated their activities. I had asked Uncle previously, "Now that the Propaganda Unit operates according to the plan of the Inter-Provincial Committee, what will be its obligations and rights as regards the local armed groups in the localities where it will be carrying out its activities?" His answer was, "There must be unified command." This was put into execution right away. During the hard and drawn-out war of resistance carried out by our people as a whole, this combat watchword was thoroughly applied and its effect remained extremely powerful.

By mid-December 1944, on the eve of the founding of the Propaganda and Liberation Unit, I received Uncle's instructions written on a small piece of paper inserted into a packet of cigarettes. The instructions read as follows: "The Vietnam Propaganda Unit for National Liberation is the first one born. I hope many others will soon come into being. Its size is small, but its prospects are brilliant. It is the embryo of the Liberation Army, and may have to move throughout the country from north to south."

Two days after the founding of the unit, we started our activities and won the first victories at Phai Khat and Na Ngan.

These two sudden attacks against the Phai Khat and Na Ngan posts, which resulted in their being annihilated, were swift and victorious operations. As they took place in a border region between Cao Bang, Bac Can, and Lang Son provinces, the news of victory spread rapidly and stirred the three provinces.

After the victory, we went to the Thien Thuat base to expand the unit into a company. Reinforcements came from various localities. To see our new company standing in neat rows and armed with new rifles and shining bayonets filled us with jubilation and confidence. After our first victories at Phai Khat and Na Ngan, we had seized a large amount of ammunition. At that time, ammunition was much more valued than guns.

Later we marched northward to Bao Lac district close to the Vietnam-China border. Our troops went through the villages situated high on the mountains and inhabited by the Man people. Everywhere we went, we were welcomed and cheered by the local people, especially by Man mothers who showed high esteem for the revolutionary troops, greeting us most affectionately and feasting us. At Bao Lac, we launched a sudden attack against the Dong Mu post. Our troops sang joyfully while fighting. I was injured in the leg.

With our presence at Bao Lac, the imperialists might think that all of us were there. To put them off the scent, we moved rapidly and most secretly back to Hoang Hoa Tham district, on the eve of the Lunar New Year's Day. In Hoang Hoa Tham forest, houses had been built and supplies stored for us by the local people, many of whom, old as they were, left their families to enjoy the New Year's Day festival with us in the forest.

Vu Anh, Pham Van Dong, and others of the Cao-Bac-Lang Inter-Provincial Committee also came to visit our troops. We discussed the continuation of the Southward March. Immediately after their departure, we learned that the Japanese coup d'état had just taken place on March 9, 1945.

The Vietnam Propaganda and Liberation Unit moved out from the jungle to the Kim Ma Plain in broad daylight, unfurling their golden-starred red flag. The population was overjoyed.

We marched southward, toward the delta. In every locality we passed through, we set up revolutionary power, disarmed the enemy, and called on the French remnant troops to cooperate with us in fighting the Japanese. New units of the revolutionary army were organized. The Cao-Bac-Lang Inter-Provincial Committee ordered the setting-up of people's power and launched a vast guerrilla movement against the Japanese. Companies of the Liberation Army were formed in the districts of Soc Giang, Cao Bang, Bao Lac, Nguyen Binh, That Khe. Soc Giang and a number of other district towns were attacked by local armed units. At Nuoc Hai, during a drive to enroll the youth into the Liberation Army, more than three thousand volunteered.

This was an unprecedented, historic scene.

Continuing our march southward, we reached Cho Chu and then Tan Trao.

At Tan Trao, we were heartened to find that the Bac Son bases had already been expanded to there. Guerrilla warfare had already been started and revolutionary power established in all the districts of Thai Nguyen province. The Tan Trao region was under Song Hao's guidance. The Liberation forces and the National Salvation forces had thus joined.

This time we met each other in a situation different from that of earlier days. The revolution had taken a step forward. The do-or-die battle against the Japanese had been waged. In their attempts to destroy the revolution, the Japanese from Thai Nguyen and Bac Giang cities launched attack after attack against the liberated area but in vain. The movement in the Cao-Bac-Lang area was not as it had been when the French imperialists unleashed their terror campaign. The population in the liberated area now had revolutionary power and the people throughout the country had heroically risen against the Japanese.

The Southward March reached Tan Trao, thus enabling the Cao Bang and Bac Son centers to link up, and the door was wide open for us to advance toward the delta.

On April 15, 1945, the Central Committee convened the Revolutionary Military Conference of North Vietnam at Hiep Hoa district, Bac Giang province. On our way back to Cho Chu after the conference, we stopped to attend a meeting on May Day. At that time the German fascists had already surrendered to the Allies in Europe. It was also reported that Uncle had crossed the border from China and was coming to us, by the road he had himself planned for the Propaganda Unit.

We hurriedly set out to meet him, our horses galloping, and not thinking of taking a rest. We reached Deo Re, passed Nghia Ta, and met him at Ha Kien where he had just arrived.

This was the first time I had met him since the day he entrusted me with organizing the Propaganda Unit. How many hardships we had undergone, how many successes won since then! I hastened to report to him, "The liberated area has been expanded. . . ." I told him what had been going on since he ordered the founding of the Vietnam Propaganda and Liberation Unit, about the steady development of the popular movement in the regions we had passed through. He listened attentively and calmly, his face beaming with joy.

He said that the world situation was also favorable to us. Furthermore, we had to choose in the Cao-Bac-Lang or Tuyen Quang–Thai Nguyen areas a place where the population was reliable, a place dotted with strong revolutionary organizations and favorable geographical conditions; in short, a place that could be used as a center for promoting relations with the outside world on the one hand and with other parts of the country on the other. That should be done immediately. Many urgent tasks demanded it.

I returned to Kim Quan Thuong and conferred with Song Hao. We suggested Tan Trao, a region with steep mountains and deep forests situated between Tuyen Quang and Thai Nguyen provinces, far from the highway. There in Tan Trao, revolutionary power had been set up, and the people were enthusiastically supporting the revolution. Learning that revolutionary bodies would come to stay in their locality, members of various people's organizations for national salvation came in great numbers, helping us in many ways, building houses for the leading organs, for the anti-Japanese military and political school, and so on.

Uncle arrived at Tan Trao. The period from 1941 to 1945 were years of hardship in fighting our way from Pac Bo to Tan Trao during which the population of Cao Bang, Bac Can, Lang Son, Tuyen Quang, and Thai Nguyen provinces, especially in Bac Son and Vu Nhai districts, fought heroically and made of the Viet Bac zone a nucleus of the national anti-Japanese movement.

After listening to a detailed report on the situation, Uncle reviewed the decision of the North Vietnam Revolutionary Military Conference held in April. He said, "The division of provinces into so many military zones is too cumbersome and unfavorable for achieving a common command." Now, as the liberated area covered many provinces—Cao Bang, Bac Can, Lang Son, Ha Giang, Tuyen Quang, and Thai Nguyen—it would be better to include them in one base named the "Liberated Area"; our troops would then be called "Liberation Army." On June 4, 1945, he suggested that a draft amendment be made with regard to the decision of the North Vietnam Military Conference on the founding of the Liberated Area and that a conference of all cadres in the area be convened to discuss the formation of a unified command. But the war zones in the Liberated Area were practically in a state of emergency; no one could afford to come. I was the only man to assume permanent duty at the Provisional Command Committee of the Liberated Area set up in Tan Trao, maintaining, on the one hand, contact with Cao Bang, Bac Son, and abroad, and on the other, with the zones where Le Thanh Nghi and Tran Dang Ninh were working, with the Central Committee and the other parts of the country. Every day, I came to Uncle's office to report on the situation and to discuss with him the work to be done. Only after a telephone set had been captured in an attack against Tam Dao post by the Liberation troops, could we have a three-hundred-yard telephone line between his office and mine.

For more than two months, events occurred rapidly. In Tan Trao, in view of the new situation and of our new tasks, we published the paper *Vietnam Moi* (New Vietnam).

According to the Central Committee decision, active preparations should be made for the convening of the Party National Conference and the Congress of People's Representatives. Uncle urged that preparations should be made for these two meetings to begin in July. He said that as the situation was very pressing, the meetings should be held, even if certain delegates would not be able to come. Otherwise we could not keep pace with the general situation which was fast developing. Only in mid-August could the meetings be held despite the urgent preparations because delegates of the Party and of other democratic organizations within the Vietminh Front could not reach Tan Trao before that time.

Though very busy, Uncle kept on working most industriously, paying special care to concrete details. He himself wrote and typed letters and documents, giving each item a serial number. Messengers and letters kept on streaming to all parts of the country and assumed a more and more pressing character.

Right in the midst of such pressure of work, Uncle fell ill. For days, he had felt tired and had fever, but he continued to work. Every time I came to discuss work with him and inquired about his health he simply said that I should come as usual as he was quite well. But I saw that his health had declined seriously, and he looked very haggard. One day when I came, he was in bed with an attack of fever accompanied by delirium. We only had some tablets of aspirin and quinine, which had no curative effect on him. Usually he lay down only during rest hours, but now he had to keep to his bed. Of his closest collaborators, I was then the only one to be with him at Tan Trao. One day, seeing that he was seriously ill, I asked permission to stay the night with him. Only after I had insisted, saying that I was not very busy that night, did he open his eyes and nod lightly. That night, in his hut on the flank of a mountain deep in the jungle, every time the coma passed, he talked about the situation: "Now, the favorable moment has come, whatever sacrifice we have to make, whatever obligation we have to meet, even if we have to fight a battle scorching the whole of Truong Son range we will fight it until independence is won." Each time he recalled something, he wanted us to keep it in mind. We dared not think that these were his last words. But later we realized that, feeling himself worn out, he really wanted to remind us about work, and only work. He said that to consolidate the movement it was necessary always to foster the activists and local cadres. He said, "In guerrilla warfare we must strive to develop the movement when it is at high tide. Meanwhile we must do our utmost to consolidate our bases, which would be our foothold in case of reverse."

Throughout that night, at close intervals, he fell into a coma. On the morrow, I wrote an urgent letter to the Central Committee. I also tried to find some medicines from among the local inhabitants. On being told that there was nearby an eastern physician of the Tho minority who was very skillful in curing fever, I immediately sent for him. He felt Uncle's pulse and forehead, and gave him a medicine which was a tubercle he had dug out in the forest. The tubercle was to be burned and taken with light rice gruel. After some days of this treatment his fever gradually abated, and soon he could resume his daily work. On the day he attended the Party National Conference held in early August, he still looked very pale and gaunt.

The situation at home and abroad and the development of the revolutionary movement were very pressing.

The Party National Conference and the Congress of People's Representatives wound up. From Tan Trao the order for general insurrection was dispatched throughout the country. I received the order from the Central Committee to prepare for the combat. On August 16, with the Liberation Army I left Tan Trao to attack the Japanese at Thai Nguyen, which was the first town to be freed from the enemy's hands on our march to Hanoi.

The situation was fast developing. While besieging the Japanese in Thai Nguyen, we received news that the insurrection had already taken place in many localities. People's power had already been established in Hanoi. According to a new decision, a part of the Liberation Army continued its operations against Thai Nguyen, while the rest, among which I was, went straight to Hanoi.

All through that night we marched from Thai Nguyen to Lu Van, passing through immense ricefields, now and again looking at the starlit sky that stretched over the interminable row of telegraph poles which flanked our road. There was a forest of golden-starred red flags everywhere. How moving and enthusiastic was the sight of the fatherland recovering independence! This was the second time I had such unaccustomed feelings since the day when the Japanese coup d'état had overthrown the French. Our Propaganda and Liberation Unit left the Hoang Hoa Tham forest and marched in broad daylight across the Kim Ma Plain, with the golden-starred red flag fluttering over our heads.

The August revolution triumphed. The whole country was seething with jubilation at the turning point of our national history. But in these very first days of the revolution all sorts of complicated problems emerged. Uncle returned to Hanoi. He had not yet recovered from the illness he suffered previously in Tan Trao. Nevertheless, he had to attend conferences, receive all sorts of visitors and deal with so many affairs. Each day, he was busy until noon or 1:00 P.M. When he took meals (the same as those served to office workers) they were usually cold. After meals he would sit at his desk, leaning against the back of his chair, have a nap, then resume his day's work (exchanging views with the Standing Bureau of the Central Committee and so on) until late into the night. But he was always lively and clear-sighted in dealing with everything. Only on seeing his forehead covered with sweat while he dozed off, could one realize that he was utterly exhausted.

Just as he had said years previously, our Vietnam Liberation Army would have to go from north to south. After the triumph of the revolution, liberation troops emerged in every locality and in the first days of the revolution, when the French colonialists coming at the heels of the British troops started war in South Vietnam, many units of the Vietnam Liberation Army got ready to go south. These were not merely platoons of some dozens as before but thousands of young patriots from every locality who, responding to the appeal of the revolution, resolutely went south to fight the aggressors. Throughout the country, every day witnessed moving, encouraging scenes of these youths piling into long trains which took them to the southern part of their fatherland to fight together with their compatriots there for national independence. The soil in South Vietnam was thus soaked with the blood of the combatants of the Vietnam Liberation Army.

Then came the national resistance. All through that protracted and hard war, the Vietnam army enjoyed uncle's solicitude just as it did at its inception when it was only a small armed unit in the liberated area. It may be rightly said that our army, which stems from the people, has been brought up according to the ideas and way of life of the Party and of Uncle.

He was used to prompt and timely decisions. In the winter of 1947, French troops parachuted into many localities of Viet Bac (northern Vietnam) with the aim of striking deep in our base. When the battle was raging, a report on the military situation was presented to the Standing Bureau of the Central Committee and to him, with the proposal to set up "independent companies" * in order to step up guerrilla warfare in accordance with the situation at the battlefront. The proposal was immediately approved.

When the Central Committee decided on the launching of the Cao-Lang border campaign in 1950, Uncle gave orders to the troops "only to win"; then he went straight to the front, visited nearly all the army units, and stayed at the front during the whole campaign. His living quarters, which shifted according to the movement of the battle, was a canvas tent set up in the open.

Again, when the northwest campaign started, Uncle gave instructions to issue the *Eight-Point Order of the Government of the Democratic Republic of Vietnam* to the troops entrusted with liberating the western area. Many cadres who took part in that campaign still keep fresh in their memory his presence at the conference which was to decide on the launching of the campaign. That was an unforgettable event. It rained heavily for days prior to the holding of the conference. Streams swelled, cutting the roads. He had to ford swollen and fast-running streams to come to the conference. He told us all that had happened and how resolute he was to get across the streams. Many local people who had come to

---

* In autumn-winter 1947, the Central Committee decided to launch widespread guerrilla warfare in all French-occupied areas. One part of the regular army was scattered in independent companies, whose task was to penetrate deep into the enemy rear to carry out propaganda and armed activities.

the place before him and did not know what to do followed his example, and all succeeded in reaching the opposite bank. Knowing that fording swollen streams in rainy days was not an easy thing, and seeing that he came to the conference in time, all of us were moved by the solicitude he showed to the army. Moreover, we considered it a most valuable lesson for us before we went to the battlefront. That lesson was, as he often said, "Determination, determination; with determination one can do everything successfully."

He is the incarnation of a great energy, an energy which possesses a great mobilizing force and of which nothing can stand in the way. On that very first day when I met him in Kunming I got an impression which I failed to distinguish, the impression of standing before a man endowed with a simple, lucid, resolute, and steady mind. And today, he is still that kind of man.

Several years ago, at the setting-up of the Vietnam Propaganda and Liberation Unit, he again and again advised us to be active, quick in taking initiative, to act secretly during the combat, to come unseen and to go unnoticed, and to go throughout the country from north to south. More than nine years later, when the revolutionary army had become a full-fledged and powerful fighting force, just when our troops had triumphed at Dien Bien Phu and enemy troops had capitulated, we received his message saying, among other things, "Though great is the victory it is only the beginning."

Every piece of advice of his at a given time has its particular meaning. But there is one common thing we have found in his teachings, several years ago or at the time of the Dien Bien Phu victory, and that is the spirit inherent in them: consistency, calmness, firmness, simplicity, steadfastness, perseverance in the fight until victory, upholding the great spirit of the Party, of the working class, and of our people as a whole.

The War of Liberation, 1945-1954

I. A Few Historical and Geographical Considerations

Vietnam is one of the oldest countries in Southeast Asia.

Stretching like an immense S along the edge of the Pacific, it includes Bac Bo, or North Vietnam, which, with the Red River delta, is a region rich in agricultural and industrial possibilities; Nam Bo, or South Vietnam, a vast alluvial plain furrowed by the arms of the Mekong and especially favorable to agriculture; and Trung Bo, or Central Vietnam, a long narrow belt of land joining them. To describe the shape of their country, the Vietnamese like to recall an image familiar to them: that of a shoulder pole carrying a basket of paddy at each end.

Vietnam extends over nearly three hundred and thirty thousand square miles and has a population of approximately thirty million inhabitants. During its thousands of years of history, the Vietnamese have always maintained a heroic tradition of struggle against foreign aggression. During the thirteenth century in particular, they succeeded in thwarting attempts at invasion by the Mongols who had extended their domination over the whole of feudal China.

From the middle of the nineteenth century, the French imperialists began the conquest of the country. Despite resistance lasting dozens of years, Vietnam was progressively reduced to colonial status, thereafter to be integrated in "French Indochina" with Cambodia and Laos. But from the first day of French aggression, the national liberation movement of the Vietnamese people developed unceas-

---

This is an edited condensation of the essay entitled "The Vietnamese People's War of Liberation Against the French Imperialists and the American Interventionists" and included in the collection, *People's War, People's Army* (Hanoi, Foreign Languages Publishing House, 1961), pp. 11–37.

ingly. The repression used to stifle this movement only increased it the more; so much so, that after the First World War, it began to take on a powerful mass character. It had already won over wide circles of the intellectual and petty bourgeois levels, while penetrating deeply into the peasant masses and the newly forming working class. The year 1930 saw another step forward with the founding of the Indochinese Communist Party, now the Vietnam Workers Party, which took up the leadership of the national democratic revolution of the Vietnamese people against the imperialists and the feudal landlord class.

Just after the start of the Second World War in 1939, France was occupied by the Nazis, while Vietnam was progressively becoming a colony of the Japanese fascists. The Party appreciated in good time the situation created by this new development. Estimating that a new cycle of war and revolution had begun, it set the task for the whole nation to widen the anti-imperialist National United Front, the preparation of armed insurrection, and the overthrow of the French and Japanese imperialists in order to reconquer national independence. The Vietnam Doc Lap Dong Minh (League for the Independence of Vietnam, abbreviated to Vietminh) was founded and drew in all patriotic classes and social strata. Guerrilla warfare was launched in the high region of Bac Bo, and a free zone was formed.

In August 1945, the capitulation of the Japanese forces before the Soviet army and the Allied forces put an end to the world war. The defeat of the German and Japanese fascists was the beginning of a great weakening in the capitalist system. After the great victory of the Soviet Union, many people's democracies came into existence. The socialist system was no longer confined within the frontiers of a single country. A new historic era was beginning throughout the world.

In view of these changes, in Vietnam the Indochinese Communist Party and the Vietminh called the whole Vietnamese nation to general insurrection. Everywhere the people rose up together. Demonstrations and shows of force followed each other uninterruptedly. In August, the revolution broke out, neutralizing the bewildered Japanese troops, overthrowing the pro-Japanese feudal authorities, and installing people's power in Hanoi and throughout the country; in the towns as well as in the countryside, in Bac Bo as well as in Nam Bo. In Hanoi, the capital, on September 2, the provisional government was formed around President Ho Chi Minh; it presented itself to the nation, proclaimed the independence of Vietnam, and called on the nation to unite, to hold itself in readiness to defend the country, and to oppose all attempts at imperialist aggression. The Democratic Republic of Vietnam was born, the first people's democracy in Southeast Asia.

But the imperialists intended to extinguish the republican regime at its first breath and once again transform Vietnam into a colony. Three weeks had hardly passed when, on September 23, 1945, the French Expeditionary Corps opened fire in Saigon. The whole Vietnamese nation then rose to resist foreign aggression. From that day began a war of national liberation which was to be carried on for nine years at the cost of unprecedented heroism and amidst unimaginable difficulties, to end with the shining victory of our people and the crushing defeat of the aggressive imperialists at Dien Bien Phu.

But while the Vietnamese people were closing their ranks around the provisional government in the amazing enthusiasm aroused by the August revolution, a new factor intervened which was to make the political situation more difficult and more complex. According to the terms of an agreement between the Allies, in order to receive the Japanese surrender, the Chinese Kuomintang forces entered Vietnam north of the sixteenth parallel en masse, while the British forces landed in the South. The Chiang Kai-shek troops took advantage of the opportunity to pillage the population and sack the country, while using every means to help the most reactionary elements among the Vietnamese bourgeois and landlords—the members of the Vietnam Quoc Dan Dang (the Vietnamese Kuomin-

82 *The Military Art of People's War*

tang) and the pro-Japanese Phuc Quoc (Vietnamese National Restoration Party)—to stir up trouble throughout the country. After occupying the five frontier provinces, they provoked incidents even in the capital and feverishly prepared to overthrow people's power. In the South, the British actively exerted themselves to hasten the return of the French imperialists. Never before had there been so many foreign troops on the soil of Vietnam. But never before either had the Vietnamese people been so determined to rise up in combat to defend their country.

II. Summary of the Progress of the War of National Liberation

At the outset of the war, the French imperialists' scheme was to rely upon the British troops to reconquer Nam Bo and afterward to use it as a springboard for preparing their return to the North. They had shamefully capitulated before the Japanese fascists, but after the end of the world war, they considered the resumption of their place at the head of their former colony as an indisputable right. They refused to admit that in the meantime the situation had changed radically.

In September 1945, French colonial troops armed by the British and soon strengthened by the French Expeditionary Corps under the command of General Leclerc,* launched their aggression in Saigon, with the direct support of the British army. The population of Nam Bo immediately rose up to fight. In view of the extreme weakness of its forces at the beginning, people's power had to withdraw to the countryside after waging heroic street fights in Saigon and in the large towns. Almost all the towns and important lines of com-

---

* Appointed commander of French forces in the Far East at the conclusion of World War II, Marshal Philippe de Hautecloque "Leclerc" served as commander in chief in Indochina from 1945 to 1947. He began the French reconquest of Indochina on October 25, 1945, predicting that he would conclude his "mopping-up operations" in a month.

The War of Liberation, 1945–1954

munication in Nam Bo and the south of Trung Bo gradually fell into the hands of the adversary.

The colonialists thought they were on the point of achieving the reconquest of Nam Bo, and General Leclerc declared that occupation and pacification would be completed in ten weeks. But events took quite a different turn. Confident of the support of the whole country, the southern population continued the fight. In all the campaigns of Nam Bo the guerrilla forces went from strength to strength, their bases were being consolidated and extended, and people's power was maintained and strengthened during the nine years of the resistance, until the re-establishment of peace.

Knowing that the invasion of Nam Bo was only the prelude to a plan of aggression by the French imperialists, our Party guided the whole nation toward preparing a long-term resistance. In order to assemble all the forces against French imperialism, the Party advocated uniting all the elements that could be united, neutralizing all those that could be neutralized, and widening the National United Front by the formation of the Lien Viet* (Vietnam People's Front). It urgently organized general elections with universal suffrage in order to form the first National Assembly of the Democratic Republic of Vietnam, which was responsible for passing the Constitution and forming a widely representative resistance government grouping the most diverse elements, including even those of the Vietnam Quoc Dan Dang (the Vietnamese Kuomintang). At that time, we avoided all incidents with the Chiang Kai-shek troops.

The problem then before the French Expeditionary Corps was to know whether it would be easy for them to return to North Vietnam by force. It was certainly not so, because our forces were

---

* In *The Struggle for Indochina, 1940–1955,* Ellen Hammer states that the Lien Viet was formed in Hanoi in May 1946 and included representatives from many important political groups, including the pro-Kuomintang VNQDD. (See Hammer, pp. 175–176.) The Vietminh gradually merged with the Lien Viet.

more powerful there than in the South. For its part, our government intended doing everything in its power to preserve peace so as to enable the newly created people's power to consolidate itself and to rebuild the country devastated by long years of war. It was thus that negotiations which ended in the preliminary agreement of March 6, 1946,* took place between the French colonialists and our government. According to the terms of this convention, limited contingents of French troops were allowed to station in a certain number of localities in North Vietnam in order to cooperate with the Vietnamese troops in taking over from the repatriated Chiang Kai-shek forces. In exchange, the French government recognized Vietnam as a free state, having its own government, its own national assembly, its own army and finances, and promised to withdraw its troops from Vietnam within the space of five years. The political status of Nam Bo was to be decided by a referendum.

Relations between the Democratic Republic of Vietnam and France were then at a crossroads. Would there be a move toward consolidation of peace or a resumption of hostilities? The colonialists considered the preliminary agreement as a provisional expedient enabling them to introduce part of their troops into the North of Vietnam, a delaying stratagem for preparing the war they intended to continue. Therefore, the talks at the Dalat Conference† led to no result, and those at the Fontainebleau Conference‡ resulted only

---

* Two agreements were signed. The first was agreed between Jean Sainteny, French commissioner in northern Indochina, and Ho Chi Minh and Vu Hong Khanh (of the VNQDD). The second was a military annex, signed by Sainteny and General Raoul Salan and Giap.

† The first Dalat Conference, in which Giap participated actively, began on April 18, 1946. Its purpose was to move beyond the generalities of the March 6 accord in determining the future status of Indochina. A second Dalat Conference was called on August 1, to which the French invited representatives from Laos and Cambodia, as well as their South Vietnamese placemen. Little that was constructive was accomplished at either meeting.

‡ The Fontainebleau Conference began on July 6, 1946, and continued into August, when the negotiations broke down completely. The Vietnamese

The War of Liberation, 1945-1954

in the signing of an unstable modus vivendi. During the whole of this time, the colonialist partisans of war were steadily pursuing their tactics of local encroachments. Instead of observing the armistice, they continued their mopping-up operations in Nam Bo and set up a local puppet government* there; in Bac Bo they increased provocations and attacked a certain number of provinces, pillaging and massacring the population of the Hon Gai mining area, and everywhere creating an atmosphere of tension preparatory to attacks by force.

Loyal to its policy of peace and independence, our government vainly endeavored to settle conflicts in a friendly manner, many times appealing to the French government then presided over by the SFIO (Socialist Party) to change their policy in order to avoid a war detrimental to both sides. At the same time, we busied ourselves with strengthening our rear with a view to resistance. We obtained good results in intensifying production. We paid much attention to strengthening national defense. The liquidating of the reactionaries of the Vietnam Quoc Dan Dang was crowned with success, and we were able to liberate all the areas which had fallen into their hands.

In November 1946 the situation worsened. The colonialists in Haiphong seized the town by a *coup de force*. After engaging in street fights, our troops withdrew to the suburbs. In December the colonialists provoked tension in Hanoi, massacred civilians, seized

---

delegation was led by Ho and Pham Van Dong and included several other cabinet ministers. When the delegation returned to Vietnam, Ho stayed on, hoping to salvage something out of the talks. The only result was the ill-fated modus vivendi which he signed with the French on September 14. It was confined to cultural and economic questions and immediate problems of public order.

* France recognized a "free republic" of Cochin China on June 1, 1946, with Nguyen Van Xuan, a colonel in the French Army, as vice president and Dr. Nguyen Van Thinh, a French citizen, as president. This action violated the French pledge of March 6 to adhere to the results of a referendum on the status of southern Vietnam.

a number of public offices, sent an ultimatum demanding the disarming of our self-defense groups and the right to ensure order in the town, and finally provoked armed conflict. Obstinately, the colonialists chose war which led to their ruin.

On December 19, resistance broke out throughout the country. The next day, in the name of the Party and the government, President Ho Chi Minh called on the whole people to rise up to exterminate the enemy and save the country, to fight to the last drop of blood, and whatever the cost, to refuse re-enslavement.

At the time when hostilities became generalized throughout the country, what was the balance of forces? From the point of view of materiél, the enemy was stronger than us. Our troops were thus ordered to fight the enemy wherever they were garrisoned so as to weaken them and prevent them spreading out too rapidly, and thereafter, when conditions became unfavorable to us, to make the bulk of our forces fall back toward our rear in order to keep our forces intact with a view to a long-term resistance. The most glorious and most remarkable battles took place in Hanoi, where our troops succeeded in firmly holding a huge sector for two months before withdrawing from the capital unhurt.

The whole Vietnamese people remained indissolubly united in a fight to the death in those days when the country was in danger. Replying to the appeal by the Party, they resolutely chose the path of freedom and independence. The central government, having withdrawn to bases in the mountainous region of Viet Bac, formed military zones, soon united in interzones, and the power of local authorities was strengthened for mobilizing the whole people and organizing the resistance. Our government continued appealing to the French government not to persist in their error and to reopen peaceful negotiations. But the latter, under the pretext of negotiation, demanded the disarming of our troops. We replied to the colonialists' obstinacy by intensifying the resistance.

In fact, the French High Command began regrouping forces to

prepare a fairly big lightning offensive in the hope of ending the war. In October 1947, they launched a big campaign against our principal base, Viet Bac, in order to annihilate the nerve center of the resistance and destroy our regular forces. But this large-scale operation ended in a crushing defeat. The forces of the Expeditionary Corps suffered heavy losses without succeeding in causing anxiety to our leading organizations or impairing our regular units. It was a blow to the enemy's strategy of a lightning war and a rapid solution. Our people were all the more determined to persevere along the path of a long-term resistance.

From 1948, realizing that the war was being prolonged, the enemy changed their strategy. They used the main part of their forces for "pacification" and for consolidating the already occupied areas, in Nam Bo especially, applying the principle: fight Vietnamese with Vietnamese, feed war with war. They set up a puppet central government, actively organized supplementary local units, and indulged in economic pillage. They gradually extended their zone of occupation in the North and placed under their control the major part of the Red River delta. During all these years, the French Expeditionary Corps followed a procedure of great dispersion, scattering their forces in thousands of military posts to occupy territory and control localities. But ever growing military and financial difficulties gradually induced the French imperialists to let the American imperialists interfere in the conflict.

The enemy altered their strategy, and we then advocated the wide development of guerrilla warfare, transforming the former's rear into our front line. Our units operated in small pockets, with independent companies penetrating deeply into the enemy-controlled zone to launch guerrilla warfare, establish bases, and protect local people's power. It was an extremely hard war generalized in all domains: military, economic, and political. The enemy mopped up; we fought against mopping-up. They organized supplementary local Vietnamese troops and installed puppet authorities; we firmly upheld local people's power, overthrew straw men, eliminated traitors, and carried out active propaganda to bring about the disintegration of the supplementary forces. We gradually formed a network of guerrilla bases. On the map showing the theater of operations, besides the free zone, "red zones," which ceaselessly spread and multiplied, began to appear right in the heart of the occupied areas. The soil of the fatherland was being freed inch by inch right in the enemy's rear lines. There was no clearly defined front in this war. It was wherever the enemy was. The front was nowhere, it was everywhere. Our new strategy created serious difficulties for the enemy's plan to feed war with war and to fight Vietnamese with Vietnamese and finally brought about their defeat.

The center of gravity of the front was gradually moving toward the enemy's rear. During this time, the free zone was continually being consolidated. Our army was growing in the struggle. The more our guerrillas developed and the more our local units grew, the more we found ourselves able to regroup our forces. At the end of 1948 and the beginning of 1949, for the first time we launched small campaigns which inflicted considerable losses on our adversary. The imperialists were beginning to feel great anxiety. The commission of inquiry presided over by General Revers* made a fairly pessimistic report, concluding that it was necessary to ask the United States for more aid. The year 1949 saw the brilliant triumph of the Chinese Revolution and the birth of the People's Republic of China. This great historic event, which altered events in Asia and throughout the world, exerted a considerable influence on the war of liberation of the Vietnamese people. Vietnam was no longer in the grip of enemy encirclement, and was henceforth geographically linked to the socialist bloc.

---

* General Georges Revers, chief of staff of the French Army, was sent to investigate the military situation in Indochina in 1949. His critical assessment not only prompted requests for United States aid but also recommended the use of the Bao Dai "alternative" then being urged by Washington.

The War of Liberation, 1945–1954

At the beginning of 1950, the Democratic Republic of Vietnam was officially recognized by the People's Republic of China, the Soviet Union, and by fraternal countries. The following year, the second Congress of the Indochinese Communist Party decided to alter the name of the Party and founded the Vietnam Workers Party. The Vietminh and the Lien Viet were amalgamated. In 1953, the Party and the government decided to carry out agrarian reform in order to liberate productive forces and give a more vigorous impulse to the resistance. All these facts contributed to shaping to our advantage the course of our struggle.

In effect, 1950 marked the opening of a new phase in the evolution of our long resistance. During the winter, in the frontier campaign, for the first time, we opened a relatively big counterattack which resulted in the liberation of the provinces of Cao Bang, Lang Son, and Lao Cai. Immediately afterward, we began a series of offensive operations on the delta front. The enemy, routed, sent General de Lattre de Tassigny* to Indochina. The military aid granted by the United States following an agreement signed in 1950 was on the increase. The aggressive war waged by the French colonialists gradually became a war carried out with "United States dollars" and "French blood." It was really a "dirty war."

De Lattre's plan, approved by Washington, provided for a strong line of bunkers in the Red River delta to stop our progress, and for a regrouping of forces in order to launch violent mopping-up operations so as at all costs to "pacify" the rear and create the right conditions for an offensive which would enable the French forces to recapture the initiative while attacking our free zone. In October 1951, the enemy occupied Hoa Binh. We replied by immediately launching the Hoa Binh campaign. On the one hand, we contained and overwhelmed the adversary's forces on the "opposite" front;

---

* A war hero of the Free French in World War II, Marshal Jean de Lattre de Tassigny served as commander in chief in Indochina from December 1950 to January 1952 (when he died of cancer shortly after leaving the field). He served concurrently as high commissioner.

on the other hand, we took advantage of their exposed disposition of troops to get our divisions to strike direct blows at their rear in the Red River delta. Our large guerrilla bases were extending further still, freeing nearly two million inhabitants. Hoa Binh was released. De Lattre's plan was checked.

In 1952, we launched a campaign in the northwestern zone and freed vast territories as far as Dien Bien Phu. At the beginning of 1953, units of Vietnamese volunteers cooperating with the Pathet Lao liberation army, began the campaign in upper Laos which brought about the liberation of Samneu.

In short, the face of the various theaters of operations was as follows:

The main front was that of North Vietnam where most of the big battles were taking place. At the beginning of 1953, almost the whole of the mountainous region, say, more than two-thirds of the territory of North Vietnam, had been liberated. The enemy still occupied Hanoi and the Red River delta, but outside the large towns and the important lines of communication, our enlarged guerrilla bases—our free zone—already embraced nearly two-thirds of the villages and localities situated in the enemy rear. In Central and South Vietnam, we still firmly held vast free zones while continuing powerfully to develop our guerrilla bases in the occupied zone.

The face of the theaters of operations had greatly altered: the zone of enemy occupation had been gradually reduced, whereas the main base of the resistance—the free zone of North Vietnam—had gone on extending and being consolidated day by day. Our forces constantly maintained the initiative in operations. The enemy found themselves driven into a very dangerous impasse.

The French imperialists were getting more and more bogged down in their unjust war of aggression. American aid, which covered 15 percent of the expenditure on this war in 1950 and 1951, rose to 35 percent in 1952, 45 percent in 1953, soon to reach 80 percent in

1954.* But the situation of the French Expeditionary Corps remained without much hope. In autumn 1953, taking advantage of the armistice in Korea, the American and French imperialists plotted to increase their armed forces in Indochina in the hope of prolonging and extending hostilities.

They decided on the Navarre plan which proposed to crush the main part of our forces, to occupy the whole of Vietnam, to transform it into a colony and a Franco-American military base, and to end the war victoriously within eighteen months. It was, in fact, the plan of the "war-to-the-end" men, Laniel† and Dulles. In order to realize the first phase of this plan, General Navarre‡ assembled in the North more than half the entire mobile forces of the Indochinese theater, including reinforcements newly arrived from France, launched attacks against our free zone, and parachuted troops into Dien Bien Phu to turn it into the springboard for a future offensive.

The enemy wanted to concentrate their forces. We compelled them to disperse. By successively launching strong offensives on the points they had left relatively unprotected, we obliged them to scatter their troops all over the place in order to ward off our blows, and thus created favorable conditions for the attack at Dien Bien Phu, the most powerful entrenched camp in Indochina, considered invulnerable by the Franco-American general staff. We decided to take the enemy by the throat at Dien Bien Phu. The major part of our forces were concentrated there. We mobilized the entire potential of the population of the free zone in order to guarantee victory for our front line. After fifty-five days and fifty-five nights of fighting, the

---

* See Hammer, *The Struggle for Indochina*, pp. 313–314.

† Joseph Laniel was elected premier of France as a conservative Independent in late June 1953. His government fell a year later, during the negotiations at Geneva.

‡ General Henri-Eugene Navarre replaced Salan as commander in chief in Indochina in the spring of 1953.

Vietnam People's Army accomplished the greatest feat of arms of the whole war of liberation: the entire garrison at Dien Bien Phu was annihilated. This great campaign, which altered the course of the war, contributed decisively to the success of the Geneva Conference.

In July 1954, the signing of the Geneva agreements re-established peace in Indochina on the basis of respect for the sovereignty, independence, unity, and territorial integrity of Vietnam, Cambodia, and Laos. It is following these agreements that North Vietnam, with a population of sixteen million inhabitants, is today entirely free. This success crowned nearly a century of struggle for national liberation, and especially the nine long and hard years of resistance war waged by the Vietnamese people. It was a crushing defeat for the French and American imperialists as well as for their lackeys. But at present, half of our country is still living under the yoke of the American imperialists and the Ngo Dinh Diem authorities. Our people's struggle for national liberation is not yet finished; it is continuing by peaceful means.

III. The Fundamental Problems of Our War of Liberation

The Vietnamese people's war of liberation was a just war, aiming to win back the independence and unity of the country, to bring land to our peasants and guarantee them the right to it, and to defend the achievements of the August revolution. That is why it was first and foremost a *people's war*. To educate, mobilize, organize, and arm the whole people in order that they might take part in the resistance was a crucial question.

The enemy of the Vietnamese nation was aggressive imperialism, which had to be overthrown. But the latter, having long since joined up with the feudal landlords, the anti-imperialist struggle could definitely not be separated from antifeudal action. On the other hand, in a backward colonial country such as ours where the peasants make up the majority of the population, a people's war is essentially *a peasants' war under the leadership of the working class.* Owing to this fact, a general mobilization of the whole people is neither more nor less than the mobilization of the rural masses. The problem of land is of decisive importance. From an exhaustive analysis, the Vietnamese people's war of liberation was essentially a people's national democratic revolution carried out under armed force and had a twofold fundamental task: the overthrowing of imperialism and the defeat of the feudal landlord class, the anti-imperialist struggle being the primary task.

A backward colonial country which had just risen up to proclaim its independence and install people's power, Vietnam only recently possessed armed forces; these forces were equipped with very mediocre arms and had no combat experience. Her enemy, on the other hand, was an imperialist power which had retained a fairly considerable economic and military potentiality despite the recent German occupation and benefited, furthermore, from the active support of the United States. The balance of forces decidedly showed up our weaknesses against the enemy's power. The Vietnamese people's war of liberation had, therefore, to be a hard and long-lasting war in order to succeed in creating conditions for victory. All the conceptions born of impatience and aimed at obtaining speedy victory could only be gross errors. It was necessary to grasp firmly the strategy of a long-term resistance, and to exalt the will to be self-supporting in order to maintain and gradually augment our forces while nibbling at and progressively destroying those of the enemy; it was necessary to accumulate thousands of small victories to turn them into a great success, thus gradually altering the balance of forces, in transforming our weakness into power and carrying off final victory.

At an early stage, our Party was able to discern the characteristics of this war: a people's war and a long-lasting war, and it was by proceeding from these premises that, during the whole of hostilities and in particularly difficult conditions, the Party solved all the problems of the resistance. This judicious leadership by the Party led us to victory.

Our strategy was, as we have stressed, to wage a long-lasting battle. A war of this nature in general entails several phases; in principle, starting from a stage of contention, it goes through a period of equilibrium before arriving at a general counteroffensive. In effect, the way in which it is carried on can be more subtle and more complex, depending on the particular conditions obtaining on both sides during the course of operations. Only a long-term war could enable us to utilize to the maximum our political trump cards, to overcome our material handicap, and to transform our weakness into strength. To maintain and increase our forces was the principle to which we adhered, contenting ourselves with attacking when success was certain, refusing to give battle likely to incur losses to us or to engage in hazardous actions. We had to apply the slogan: to build up our strength during the actual course of fighting.

The forms of fighting had to be completely adapted, that is, to raise the fighting spirit to the maximum and rely on heroism of our troops to overcome the enemy's material superiority. In the main, especially at the outset of the war, we had recourse to guerrilla fighting. In the Vietnamese theater of operations, this method carried off great victories: it could be used in the mountains as well as in the delta, it could be waged with good or mediocre material and even without arms, and was to enable us eventually to equip ourselves at the cost of the enemy. Wherever the Expeditionary Corps came, the entire population took part in the fighting; every commune had its fortified village, every district had its regional troops fighting under the command of the local branches of the Party and the people's administration, in liaison with regular forces in order to wear down and annihilate the enemy forces.

Thereafter, with the development of our forces, guerrilla warfare changed into a mobile warfare—a form of mobile warfare still strongly marked by guerrilla warfare—which would afterward become the essential form of operations on the main front, the northern front. In this process of development of guerrilla warfare and of accentuation of the mobile warfare, our people's army constantly grew and passed from the stage of combats involving a section or company, to fairly large-scale campaigns bringing into action several divisions. Gradually, its equipment improved, mainly by the seizure of arms from the enemy—the matériel of the French and American imperialists.

From the military point of view, *the Vietnamese people's war of liberation proved that an insufficiently equipped people's army, but an army fighting for a just cause, can, with appropriate strategy and tactics, combine the conditions needed to conquer a modern army of aggressive imperialism.*

Concerning the management of a war economy within the framework of an agriculturally backward country undertaking a long-term resistance as was the case in Vietnam, the problem of the rear lines arose under the form of building resistance bases in the countryside. The raising and defense of production, and the development of agriculture, were problems of great importance for supplying the front as well as for the progressive improvement of the people's living conditions. The question of manufacturing arms was not one which could be set aside.

In the building of rural bases and the reinforcement of the rear lines for giving an impulse to the resistance, the agrarian policy of the Party played a determining role. Therein lay the antifeudal task of the revolution. In a colony where the national question is essentially the peasant question, the consolidation of the resistance forces was possible only by a solution to the agrarian problem.

The August revolution overthrew the feudal state. The reduction of land rents and rates of interest decreed by people's power bestowed on the peasants their first material advantages. Land monopolized by the imperialists and the traitors was confiscated and shared out.

Communal land and ricefields were more equitably distributed. From 1953, deeming it necessary to promote the accomplishment of antifeudal tasks, the Party decided to achieve agrarian reform even during the course of the resistance war. Despite the errors which blemished its accomplishment, it was a correct line crowned with success; it resulted in real material advantages for the peasants and brought to the army and the people a new breath of enthusiasm in the war of resistance.

Thanks to this just agrarian policy, the life of the people, in the hardest conditions of the resistance war, in general improved, not only in the vast free zones of the North, but even in the guerrilla bases in South Vietnam.

The Vietnamese people's war of liberation brought out the importance of building resistance bases in the countryside and the close and indissoluble relationships between the anti-imperialist revolution and the antifeudal revolution.

From the political point of view, the question of unity among the people and the mobilization of all energies in the war of resistance were of paramount importance. It was at the same time a question of the National United Front against the imperialists and their lackeys, the Vietnamese traitors.

In Vietnam, our Party carried off a great success in its policy of establishing a Front. As early as during the difficult days of the Second World War, it formed the League for the Independence of Vietnam. At the time of and during the early years of the war of resistance, it postponed the application of its watchwords on the agrarian revolution, limiting its program to the reduction of land rents and interest rates, which enabled us to neutralize part of the landlord class and to rally around us the most patriotic of them.

From the early days of the August revolution, the policy of broad front adopted by the Party neutralized the wavering elements among the landlord class and limited the acts of sabotage by the partisans of the Vietnam Quoc Dan Dang.

Thereafter, in the course of development of the resistance war, when agrarian reform had become an urgent necessity, our Party applied itself to making a differentiation within the heart of the landlord class by providing in its political line for different treatment for each type of landlord according to the latter's political attitude on the principle of liquidation of the regime of feudal appropriation of land.

The policy of unity among nationalities adopted by the National United Front also achieved great successes, and the program of unity with the various religious circles attained good results.

The National United Front was to be a vast assembly of all the forces capable of being united, neutralizing all those which could be neutralized, dividing all those it was possible to divide in order to direct the spearhead at the chief enemy of the revolution, invading imperialism. It was to be established on the basis of an alliance between workers and peasants and placed under the leadership of the working class. In Vietnam, the question of an alliance between workers and peasants was backed by a dazzling history and firm traditions, the party of the working class having been the only political party to fight resolutely in all circumstances for national independence, and the first to put forward the watchword "land to the tillers" and to struggle determinedly for its realization. However, in the early years of the resistance a certain underestimation of the importance of the peasant question hindered us from giving all the necessary attention to the worker-peasant alliance. This error was subsequently put right, especially from the moment when the Party decided, by means of accomplishing agrarian reform, to make the peasants the real masters of the countryside. At present, after the victory of the resistance and of agrarian reform, when the Party has restored independence to half the country and brought land to the peasants, the bases of the worker-peasant alliance will daily go from strength to strength.

The war of liberation of the Vietnamese people proves that, in the face of an enemy as powerful as he is cruel, victory is possible only by uniting the whole people within the bosom of a firm and wide national united front based on the worker-peasant alliance.

IV. The Factors of Success

The Vietnamese people's war of liberation has won great victories. In North Vietnam, entirely freed, the imperialist enemy has been overthrown, the landlords have been eliminated as a class, and the population is advancing with a firm tread on the path of building socialism to make of the North a firm base of action for the reunification of the country.

The Vietnamese people's war of liberation was victorious because it was a just war, waged for independence and the reunification of the country, in the legitimate interests of the nation and the people and which by this fact succeeded in leading the whole people to participate enthusiastically in the resistance and to consent to make every sacrifice for its victory.

The Vietnamese people's war of liberation won this great victory because we had a revolutionary armed force of the people, the heroic *Vietnam People's Army*. Built in accordance with the political line of the Party, this army was animated by an unflinching combative spirit, and accustomed to a style of persevering political work. It adopted the tactics and strategy of a people's war. It developed from nothing by combining the best elements among the workers, peasants, and revolutionary students and intellectuals, stemming from the patriotic organizations of the popular masses. Born of the people, it fought for the people. It is an army led by the Party of the working class.

The Vietnamese people's war of liberation was victorious because we had a wide and firm *National United Front,* comprising all the revolutionary classes, all the nationalities living on Vietnamese soil, all the patriots. This Front was based on the alliance between workers and peasants, under the leadership of the Party.

The War of Liberation, 1945-1954

The Vietnamese people's war of liberation ended in victory because of the existence of *people's power* established during the August revolution and thereafter constantly consolidated. This power was the government of alliance between classes, the government of the revolutionary classes, and above all of the workers and peasants. It was the dictatorship of people's democracy, the dictatorship of the workers and peasants, in fact, under the leadership of the Party. It devoted its efforts to mobilizing and organizing the whole people for the resistance; it brought the people material advantages not only in the free zones but also in the guerrilla bases behind the enemy's back.

The Vietnamese people's war of liberation attained this great victory for the reasons we have just enumerated, but above all because it was *organized and led by the Party of the working class: the Indochinese Communist Party, now the Vietnam Workers Party*. In the light of the principles of Marxism-Leninism, it was this Party which proceeded to make an analysis of the social situation and of the balance of forces between the enemy and ourselves in order to determine the fundamental tasks of the people's national democratic revolution, to establish the plan for the armed struggle and decide on the guiding principle: long-term resistance and self-reliance. It was the Party which found a correct solution to the problems arising out of the setting-up and leadership of a people's army, people's power, and a national united front. It also inspired in the people and the army a completely revolutionary spirit which instilled into the whole people the will to overcome all difficulties, to endure all privations, the spirit of a long resistance, of resistance to the end. Our Party, under the leadership of President Ho Chi Minh, is the worthy Party of the working class and the nation. President Ho Chi Minh, leader of the Party and the nation, is the symbol of this gigantic uprising of the Vietnamese people.

If the Vietnamese people's war of liberation ended in a glorious victory, it is because we did not fight alone, but with the *support of progressive peoples the world over, and more especially the peoples* of the fraternal countries, with the Soviet Union at the head. The victory of the Vietnamese people cannot be divided from this support; it cannot be disassociated from the brilliant successes of the socialist countries and the movement of national liberation; neither can it be detached from the victories of the Soviet Red Army during the Second World War, nor from those of the Chinese people during the last few years. It cannot be isolated from the sympathy and support of progressive peoples throughout the world, among whom are the French people under the leadership of their Communist Party, and the peoples of Asia and Africa.

The victory of the Vietnamese people is that of a small and weak nation, one possessing no regular army, which rose up to engage in an armed struggle against the aggression of an imperialist country with a modern army and benefiting from the support of the American imperialists. This colonial country has established and maintained a regime of people's democracy, which will open up to it the path to socialism. That is one of the great historic events in the national liberation movement and in the proletarian revolutionary movement, in the new international position born of the Second World War, in the period of transition from capitalism to socialism, in the time of the disintegration of imperialism. The Vietnamese people's war of liberation has contributed to making obvious this new historic truth: in the present international situation, a weak people which rises up resolutely to fight for its freedom is sure to triumph over all enemies and to achieve victory.

This great truth enlightens and encourages the Vietnamese people on the path of struggle for peace, socialism, and the reunification of the country. This path will certainly lead it to new victories.

People's War, People's Army

Even to this day, bourgeois strategists have not yet overcome their surprise at the outcome of the war in Indochina. How could the Vietnamese nation have defeated an imperialist power such as France which was backed by the United States? They try to explain this extraordinary fact by the correctness of strategy and tactics, by the forms of combat and the heroism of the Vietnam People's Army. Of course all these factors contributed to the happy outcome of the resistance. But if the question is put: "Why were the Vietnamese people able to win?" the most precise and most complete answer must be: "The Vietnamese people won because their war of liberation was a people's war."

When the resistance war spread to the whole country, the Indochinese Communist Party emphasized in its instructions that our resistance war must be the work of the entire people. Therein lies the key to victory.

Our resistance war was a people's war, because its political aims were to smash the imperialist yoke in order to win back national independence, to overthrow the feudal landlord class in order to bring land to the peasants; in other words, to radically solve the two fundamental contradictions of Vietnamese society—the contradiction between the nation and imperialism on the one hand, and the contradiction between the people, especially between the peasants and the feudal landlord class, on the other—and to pave the socialist path for the Vietnamese revolution.

This is an edited condensation of the famous essay, "People's War, People's Army," published in the collection of the same name (Hanoi, Foreign Languages Publishing House, 1961), pp. 41a–64. The article was written in December 1959; it was originally published on the occasion of the fifteenth anniversary of the founding of the Vietnam People's Army.

Holding firmly to the strategy and tactics of the national democratic revolution, the Party pointed out to the people the aims of the struggle: independence and democracy. It was, however, not enough to have objectives entirely in conformity with the fundamental aspirations of the people. It was also necessary to bring everything into play to enlighten the masses of the people, educate and encourage them, organize them in fighting for national salvation. The Party devoted itself entirely to this work, to the regrouping of all the national forces, and to the broadening and strengthening of a national united front, the Vietminh, and later the Lien Viet which was a magnificent model of the unity of the various strata of the people in the anti-imperialist struggle in a colonial country. In fact, this Front united the patriotic forces of all classes and social strata, even progressive landlords; all nationalities in the country, majority as well as minority; patriotic believers of each and every religion. "Unity, the great unity, for victory, the great victory"; this slogan launched by President Ho Chi Minh became a reality, a great reality during the long and hard resistance.

We waged a people's war, and that in the framework of a long-since colonized country. Therefore, the national factor was of primary importance. We had to rally all the forces likely to overthrow the imperialists and their lackeys. On the other hand, this war proceeded in a backward agricultural country where the peasants, making up the great majority of the population, constituted the essential force of the revolution and of the resistance war. Consequently, the relation between the national question and the peasant question had to be clearly defined, with the gradual settlement of the agrarian problem, so as to mobilize the broad peasant masses, one of the essential and decisive factors for victory. Always solicitous about the interests of the peasantry, the Party began by advocating reduction of land rent and interest. Later on, as soon as the stabilization of the situation allowed it, the Party carried out with great firmness the mobilization of the masses for land reform in order to bring land to the tillers, thereby to maintain and strengthen the resistance.

During the years of war, various erroneous tendencies appeared. Either we devoted our attention only to the organization and growth of the armed forces while neglecting the mobilization and organization of large strata of the people; or we mobilized the people for the war without heeding seriously their immediate everyday interests; or we thought of satisfying the immediate interests of the people as a whole, without giving due attention to those of the peasants. The Party resolutely fought all these tendencies. To lead the resistance to victory, we had to look after the strengthening of the army, while giving thought to mobilizing and educating the people, broadening and consolidating the National United Front. We had to mobilize the masses for the resistance while trying to satisfy their immediate interest in improving their living conditions, essentially those of the peasantry. A very broad national united front was indispensable, on the basis of the worker-peasant alliance and under the leadership of the Party.

The imperatives of the people's war in Vietnam required the adoption of appropriate strategy and tactics on the basis of the enemy's characteristics and of our own, of the concrete conditions of the battlefields and balance of forces facing each other: in other words, the strategy and tactics of a people's war, in an economically backward, colonial country.

First of all, this strategy must be the *strategy of a long-term war*. It does not mean that all revolutionary wars, all people's wars, must necessarily be long-term wars. If from the outset the conditions are favorable to the people and the balance of forces turn in favor of the revolution, the revolutionary war can end victoriously in a short time. But the war of liberation of the Vietnamese people started in quite different conditions: we had to deal with a much stronger enemy. It was obvious that this balance of forces took away from us the possibility of giving decisive battles from the opening of the hostilities and of checking the aggression from the first landing operations on our soil. In a word, it was impossible for us to defeat the enemy swiftly.

It was only by a long hard resistance that we could wear out the enemy forces little by little while strengthening ours, progressively turn the balance of forces in our favor, and finally win victory. We did not have any other way.

This strategy and slogan of long-term resistance was decided upon by the Indochinese Communist Party from the first days of the war of liberation. It was in this spirit that the Vietnam People's Army, after fierce street battles in the big cities, beat strategic retreats to the countryside on its own initiative in order to maintain its bases and preserve its forces.

The long-term revolutionary war must include several different stages: stage of contention, stage of equilibrium, and stage of counteroffensive. Practical fighting was, of course, more complicated. There had to be many years of more and more intense and generalized guerrilla fighting to realize the equilibrium of forces and develop our war potentiality. When the conjunctures of events at home and abroad allowed it, we went over to counteroffensive first by a series of local operations, then by others on a larger scale which were to lead to the decisive victory of Dien Bien Phu.

The application of this strategy of long-term resistance required a whole system of education, a whole ideological struggle among the people and Party members, a gigantic effort of organization in both military and economic fields, extraordinary sacrifices and heroism from the army as well as from the people, at the front as well as in the rear. Sometimes erroneous tendencies appeared, trying either to bypass the stages to end the war earlier, or to throw important forces into military adventures. The Party rectified them by a stubborn struggle and persevered in the line it had fixed. In the difficult hours, certain hesitations revealed themselves, and the Party faced them with vigor and with determination in the struggle and faith in final victory.

The long-term people's war in Vietnam also called for appropriate forms of fighting: appropriate to the revolutionary nature of the war as well as to the balance of forces which revealed at that time an overwhelming superiority of the enemy over the still very weak material and technical bases of the People's Army. *The adopted form of fighting was guerrilla warfare.* It can be said that the war of liberation of the Vietnamese people was a long and vast guerrilla war proceeding from simple to complex then to mobile war in the last years of the resistance.

Guerrilla war is the war of the broad masses of an economically backward country standing up against a powerfully equipped and well-trained army of aggression. Is the enemy strong? One avoids him. Is he weak? One attacks him. To his modern armament, one opposes a boundless heroism to vanquish either by harassing or by combining military operations with political and economic action; there is no fixed line of demarcation, the front being wherever the enemy is found.

Concentration of troops to realize an overwhelming superiority over the enemy where he is sufficiently exposed in order to destroy his manpower; initiative, flexibility, rapidity, surprise, suddenness in attack and retreat. As long as the strategic balance of forces remains disadvantageous, resolutely to muster troops to obtain absolute superiority in combat in a given place, and at a given time. To exhaust the enemy forces little by little by small victories and at the same time to maintain and increase ours. In these concrete conditions it proves absolutely necessary not to lose sight of the main objective of the fighting, that is, the destruction of the enemy manpower. Therefore, losses must be avoided even at the cost of losing ground. And that for the purpose of recovering, later on, the occupied territories and completely liberating the country.

In the war of liberation in Vietnam, guerrilla activities spread to all the regions temporarily occupied by the enemy. Each inhabitant was a soldier, each village a fortress, each Party cell and each village administrative committee a staff.

The people as a whole took part in the armed struggle, fighting according to the principles of guerrilla warfare, in small packets, but always in pursuance of the one and same line, and the same instructions, those of the Central Committee of the Party and the government.

At variance with numerous other countries which waged revolutionary wars, Vietnam, in the first years of its struggle, did not and could not engage in pitched battles. It had to rest content with guerrilla warfare. At the cost of thousands of difficulties and countless sacrifices, this guerrilla war developed progressively into a form of mobile war that daily increased in scale. While retaining certain characteristics of guerrilla war, it involved regular campaigns with greater attacks on fortified positions. Starting from small operations with the strength of a platoon or a company to annihilate a few men or a group of enemy soldiers, our army went over, later, to more important combats with a battalion or regiment to cut one or several enemy companies to pieces, finally coming to greater campaigns bringing into play many regiments, then many divisions, to end at Dien Bien Phu where the French Expeditionary Corps lost sixteen thousand men of its crack units. It was this process of development that enabled our army to move forward steadily on the road to victory.

People's war, long-term war, guerrilla warfare developing step by step into mobile warfare, such are the most valuable lessons of the war of liberation in Vietnam. It was by following that line that the Party led the resistance to victory. After three thousand days of fighting, difficulties and sacrifices, our people defeated the French imperialists and American interventionists. At present, in the liberated half of our country, sixteen million of our compatriots, by their creative labor, are healing the horrible wounds of war, reconstructing the country and building socialism. In the meantime, the struggle is going on to achieve the democratic national revolution throughout the country and to reunify the fatherland on the basis of independence and democracy.

People's War, People's Army

After this account of the main lines of the war of liberation waged by the Vietnamese people against the French and American imperialists, I shall speak of the Vietnam People's Army.

Being the armed forces of the Vietnamese people, it was born and grew up in the flames of the war of national liberation. Its embryo was the self-defense units created by the Nghe An soviets, which managed to hold power for a few months in the period of revolutionary upsurge in the years 1930–1931. But the creation of revolutionary armed forces was positively considered only at the outset of World War II when the preparation for an armed insurrection came to the forefront of our attention. Our military and paramilitary formations appeared at the Bac Son uprising and in the revolutionary bases in Cao Bang region. Following the setting-up of the first platoon of National Salvation, on December 22, 1944, another platoon-strong unit was created: the Propaganda Unit of the Vietnam Liberation Army. Our war bases organized during our illegality were at the time limited to a few districts in the provinces of Cao Bang, Bac Can, and Lang Son in the jungle of the North. As for the revolutionary armed forces they still consisted of people's units of self-defense and of a few groups and platoons completely free from production work. Their number increased quickly, and there were already several thousands of guerrillas at the beginning of 1945, at the time of the *coup de force* by the Japanese fascists over the French colonialists. After establishing people's power in the rural regions of the six provinces in Viet Bac that were established as a free zone, the existing armed organizations merged to form the Vietnam Liberation Army.

During the August insurrection, side by side with the people and the self-defense units, the Liberation Army took part in the conquest of power. By incorporating the paramilitary forces regrouped in the course of the glorious days of August, it saw its strength increase rapidly. With heterogeneous matériel wrested from the Japanese and their Bao An troops*—rifles alone consisted of sixteen different types including old French patterns and even rifles of the tsarist forces taken by the Japanese—this young and poorly equipped army soon had to face the aggression of the French Expeditionary Corps which had modern armaments. Such antiquated equipment required from the Vietnamese Army and people complete self-sacrifice and superhuman heroism.

Should the enemy attack the regions where our troops were stationed, the latter would give battle. Should he ferret about in the large zones where there were no regular formations, the people would stay his advance with rudimentary weapons: sticks, spears, scimitars, bows, flintlocks. From the first days, there appeared three types of armed forces: paramilitary organizations or guerrilla units, regional troops, and regular units. These formations were, in the area of organization, the expression of the general mobilization of the people in arms. They cooperated closely with one another to annihilate the enemy.

Peasants, workers, and intellectuals crowded into the ranks of the armed forces of the revolution. Leading cadres of the Party and the state apparatus became officers from the first moment. The greatest difficulty to be solved was the equipment problem. Throughout Vietnam there was no factory manufacturing war matériel. For nearly a century, possession and use of arms were strictly forbidden by the colonial administrations. Importation was impossible, the neighboring countries being hostile to the Democratic Republic of Vietnam. The source of supply could only be the battlefront: take the matériel from the enemy and turn it against him. While carrying on the aggression against Vietnam the French Expeditionary Corps fulfilled another task: it became, unwittingly, the supplier of the Vietnam People's Army with French, even United States arms. In spite of their enormous efforts, the arms factories set up later on with make-

---

* Local Vietnamese militia units established under the auspices of the Japanese puppet government.

shift means were far from being able to meet all our needs. A great part of our military materials came from war booty.

As I have stressed, the Vietnam People's Army could at first bring into combat only small units such as platoons or companies. The regular forces were, at a given time, compelled to split up into companies operating separately to promote the extension of guerrilla activities while mobile battalions were maintained for more important actions. After each victorious combat, the people's armed forces marked a new step forward.

Tempered in combat and stimulated by victories, the guerrilla formations created conditions for the growth of the regional troops. And the latter, in their turn, promoted the development of the regular forces. For nine successive years, by following this heroic path bristling with difficulties, our People's Army grew up with a determination to win at all costs. It became an army of hundreds of thousands strong, successively amalgamating into regiments and divisions and directing toward a progressive standardization in organization and equipment. This force, ever more politically conscious, and better trained militarily, succeeded in fighting and defeating the five hundred thousand men of the French Expeditionary Corps who were equipped and supplied by the United States.

The Vietnamese army is indeed a national one. In fighting against imperialism and the traitors in its service, it has fought for national independence and the unity of the country. In its ranks are the finest sons of Vietnam, the most sincere patriots from all revolutionary classes, from all nationalities—majority as well as minority people. It symbolizes the irresistible rousing of the national conscience, the union of the entire Vietnamese people in the fight against imperialist aggression to save the country.

Our army is a *democratic army* because it fights for the people's democratic interests and for the defense of people's democratic power. Impregnated with the principles of democracy in its internal political life, it submits to a rigorous discipline, but one freely consented to.

Our army is a *people's army* because it defends the fundamental interests of the people, in the first place those of the toiling people, workers and peasants. As regards social composition, it comprises a great majority of picked fighters of peasant and worker origin, and intellectuals faithful to the cause of the revolution.

It is *the true army of the people, of toilers, the army of workers and peasants, led by the Party of the working class*. Throughout the war of national liberation, its aims of struggle were the very ones followed by the Party and people: independence of the nation, and land to the tillers. Since the return of peace, as a tool of proletarian dictatorship its mission is to defend the socialist revolution and socialist building in the North, to support the political struggle for the peaceful reunification of the country, and to contribute to the strengthening of peace in Indochina and Southeast Asia.

In the first of the ten points of his Oath of Honor, the fighter of the Vietnam People's Army swears:

"To sacrifice himself unreservedly for the fatherland, fight for the cause of national independence, democracy and socialism, under the leadership of the Vietnam Workers Party and of the government of the Democratic Republic, to build a peaceful, reunified, independent, democratic and prosperous Vietnam and contribute to the strengthening of peace in Southeast Asia and the world."

This is precisely what makes the Vietnam People's Army a true child of the people. The people, in return, give it unsparing affection and support. Therein lies the inexhaustible source of its power.

The Vietnam People's Army has been created by the Party, which ceaselessly trains and educates it. It has always been and will always be under the *leadership of the Party* which, alone, has made it into a revolutionary army, a true people's army. Since its creation and in the course of its development, this leadership by the Party has been made concrete on the organizational plane. The army has always had its political commissars. In the units, the military and political chiefs assume their responsibilities under the leadership of the Party committee at the corresponding echelon.

The People's Army is the instrument of the Party and of the revolutionary state for the accomplishment, in armed form, of the tasks of the revolution. Profound awareness of the aims of the Party, boundless loyalty to the cause of the nation and the working class, and a spirit of unreserved sacrifice are fundamental questions for the army, and questions of principle. Therefore, the political work in its ranks is of the first importance. *It is the soul of the army.* In instilling Marxist-Leninist ideology into the army, it aims at raising the army's political consciousness and ideological level, at strengthening the class position of its cadres and soldiers. During the liberation war, this work imbued the army with the policy of long-drawn-out resistance and the imperative necessity for the people and army to rely on their own strength to overcome difficulties. It instilled into the army the profound significance of mass mobilization in order to achieve rent reduction and agrarian reform, which had a decisive effect on the morale of the troops. In the new stage entered upon since the restoration of peace, political work centers on the line of socialist revolution in the North and of struggle for the reunification of the country.

But that is not all. Political work still bears upon the correct fulfillment in the army of the programs of the Party and government, and the setting-up of good relations with the population and between officers and men. It aims at maintaining and strengthening combativeness, uniting true patriotism with proletarian internationalism, developing revolutionary heroism and the great tradition of our army summed up in its slogan: "Resolved to fight, determined to win." Political work is the work of propaganda among and education of the masses; it is, furthermore, the organizational work of the Party in the army. We have always given particular attention to the strengthening of organizations of the Party in the units. From 35 to 40 percent of officers and armymen have joined it; among the officers, the percentage even exceeds 90 percent.

The Vietnam People's Army is always concerned to establish and maintain *good relations between officers and men as well as between the officers themselves.* Originating from the working strata, officers and men also serve the people's interests and unstintingly devote themselves to the cause of the nation and the working class. Of course every one of them has particular responsibilities which devolve upon him. But relations of comradeship based on political equality and fraternity of class have been established between them. The officer likes his men; he must not only guide them in their work and studies but take an interest in their life and take into consideration their desires and initiatives. As for the soldier, he must respect his superiors and correctly fulfill all their orders. The officer of the People's Army must set a good example from all points of view: to show himself to be resolute, brave, to ensure discipline and internal democracy, to know how to achieve perfect unity among his men. He must behave like a chief, a leader, vis-à-vis the masses in his unit. The basis of these relations between armymen and officers, like those between officers or between soldiers, is solidarity in the fight, and mutual affection of brother-in-arms, love at the same time pure and sublime, tested and forged in the battle, in the struggle for the defense of the fatherland and the people.

The Vietnam People's Army practices a strict discipline, allied to a wide internal democracy. Point two of its Oath of Honor requires: "The fighter must rigorously carry out the orders of his superiors and throw himself body and soul into the immediate and strict fulfillment of the tasks entrusted to him." Can we say that guerrilla warfare does not require severe discipline? Of course not. It is true that it asks the commander and leader to allow each unit or each region a certain margin of initiative in order to undertake every positive action that it might think opportune. But a centralized leadership and a unified command at a given degree always proved to be necessary. He who speaks of the army speaks of strict discipline.

Such a discipline is not in contradiction with the internal democracy of our troops. In cells, in executive committees of the Party at various levels, as well as in plenary meetings of fighting units, the application of principles of democratic centralism is the rule. The facts have proved that the more democracy is respected within the units, the more unity will be strengthened, discipline raised, and orders carried out. The combativeness of the army will thereby be all the greater.

The restoration of peace has created in Vietnam a new situation. The North is entirely liberated, but the South is still under the yoke of American imperialists and the Ngo Dinh Diem clique, their lackeys. North Vietnam has entered the stage of socialist revolution while the struggle is going on to free the South from colonial and feudal fetters. To safeguard peace and socialist construction, to help in making the North a strong rampart for the peaceful reunification of the country, the problem of forces of national defense should not be neglected. The People's Army must face the bellicose aims of the American imperialists and their lackeys and step by step become a regular and modern army.

First of all, it is important to stress that, in the process of its transformation into a regular and modern army, our army always remains a revolutionary army, a people's army. That is the fundamental characteristic that makes the people's regular and modern army in the North differ radically from Ngo Dinh Diem's army, a regular and modern army too, but antirevolutionary, antipopular, and in the hands of the people's enemies. The People's Army must necessarily see to the strengthening of the leadership of Party and political work. It must work further to consolidate the solidarity between officers and men, between the troops and the people, to raise the spirit of self-conscious discipline, while maintaining internal democracy. Taking steps to that end, the Party has, during the last years, given a prominent place to the activities of its organizations as well as to the political work in the army. Officers, warrant officers, and armymen, all of them have taken political courses to improve their understanding of the tasks of socialist revolution and the struggle for national reunification, consolidating their class standpoint and strengthening Marxist-Leninist ideology. This is a particularly important question, more especially as the People's Army has grown up in an agricultural country, and has in its ranks a great majority of toiling peasants and urban petty bourgeois. Our fighters have gone through a dogged political education and their morale has been forged in the combat. However, the struggle against the influence of bourgeois and petty bourgeois ideology remains necessary. Thanks to the strengthening of ideological work, the army has become an efficacious instrument in the service of proletarian dictatorship and has been entirely faithful to the cause of socialist revolution and national reunification. The new advances realized by it in the political plan have found their full expression in the movement "with giant strides, let us overfulfill the norms of the program," a broad mass movement which is developing among the working people in North Vietnam.

It is essential actively and firmly to continue, on the basis of a constant strengthening of political consciousness, the progressive transformation of the People's Army into a regular and modern army. Thanks to the development realized during the last years of the resistance war, our army, which was made up of infantrymen only, is now an *army composed of different branches*. If the problem of improvement of equipment and technique is important, that of cadres and soldiers capable of using them is more important. Our army has always been concerned with the training of officers and warrant officers of worker and peasant origin or revolutionary intellectuals tested under fire. It helps them increase their cultural and technical worth to become competent officers and warrant officers of a regular and modern army.

To raise the fighting power of the army, to bring about a strong centralization of command and a close cooperation between the different branches, it is indispensable to enforce *regulations fitted to a regular army*. It is not that nothing has been done in this field during the years of the resistance war; it is a matter of perfecting the existing regulations. The main thing is not to lose sight of the principle that any new regulation must draw its inspiration from the popular character of the army and from the absolute necessity of maintaining the leadership of the Party. Along with the general regulations, the status of officers has been promulgated; a correct system of wages has taken the place of the former regime of allowances in kind; the question of rewards and decorations has been regularized. All these measures have resulted in the strengthening of discipline and solidarity within the army, and of the sense of responsibility among officers and warrant officers as well as among soldiers.

Military training and political education are key tasks in the building of the army in peacetime. The questions of fighting regulations and of tactical concepts and appropriate tactical principles gain a particular importance. The question is to synthesize past experiences and to analyze well the concrete conditions of our army in organization and equipment, consider our economic structure, the terrain of the country—land of forests and jungles, of plains and fields. The question is to assimilate well the modern military science of the armies of the brother countries. Unceasing efforts are indispensable in the training of troops and the development of cadres.

For many years, the Vietnam People's Army was based on voluntary service: all officers and soldiers voluntarily enlisted for an undetermined period. Its ranks swelled by the affluence of youth always ready to answer the appeal of the fatherland. Since the return of peace, it has become necessary to replace voluntary service by *compulsory military service*. This substitution has met with warm response from the population. A great number of volunteers, after demobilization, returned to fields and factories; others are working in units assigned to production work, thus making an active contribution to the building of socialism. Conscription is enforced on the basis of the strengthening and development of the self-defense organizations in the communes, factories, and schools. The members of these paramilitary organizations are ready not only to rejoin the permanent army, of which they constitute a particularly important reserve, but also to insure the security and defense of their localities.

The People's Army was closely linked with the national liberation war, in the fire of which it was born and grew up. At present, its development should neither be disassociated from the building of socialism in the North, nor from the people's struggle for a reunified independent and democratic Vietnam. Confident of the people's affection and support, in these days of peace as during the war, the People's Army will achieve its tasks: to defend peace and the fatherland.

Dien Bien Phu

I. The Military Situation in Summer 1953

The winter of 1950 marked a change in the military situation in Vietnam. After their great victory in the border campaign, our forces undertook a series of important campaigns: the midland campaign, the Road No. 18 campaign, and the Ha Nam–Nam Dinh–Ninh Binh campaign in 1951; the Hoa Binh campaign in winter 1951 and spring 1952; the northwest campaign in winter 1952.

In these victorious campaigns, we put hundreds of thousands of enemy troops out of action and liberated vast areas in the mountainous regions of North Vietnam. The important provinces on the Vietnam-China border—Cao Bang, Lang Son, Lao Cai—the province of Hoa Binh on the road joining the Viet Bac to the Fourth Zone, the great part of the northwest region from the Red River to the Vietnam-Laos border, were successively liberated. Our rear was greatly expanded. In the mountainous regions of the north, the enemy occupied only Hai Ninh province in the northeast, and the town of Lai Chau and the fortified camp of Na San in the northwest.

While our main force scored successive victories on the main front, guerrilla warfare strongly developed in all the areas behind the enemy's lines in North Vietnam. Especially during the Hoa Binh campaign, our main force penetrated deep into the enemy rear on both sides of the Red River, combined its action with the local armed and semiarmed forces, enlarged the guerrilla bases and zones, and

---

This chapter has been compiled from the pamphlet "Dienbienphu" published in the collection *People's War, People's Army* (Hanoi, Foreign Languages Publishing House, 1961), pp. 153–217. The ordering of subchapters has been rearranged in integrating material from the appendix of the original edition into the main text. The text as a whole has been edited and condensed.

freed millions of our compatriots. The temporarily occupied zones of the enemy were limited to only one-third of the land and villages near the communication lines and important cities.

On the other fronts, in the enemy rear at Binh–Tri–Thien,* in the south of Central Vietnam, and in Nam Bo, guerrilla warfare was going on and developing, causing heavy losses to the enemy.

In summer 1953, the Pathet Lao† forces, combined with the Vietnam people's volunteers, launched a sudden attack on the town of Samneu. The bulk of the garrison was annihilated; the town of Samneu and vast zones of upper Laos were liberated, thus creating a new threat to the enemy.

Throughout North Vietnam, we observed that from winter 1950 onward, our forces constantly held the initiative in operations, driving the enemy more and more onto the defensive. To save this situation, the enemy made an urgent appeal to the American imperialists whose intervention in the aggressive war in Indochina had been constantly on the increase. During this period, the French government had several times changed the commanders of the French Expeditionary Corps. After the border campaign, it sent to Indochina the famous General de Lattre de Tassigny. As is known, De Tassigny strove to concentrate his troops, fortify his defense lines, and launch an attack in the direction of Hoa Binh in order to recapture the initiative in the operations, but he was finally defeated. His successor, General Salan,‡ was, in his turn, an impotent witness to severe defeats of the Expeditionary Corps on the northwest and upper Laos fronts.

It was in this critical situation that the American imperialists availed themselves of the armistice in Korea to step up their intervention in Indochina. And the "Navarre plan" expressed the new

---

* Provinces in Central Vietnam. Their full names are Quang Binh, Quang Tri, Thua Thien.
† Free Laotian movement.
‡ Commander in chief in Indochina in 1952–1953. Later staged abortive putsch against the French government in Paris in April 1961.

Franco-American scheme to prolong and extend the aggressive war in our country.

II. The Enemy's New Scheme: The "Navarre Plan"

In mid-1953, with the consent of Washington, the French government appointed General Navarre* commander in chief of the French Expeditionary Corps in Indochina.

Navarre and the French and American generals estimated that the more critical situation of the French Expeditionary Corps was due to the extreme dispersal of French forces in thousands of posts and garrisons scattered on all fronts to cope with our guerrilla warfare; as a result, they lacked a strong mobile force to face the attacks of our main force. During that time, our forces were constantly growing, our mobile forces increased day by day, the scale of our campaigns became larger and larger.

Basing their plans on this estimation, Navarre and the French and American generals mapped out a plan to save the day, hoping to reverse the situation and to win, in a short period of time, a decisive strategic success.

The Navarre plan envisaged the organization of a very strong strategic mobile force, capable of breaking all our offensives and annihilating the main part of our forces later on. For this purpose, Navarre ordered the regroupment of his picked European and African units, which were to be withdrawn from a number of posts. At the same time, new units from France, West Germany, North Africa, and Korea were rushed to the Indochina front.

In carrying out this plan, the enemy met a great contradiction, a serious difficulty: if they kept their forces scattered in order to occupy

---

* General Henri-Eugene Navarre replaced Salan as commander in chief in Indochina in spring 1953. The "Navarre plan" called for French reinforcements and for augmenting the puppet armies in order to destroy the communist forces by the end of 1955. On the basis of this plan, the United States increased its aid.

territory, it would be impossible for them to organize a strong mobile force; but if they reduced their occupation forces to regroup them, our guerrillas would take advantage of the new weakness of their position to increase their activity, their posts and garrisons would be threatened or annihilated, the local puppet authorities overthrown, and the occupied zones reduced. Navarre sought to get round the difficulty by developing the puppet forces on a large scale to replace European and African troops transferred toward the regrouping points. In fact, this treacherous idea was nothing new and had already been applied by De Tassigny. Faced with the new dangerous situation, Navarre and the French and American generals decided to organize fifty-four new battalions of puppet troops immediately and to double this number in the following year. Later on, the enemy had to acknowledge that this expedient did not help, because the increase in the puppet forces really only represented a quantitative increase at the expense of the quality of the units.

With their great mobile forces, the Franco-American imperialists conceived a rather audacious plan aimed at annihilating our main force and ending the war within eighteen months.

On the one hand, they decided to concentrate their forces in the Red River delta in autumn and winter 1953 to open barbarous mopping-up operations to destroy our guerrilla bases; on the other hand, they planned to launch attacks on our free zone in order to attract and exhaust our main forces. Simultaneously, they intended to create new battalions of puppet soldiers and to regroup new units.

After winter, that is, after the season of big operations in North Vietnam, at the beginning of 1954, availing themselves of the fact that our army would at this time be resting, they could transfer to the South the greater part of their mobile forces. At this period, the climatic conditions in the South were favorable to their activity. Their intention was to open big operations to occupy all our free zones, particularly the Fifth and Ninth zones. To occupy all these regions would be for them tantamount to removing the gravest threats faced by them. Owing to the impetus provided by these victories, they would recruit new puppet units while continuing the regrouping of their mobile forces to prepare a decisive offensive on the front in the North.

If the plan were working well, in autumn and winter 1954, they would bring back to North Vietnam their greatly increased forces, still under the influence of the enthusiasm created by their recent victories. In launching a major offensive against our bases, they would have occupied new territories, annihilated the bulk of our main forces to end the aggressive war, and would have permanently transformed the whole of Vietnam into a colony and a Franco-American military base.

According to this plan, in summer 1953 the enemy concentrated their forces. At the beginning of autumn, enemy mobile forces reached a total of eighty-four battalions in the whole of Indochina.

To carry out the first phase of the Navarre plan, the enemy concentrated in the Red River delta more than 50 percent of their mobile forces and declared that they were changing over to the offensive in order to regain the initiative in the operations. Scores of battalions launched savage mopping-up operations in the delta in order to consolidate the rear. Units of paratroops attacked Lang Son, and it was announced that we had suffered heavy losses, although in fact our losses were insignificant. They launched a great attack on Nho Quan and on the region bordering Ninh Binh and Thanh Hoa provinces and declared that the occupation of these provinces was imminent. But their troops had to withdraw with heavy losses.

In the northwest, the enemy withdrew from Na San to the delta. Formerly, Na San had been considered by them as "the second Verdun," blocking the road to the southward advance of communism, but when they had to evacuate it in order to escape destruction, they declared that Na San had lost all military interest. Before the evacuation, they saw that their myrmidons organized gangs of bandits in rather extensive areas to the north of this locality.

On November 20, 1953, the enemy dropped considerable paratroop forces into the valley of Dien Bien Phu. Their plan was to reinforce Dien Bien Phu, then to go to Tuan Giao and Son La, reoccupy Na San, and join it to Lai Chau. Thus, Dien Bien Phu would become a stronghold threatening the flank of our northwest base. This new entrenched position would force us to scatter our troops between the delta and the mountains and would protect upper Laos. It would constitute a springboard for their next big offensive, one column pushing from the plain, the other from Dien Bien Phu to the delta. Thus, Dien Bien Phu became, little by little, a key position in the Navarre plan.

It was clear that in this autumn-winter period all enemy activities had one aim: to regroup forces, to strengthen the rear, to exhaust and scatter our forces, to prepare conditions for their coming great attacks. They thought that the first phase of their plan had been successful when our autumn-winter campaign began.

III. Our Plan in Winter 1953–Spring 1954 and the Evolution of the Military Situation on the Various Fronts

After the cease-fire in Korea, we anticipated the new Franco-American war scheme to expand their forces and extend the aggressive war in Indochina. Early in summer 1953, their military situation deteriorated. Taking advantage of the serious difficulties met by the French Expeditionary Corps following its successive defeats from 1950 onward, the American imperialists intervened more openly and more actively in the war in Indochina.

On our side, the army and people were transported with the impetus of the victorious big campaign; guerrilla warfare was developing in all regions under enemy control. Our army had accumulated more fighting experience, and its tactical and technical level had been raised through the summing-up of the experience of the military campaign and the training courses. Moreover, a new factor appeared: this was the policy of systematic rent reduction, and the carrying-out of land reform decided by the Party and government. After the political course on the mobilization of the peasant masses, our cadres and armymen saw more clearly what the objective of our struggle was: national independence, and land to the tillers. Hence, their combativeness increased greatly. More than ever, our army was transported with enthusiasm, ready to go to the front to annihilate the enemy.

We were determined to break the Navarre plan and hold the new plot of the Franco-American imperialists in check. But how to do it? Faced with the new difficulties, it was necessary to analyze the situation to determine a correct line of action which ensured success.

The concrete problem was: the enemy was concentrating forces in the Red River delta and launching attacks on our free zones. Now, had we to concentrate our forces to face the enemy or to mobilize them for attacks in other directions? The problem was difficult. In concentrating our forces to fight the enemy in the delta we could defend our free zone: but here the enemy was still strong, and we could easily be decimated. On the other hand, in attacking in other directions with our main forces, we could exploit the vulnerable points of the enemy to annihilate the bulk of their forces; but our free zone would thus be threatened.

After a careful study of the situation, the Party's Central Committee issued the following slogan to break the Navarre plan: "Dynamism, initiative, mobility, and rapidity of decision in face of new situations." Keeping the initiative, we should concentrate our forces to attack strategic points which were relatively vulnerable. If we succeeded in keeping the initiative, we could achieve successes and compel the enemy to scatter their forces, and, finally, their plan to threaten our free zone could not be realized. On the other hand, if we were driven onto the defensive, not only could we not annihilate the many enemy forces, but our own force could easily suffer losses, and, finally, it would be difficult for us to break the enemy threat.

On all fronts, our winter-spring plan was the expression of this strategic conception. In October 1953, hundreds of thousands of persons were mobilized to hasten the preparations. In mid-November, our main forces went to the front. The winter-spring campaign began.

Liberation of Lai Chau

On December 10, 1953, we opened fire on the Lai Chau front. Formerly, we had annihilated or forced to surrender thousands of bandits in the regions of Muong La and Thuan Chau. On that very night, we wiped out the outpost of Paham, about twenty miles from Lai Chau. Aware of the presence of our main forces, the enemy was very afraid and ordered the garrison to withdraw from Lai Chau and to rally at Dien Bien Phu by the mountain tracks.

Our troops were ordered to march on to liberate Lai Chau, while one column attacked westward, cutting off the enemy's retreat to encircle and annihilate him.

On December 12, Lai Chau was liberated.

On December 13, we annihilated the enemy in retreat at Muong Pon. After ten days and ten nights of fighting, pursuit, and encirclement in a mountainous region, we liberated the remaining part of the zone occupied by the enemy in Lai Chau province. The enemy lost twenty-four companies.

It was the first great success of our winter-spring campaign. It strengthened the faith of our army and people. Moreover, it obliged the enemy to send reinforcements to Dien Bien Phu. It was the first miscarriage of Navarre's regrouping plan. Our troops began to encircle the fortified entrenched camp of Dien Bien Phu.

The Liberation of Thakhek and Several Regions in Middle Laos

Parallel with the preparations to attack Lai Chau, orders were given to the Vietnam people's volunteers to cooperate with the

Pathet Lao troops to launch an offensive on the middle Laos front, where the enemy was relatively vulnerable. At the beginning of December, the enemy became aware of our activity and quickly rushed reinforcements to this sector. On December 22, the Vietnamese and Laotian units carried by storm the post of Banaphao, a strong entrenched position which controlled the frontier. Other units struck deep into the enemy's rear. After a series of victories, the Vietnamese and Laotian units made very quick progress toward Thakhek, at the same time pursuing the enemy in his flight along Road No. 9.

Bewildered, the enemy withdrew from Thakhek to Seno, a military base near Savannakhet, losing on the way three battalions of infantry and one artillery unit. On December 27, the Pathet Lao units and the Vietnam people's volunteers entered Thakhek and reached the bank of the Mekong. The liberated zones were extended to Road No. 9.

This was the second important victory in the winter-spring campaign. To face our activity in time, the enemy had to withdraw mobile forces from the Red River delta and from the South, to send them to Seno. To impede the Vietnamese and Laotian units in an advance into lower Laos, they strengthened this base. Navarre was obliged to scatter his forces over several points.

The Liberation of the Bolovens Highland and the Town of Attopeu

Simultaneously with the attack on the middle Laos front, one unit of the Laotian and Vietnamese forces crossed dangerous mountainous regions and advanced into lower Laos, where it effected a junction with local armed forces.

On December 30 and 31, the Laotian and Vietnamese units defeated an enemy battalion in the region of Attopeu and liberated this town. Exploiting their victory, they advanced toward Saravane and liberated the whole Bolovens Highland to the south of Road No. 9. The enemy had to send reinforcements to Pakse.

The Liberation of Kontum and the North of the Western Highlands of Central Vietnam

In spite of defeats at various points, the enemy remained subjective in making estimations. Owing to the easy occupation of Dien Bien Phu, the enemy thought we were incapable of attacking it. According to them, the entrenched camp was too strong for our troops. Moreover, they thought that the distance which separated it from our rear created insuperable obstacles for us in the supply of food. They thought we had passed to the attack at different points because we did not know how to deal with Dien Bien Phu; they thought that shortly we would be obliged to evacuate the northwest because of supply difficulties; then they would find the means to destroy a part of our main forces and would continue execution of their plan: the occupation of Tuan Giao and Son La and the return to Na San.

It was this same subjective estimation which made them launch the Atlanta operation against the south of Phu Yen in the Fifth Zone. This well-prepared attack was the first step in the occupation of our whole free zone in the south of Central Vietnam, as foreseen by the Navarre plan.

Our strategic principle was: "Dynamism, initiative." Our troops in the Fifth Zone received the order to leave behind only a small part of their forces to cope with the enemy, while the bulk would continue their regroupment and pass to the offensive in the north of the Western Highlands. We opened the campaign on January 26. The following day, we took the Mandel subsector, the strongest subsector of the enemy. The post of Dak To was taken, and we liberated the whole north of Kontum province. On February 17, we liberated the town of Kontum, wiped out the enemy in the whole north of the Western Highlands, and advanced as far as Road No. 19. Meanwhile, we attacked Pleiku. The enemy was at a loss and had to stop the offensive in the coastal plains of the Fifth Zone and withdraw many units from middle Laos and the three Vietnamese provinces of Quang Binh, Quang Tri, and Thua Thien to reinforce the Western Highlands.

This was another victory for our forces in the winter-spring campaign. It proved once more the correctness of the guiding principle of the Central Committee. The enemy was more and more obviously driven onto the defensive. They had to mobilize forces from the Red River delta to reinforce middle Laos, and afterward from middle Laos to reinforce the Western Highlands. They had concentrated forces to make a lightning offensive against our Fifth Zone but had to stop their action in order to protect themselves against our blows.

Our offensive on the Western Highlands was victoriously carried on till June 1954 and scored many more successes, particularly the resounding victory at An Khe where we cut to pieces the Mobile Regiment No. 100 which had just returned from Korea, thus liberating An Khe. Our troops captured in this battle a large number of vehicles and a great quantity of ammunition.

The Liberation of Phong Saly and the Nam Ou River Basin, the Push Forward Toward Luang Prabang

Dien Bien Phu was encircled after the defeat of Lai Chau. The French High Command tried to effect junction between the Dien Bien Phu entrenched camp and upper Laos by increasing their occupation forces along the Nam Ou River basin as far as Muong Khoua, intending to establish liaison with Dien Bien Phu.

To put them on the wrong track, to annihilate more of their forces, to weaken them more, and oblige them to continue to scatter their troops in order to create favorable conditions for our preparations at Dien Bien Phu, orders were given to our units to combine with the Pathet Lao forces to launch an offensive in the Nam Ou River basin.

On January 26, the Vietnamese and Laotian forces attacked Muong Khoua where they destroyed one European regiment; then, exploiting this success, they wiped out the enemy in the Nam Ou River basin and came within striking distance of Luang Prabang, while one column pushed northward and liberated Phong Saly.

Before our strong offensive, the enemy had to withdraw mobile units from the Red River delta to send them to upper Laos. Thus, Navarre was obliged to scatter his forces still further.

Our Successes in the Enemy Rear in the Red River Delta, the Three Provinces of Quang Binh, Quang Tri, Thua Thien, and in Nam Bo

While the enemy was in difficulties on all fronts, our local armed forces, people's militia, and guerrillas effectively exploited the situation in the enemy rear and strongly combined activity with the front.

In the Red River delta, a series of enemy fortified camps were destroyed, and Road No. 5 was seriously threatened, being sometimes cut for weeks together. In two great attacks on the Cat Bi (March 7, 1954) and Gia Lam airfields (March 8, 1954) our armymen destroyed seventy-eight enemy planes.

At Binh–Tri–Thien, and in the southernmost part of Central Vietnam, our armymen's activity was intense; they expanded the guerrilla bases, increased propaganda work directed to the enemy and won many successes.

In Nam Bo, through the whole winter-spring period our armymen pushed forward their combined action, and obtained very great successes: more than one hundred enemy posts and watchtowers were either destroyed or evacuated, many localities were liberated, and the number of soldiers crossing to our side amounted to several thousands.

The development of hostilities until March 1954 showed that, to a great extent, the Navarre plan had collapsed. The enemy's plan to concentrate was essentially foiled. At this moment, enemy mobile forces were no longer concentrated in the Red River delta; they were scattered over several points: Luang Prabang and Muong Sai in upper Laos, Seno in middle Laos, the south of the Western Highlands in the Fifth Zone, and large forces were pinned down at Dien Bien Phu. In the Red River delta, what was left of their mobile forces amounted to only twenty regiments, but a great part of these forces was no longer mobile and had to be scattered in order to protect the communication lines, particularly Road No. 5.

The situation of hostilities developed contrary to the enemy's will.

Navarre intended to concentrate his forces in the Red River delta with a view to recovering the initiative, but we obliged him to scatter his forces everywhere and passively take measures to protect himself.

He intended to annihilate a part of our main forces, but it was not our main forces but his that suffered heavy losses. He intended to attack our free zone, but instead his rear was severely attacked by us. Thus we threatened his whole system of disposition of forces.

However, the Franco-American generals did not want to recognize this disastrous truth. They still thought our activity in winter 1953–spring 1954 had reached its peak, that our withdrawal was beginning, that we lacked the strength to continue our activity, and that their favorable moment was approaching.

As a result, in order to get back the initiative, on March 12, the enemy resumed the Atlanta plan which had been interrupted, and opened an attack by landing at Quy Nhon.

Not for a moment did they believe that on the following day, March 13, 1954, we would launch a large-scale attack on the Dien Bien Phu entrenched camp. Thus, the historic Dien Bien Phu campaign began.

IV. The Historic Dien Bien Phu Campaign

Dien Bien Phu is a large plain about eleven miles long and three to five miles wide in the mountainous zone of the northwest. It is the biggest and richest of the four plains in this hilly region close to the Vietnam-Laos frontier. It is situated at the junction of important roads, running to the northeast toward Lai Chau; to the east and southeast toward Tuan Giao, Son La, Na San; to the west toward Luang Prabang; and to the south toward Samneu. In the theater of operations of Bac Bo and upper Laos, Dien Bien Phu is a strategic position of first importance, capable of becoming an infantry and air base of extreme efficiency.

At the beginning, there were at Dien Bien Phu only ten enemy battalions, but they were gradually reinforced to cope with our offensive. When we launched the attack, the enemy forces totaled seventeen battalions and ten companies, comprising chiefly Europeans and Africans and units of highly trained paratroops. Moreover, the camp had three battalions of artillery, one battalion of sappers, one armored company, a transport unit of two hundred trucks and a permanent squadron of twelve aircraft: altogether, 16,200 men.

The forces were distributed in three subsectors which had to support one another and comprised forty-nine strongpoints. Each had defensive autonomy; several were grouped in "complex defense centers" equipped with mobile forces and artillery and were surrounded by trenches and barbed wire hundreds of feet thick. Each subsector comprised several strongly fortified defense centers.

But the most important was the central subsector situated in the middle of the Muong Thanh village, the chief town of Dien Bien Phu. Two-thirds of the forces of the garrison were concentrated here. It had several connected defense centers protecting the command post, the artillery and commissariat bases, and at the same time the airfield. To the east, well-situated hills formed the most important defense system of the subsector. Dien Bien Phu was considered by the enemy to be an unassailable and impregnable fortress.

In fact, the central subsector did have rather strong forces, and the heights in the east could not be attacked easily. Besides, the artillery and armored forces could break every attempt at intervention through the plain, a system of barbed wire and trenches would permit the enemy to decimate and repel any assault, and the mobile forces formed by the battalions of paratroops, whose action was combined with that of the defense centers, could counterattack and break any offensive. The northern subsector comprised the defense centers of Him Lam, Doc Lap, and Ban Keo. The very strong positions of Him Lam and Doc Lap were required to check all attacks of our troops coming from Tuan Giao and Lai Chau.

As for the southern subsector, also known as Hong Cum subsector, its purpose was to break any offensive coming from the south and to protect the communication way with upper Laos.

Their artillery was divided between two bases: one at Muong Thanh, the other at Hong Cum, arranged in such a way as to support each other and to support all the surrounding strong points.

Dien Bien Phu had two airfields: besides the main field at Muong Thanh, there was a reserve field at Hong Cum; they linked with Hanoi and Haiphong in an airlift which insured seventy to eighty transports of supply daily.

The reconnaissance planes and fighters of the permanent squadron constantly flew over the entire region. The planes from the Gia Lam and Cat Bi airbases had the task of strafing and bombing our army. Navarre asserted that with such powerful forces and so strong a defense system Dien Bien Phu was "an impregnable fortress. . . ." The American General O'Daniel* who paid a visit to the base

---

* Lt. Gen. John ("Iron Mike") O'Daniel was only one of many high-ranking American and French military officials who inspected Dien Bien Phu during

shared this opinion. From this subjective point of view, the enemy came to the conclusion that our troops had little chance in an attack on Dien Bien Phu. They even considered that an attack on our part would be a good opportunity for them to inflict a defeat on us.

On our side, after the liberation of Lai Chau, the attack upon Dien Bien Phu was on the agenda. We considered that the base, well entrenched as it was, also had vulnerable points. In attacking it, we faced difficulties in strategy, tactics, and supply; but these difficulties could be overcome. After having analyzed the situation, and weighed the pros and cons, we decided to attack Dien Bien Phu according to the method: to take no risks. Our tactic would be to attack each enemy defense center, each part of the entrenched camp, thus creating conditions for the launching of a general offensive to annihilate the whole camp.

Three months had passed from the occupation of Dien Bien Phu by enemy paratroops to the launching of our campaign. During that time, the enemy did their utmost to consolidate their defense system, gather reinforcements, dig new trenches, and strengthen their entrenchments.

On our side, the army and people actively prepared the offensive, carrying out the orders of the Party's Central Committee and the government; the army and people mustered all their strength to guarantee the success of the winter-spring campaign, to which Dien Bien Phu was the key. Our troops succeeded in liberating the surrounding regions, isolating Dien Bien Phu, obliging the enemy to scatter forces and thus reduce their possibilities of sending reinforcements to the battlefield. We made motor roads, cleared the tracks to haul up artillery pieces, built casemates for the artillery, prepared the ground for the offensive and encirclement; in short, transformed the relief of the battlefield terrain with a view to solving the tactical

---

the four months that the fortress was held by the French prior to the main Vietminh attacks. They unanimously judged it a sound position. (See Bernard Fall, *Street Without Joy*, p. 318.)

problems. We overcame very great difficulties. We called upon our local compatriots to supply food, to set up supply lines hundreds of miles long from Thanh Hoa or Phu Tho to the northwest, crossing very dangerous areas and very high hills. We used every means to carry food and ammunition to the front. Our troops and voluntary workers ceaselessly went to the front and actively participated in the preparations under the bombs and bullets of enemy aircraft.

In the first week of March, the preparations were completed: the artillery had solid casemates, the operational bases were established, food and ammunition were available in sufficient quantity. After having been educated in the aim and significance of the campaign, all officers and soldiers were filled with a very strong determination to annihilate the enemy, as they were persuaded that only the destruction of the Dien Bien Phu entrenched camp would bring the Navarre plan to complete failure.

On March 13, 1954, our troops received the order to launch an offensive against Dien Bien Phu.

The campaign proceeded in three phases: in the first phase we destroyed the northern subsector; in the second, the longest and bitterest one, we took the heights in the east of the central subsector and tightened our encirclement; in the third, we launched the general offensive and annihilated the enemy.

The First Phase: Destruction of the Northern Subsector

This phase began on March 13 and ended on March 17. On the night of March 13, we annihilated the very strong defense center of Him Lam which overlooked the road from Tuan Giao to Dien Bien Phu. The battle was very sharp, the enemy artillery concentrated its fire and poured scores of thousands of shells on our assaulting waves. Our troops carried the position in the night. This first victory had very deep repercussions on the development of the whole campaign.

During the night of March 14, we concentrated our forces to attack the defense center of Doc Lap, the second strong defense sector of the northern subsector which overlooked the road from Lai Chau to Dien Bien Phu. The battle went on till dawn. The enemy used every means to repel our forces, fired scores of thousands of shells and sent their mobile forces protected by tanks from Muong Thanh to support their position. Our troops fought heroically, took the strong point, and repelled the enemy reinforcements.

The third and last defense center of the northern subsector, the Ban Keo post, became isolated and was threatened by us. This was a less strong position, manned by a garrison chiefly made up of puppet soldiers. On March 17, the whole garrison left its positions and surrendered. After the loss of the northern subsector, the central subsector, now exposed on its eastern and northern flanks, was threatened.

In the fighting in the first phase, the correctness of our tactical decisions, the good organization of our defense and antiaircraft activity reduced the efficiency of the enemy artillery and air force. Besides, our artillery fire, which was very accurate, inflicted heavy losses on the enemy. The main airfield was threatened. Our antiaircraft batteries went into action for the first time and brought down enemy planes. But above all, it was by their heroic spirit, their high spirit of sacrifice, and their will to win, that our troops distinguished themselves during these battles.

The great and resounding victory which ended the first phase of operations stirred our army and people and gave each and every one faith in final victory.

As for the enemy, despite their heavy losses, they still had confidence in the power of resistance of the central subsector, in the strength of their artillery and air force. They even expected that we would suffer heavy losses and would be obliged to give up the offensive; and especially, that if the campaign was protected our supply lines would be cut and that the great logistic difficulties thus created would force us to withdraw.

The Second Phase: Occupation of the Hills in the East and Encirclement of the Central Subsector

The second phase was the most important of the campaign. We had to deal with the central subsector, in the middle of the Muong Thanh plain, and new difficulties arose in the conduct of the operations. Our troops had to work actively to complete the operations; they had to dig a vast network of trenches, from the neighboring hills to the plain, to encircle the central subsector and cut it off from the southern sector. This advance of our lines which encircled the enemy positions was made at the cost of fierce fighting. By every means the enemy tried to upset our preparations by the fire of their air force and artillery. However, our troops drew closer to their positions with irresistible power in the course of uninterrupted fighting.

During the night of March 30, the second phase began. We launched a large-scale attack of long duration to annihilate the heights in the east and a certain number of strong points in the west in order to tighten our encirclement, and to hamper and cut off the supplies to the garrison. On this night of March 30, we concentrated important forces to attack simultaneously the five fortified heights in the east. On this same night, we succeeded in capturing Hills E-1, D-1, and C-1 but could not take Hill A-1, the most important of all. The defense line constituted by these heights was the key to the defensive system of the central subsector: its loss would lead to the fall of Dien Bien Phu. Consequently, the fight here was at its fiercest. Particularly on Hill A-1, the last height which protected the command post, the battle lasted until April 4. Every inch of ground was hotly disputed. Finally, we occupied half of the position, while the enemy, entrenched in casemates and trenches, continued to resist in the other half. While this fighting was going on, the garrison received paratroop reinforcements.

On April 9, the enemy launched a counterattack to reoccupy Hill

C-1. The battle went on for four days and nights, and the position was occupied half by the enemy and half by us.

While the situation in the east was static, in the north and in the west our encirclement grew tighter and tighter. The lines of both sides drew nearer and nearer; in some points they were only ten to fifteen yards away from each other. From the occupied positions to the battlefields northward and westward, the fire of our artillery and mortars pounded the enemy without letup. Day and night the fighting went on. We exhausted the enemy by harassing them, firing constantly at their lines, and at the same time tried to take their strong points one by one with a tactic of combined nibbling advance and full-scale attack.

In mid-April, after the destruction of several enemy positions in the north and west, our lines reached the airfield, then cut it from west to east. Our encirclement grew still tighter; the fighting was still more fierce. The enemy launched several violent counterattacks supported by tanks and aircraft aimed at taking ground from us and obliging us to loosen our encirclement. On April 24, the most violent counterattack was launched with the aim of driving us off the airfield: after inflicting heavy losses on the enemy, we remained the master, and the airfield stayed in our control.

The territory occupied by the enemy shrank in size day by day, and they were driven into a one-mile square. It was threatened by our heavy fire. The enemy's supply problem became more and more critical. The airfield had been out of action for a long time; all supplies were being dropped by parachute. But as the enemy zone was so narrow, and their pilots feared our antiaircraft fire and dared not fly low, only a part of the parachutes carrying food and ammunition fell into the enemy positions, and the bulk of them fell on our ground; thus we poured shells parachuted by the enemy on the entrenched camp.

Throughout the second phase, the situation was extremely tense. The American interventionists sent more bombers and transport planes to support the Dien Bien Phu base. The enemy bombers were very active; they ceaselessly bombed our positions, dropped napalm bombs to burn down the vegetation on the heights surrounding Dien Bien Phu, and bombed points that they took for our artillery bases. Day and night they shelled our supply lines, dropped blockbusters on the roads, showered the roads with delayed-action and "butterfly" bombs,* in an endeavor to cut our supply lines. These desperate efforts did not achieve the desired results. They could not check the flow of hundreds of thousands of voluntary workers, pack horses, and transport cars carrying food and ammunition to the front. They could not stop us from carrying out our plan of encirclement, the condition of their destruction.

The French and American generals clearly saw the danger of the destruction of the Dien Bien Phu entrenched camp.

At this moment, the High Command of the French Expeditionary Corps thought of gathering together the remaining forces for an attack on our rear, in the direction of the Viet Bac base, to cut our supply lines and oblige us to withdraw for lack of food and ammunition. But it could not carry out this plan. Moreover, it feared that a still more severe defeat could be the result of so foolhardy an action. At another time it intended to regroup the Dien Bien Phu garrison in several columns which would try to break through our encirclement and open a way toward upper Laos at all costs. Finally, it had to give up this plan and continue to defend its positions.

The Third Phase: Annihilation of the Enemy

On May 1 the third phase began. From May 1 to May 6, following several successive attacks, we occupied Hill C-1, Hill A-1, which was the key of the last defensive system of the central subsector, and several other strong points from the foot of the hills in the east to the Nam Gion River, and, finally some positions in the west.

---

* Small grenadelike explosives which dropped from the air but whose downward flight was retarded by a set of wings. They would touch down gently and detonate only when stepped on or violently disturbed.

The enemy was driven into a square mile area and exposed to our fire. There was no fortified height to protect them. The problem of supply became very grave. Their situation was critical: the last hour of the entrenched camp had come.

In the afternoon of May 7, from the east and west, we launched a massive combined attack upon the headquarters at Muong Thanh. At several posts, the enemy hoisted the white flag and surrendered. At 5:30 P.M. we seized the headquarters: General de Castries* and his staff were captured.

The remaining forces at Dien Bien Phu surrendered. The prisoners of war were well treated by our troops.

The "Determined to fight and to win" banner of our army fluttered high in the valley of Dien Bien Phu. On this very night, we attacked the south subsector. The whole garrison of more than two thousand men was captured.

The historic Dien Bien Phu campaign ended in our complete victory. Our troops had fought with an unprecedented heroism for fifty-five days and fifty-five nights.

During this time, our troops were very active in all theaters of operation in coordination with the main front.

In the enemy rear in the Red River delta, they destroyed, one after another, a large number of positions and seriously threatened Road No. 5.

In the Fifth Zone, they attacked Road No. 19, annihilated the mobile Regiment No. 100, liberated An Khe, penetrated deep into the region of Cheo Reo, and threatened Pleiku and Ban Me Thuot.

Our troops were also very active in the region of Hue and in Nam Bo.

In middle Laos, the Vietnamese and Laotian units increased their activity on Road No. 9 and advanced southward.

Our troops won victories on all fronts.

---

* Fortress commandant at Dien Bien Phu. He was perhaps ill suited to the job since his military reputation rested on his work in the armored cavalry as commander of a mobile group in the Red River delta.

Such are the broad outlines of the military situation in winter 1953 and spring 1954.

On all fronts, we put out of action 112,000 enemy troops and brought down or destroyed on the ground 177 planes.

At Dien Bien Phu, we put out of action 16,200 enemy troops including the whole staff of the entrenched camp, 1 general, 16 colonels, 1,749 officers and warrant officers, brought down or destroyed 62 planes of all types, and seized all the enemy's armaments, ammunition, and equipment, as well as more than 30,000 parachutes.

These great victories of the Vietnam People's Army and people as a whole at Dien Bien Phu and on the other fronts had smashed to pieces the Navarre plan, and impeded the attempts of the Franco-American imperialists to prolong and extend the war. These great victories liberated the North of Vietnam, contributed to the success of the Geneva Conference and the restoration of peace in Indochina on the basis of respect of the sovereignty, independence, national unity, and territorial integrity of Vietnam and of the two friendly countries, Cambodia and Laos.

These are glorious pages of our history, of our People's Army and our people. They illustrate the striking success of our Party in leading the movement for national liberation against the French imperialists and the American interventionists.

Strategic Direction

The strategic direction of the Dien Bien Phu campaign and of the winter 1953–spring 1954 campaign in general *was a typical success of the revolutionary military line of Marxism-Leninism applied to the actual conditions of the revolutionary war in Vietnam.*

The enemy's strategy in the Navarre plan was aimed at solving the great difficulties of the aggressive war, in an attempt to save their situation and win a decisive victory.

Our strategy, applied in this winter-spring campaign, was the strategy of a people's war and of a revolutionary army. Starting from a thorough analysis of the enemy's contradictions, and developing to the utmost the offensive spirit of an army still weak materially but particularly heroic, it aimed at concentrating our forces in the enemy's relatively exposed sectors, at annihilating their manpower and liberating a part of the territory, compelling them to scatter their forces, thus creating favorable conditions for a decisive victory.

The war unleashed by the Franco-American imperialists was an unjust war of aggression. This colonial war had no other aim than to occupy and dominate our country. The aggressive nature and object of the war forced the enemy to scatter his forces to occupy the invaded localities. The carrying-out of the war was for the French Expeditionary Corps a continuous process of dispersal of forces. The enemy divisions were split into regiments, then into battalions, companies, and platoons, to be stationed at thousands of points and posts on the various battlefronts of the Indochina theater of operations. The enemy found himself face to face with a *contradiction:* without scattering his forces, it was impossible for him to occupy the invaded territory; in scattering his forces, he put himself in difficulties. His scattered units would fall easy prey to our troops; his mobile forces would be more and more reduced; and the shortage of troops would be all the more acute. On the other hand, if he concentrated his forces to move from the defensive position and cope with us with more initiative, the occupation forces would be weakened and it would be difficult for him to hold the invaded territory. Now if the enemy gives up occupied territory, the very aim of the war of reconquest is defeated.

Throughout the resistance war, while the enemy's forces were more and more scattered, *our strategic line was to extend guerrilla warfare everywhere.* And in each theater of operations, we chose the positions where the enemy was relatively weak to concentrate our forces there and annihilate his manpower. As a result, the more we fought, the stronger we became; our forces grew with every passing day. *And parallel with the process of the enemy's dispersal of forces, our people's revolutionary armed forces unceasingly intensified and extended guerrilla activities, while without cease carrying on the work of concentration and building up regular units. In the fighting, in the course of the formation of our forces, we went gradually from independent companies operating separately to mobile battalions, then from battalions to regiments and divisions.* The first appearance of our divisions in the battles in the Vietnam-China border region marked our first major victory, which drove the enemy into a disadvantageous situation.

It was after the frontier campaign that General de Lattre de Tassigny was dispatched to Vietnam to save the situation. De Tassigny had seen the problem. He was aware of the too great dispersal of French forces and of the danger arising from our guerrilla warfare. So he energetically regrouped his forces and launched extremely fierce and barbarous mopping-up operations to "pacify" the areas behind the enemy's lines in the Red River delta. But he found himself very soon face to face with the same insoluble contradiction. By concentrating his forces he found it impossible to extend occupied territory. De Tassigny had, in the end, to resign himself to scattering his forces to launch the famous offensive on Hoa Binh. The results were not long in coming. While his crack troops suffered very heavy losses at Hoa Binh, our guerrilla bases in the delta were restored and extended very considerably.

In 1953, when the Navarre plan was being worked out, the French imperialists also found themselves faced with the same dilemma: lack of forces to win back the initiative, to attack and annihilate our main forces. They set themselves the task of building up their fighting forces again at all costs, and, in fact, they did concentrate big forces in the Red River delta. With these forces, they hoped to wear out our main forces, compel us to scatter our army between the delta and the mountainous regions, with a view to carrying out their plan gradually and preparing for a big decisive offensive.

Faced with this situation, our Party's Central Committee made a thorough and clear-sighted analysis of the enemy's designs and of the characteristics of the theater of operations. *The thorough understand-*

ing of the contradictions and general laws of the aggressive war enabled us to detect the enemy's great weakness arising from the concentration of his forces. Always convinced that the essential thing was to destroy the enemy's manpower, the Central Committee worked out its plan of action on the basis of scientific analysis: to concentrate our forces to move to the offensive against important strategic points where the enemy's forces were relatively weak in order to wipe out a part of his manpower, at the same time compelling him to scatter his forces to cope with us at vital points which he had to defend at all costs. Our strategic directives were: dynamism, initiative, mobility, and rapidity of decision in the face of new situations.

The Central Committee's strategic direction proved itself correct and clear-sighted: while the enemy was concentrating big forces in the delta to threaten our free zone, instead of leaving our main forces in the delta or scattering our forces in the free zone to defend it by a defensive action, we regrouped our forces and boldly attacked in the direction of the northwest. Indeed, our divisions marched on the northwest with an irresistible impetus, swept away thousands of local bandits at Son La and Thuan Chau, liberated Lai Chau, cutting to pieces the greater part of the enemy's column which fled from Lai Chau. Simultaneously, we encircled Dien Bien Phu, thus compelling the enemy to carry out in haste a movement of forces to reinforce Dien Bien Phu in order to save it from being wiped out. Besides the Red River delta, Dien Bien Phu became a second point of concentration of enemy forces.

Concurrently with our offensive in the northwest, the Laos-Vietnam joint forces launched a second offensive in an important direction where the enemy was relatively exposed, the middle Laos front.

Several enemy mobile units were annihilated, and the town of Thakhek was liberated. The joint forces pushed on in the direction of Seno, an important enemy air base in Savannakhet. The enemy had to rush forces in haste from the Red River delta and from all

Dien Bien Phu 143

other battlefields to reinforce Seno, thus turning it into a third point of concentration of his forces.

Early in 1954, while the enemy was feverishly making preparations for his offensive against our free territory in the Fifth Zone, our plan was to leave only a small part of our forces to protect our rear and to concentrate big forces to attack on the Western Highlands, which was an important strategic position where the enemy was relatively exposed. Our advance to the Western Highlands was accompanied by resounding victories: important enemy units were wiped out, the town and whole province of Kontum were liberated. Our troops made a raid on Pleiku, compelling the enemy to dispatch more troops there in reinforcement, turning Pleiku and various bases on the Western Highlands into a fourth point of concentration of French forces.

During the same period, to create a diversion in order to secure conditions for our troops to step up preparations at Dien Bien Phu, the Laos-Vietnam joint forces had, from Dien Bien Phu, launched an offensive in upper Laos. Several enemy units were wiped out, and the vast Nam Ou basin was liberated. The enemy was compelled to rush more forces to Luang Prabang, which became the fifth point of concentration of French forces.

In the first phase of the winter-spring campaign, after three months' activity by our army, the enemy had suffered great losses on all battlefields. Many vast areas of strategic importance had been liberated and the Navarre plan of regroupment of forces was foiled. The enemy, who had made great efforts to regroup fairly strong mobile forces on a single battlefield—the Red River delta—was compelled to change his plan by concentrating his forces on a smaller scale at many different points. In other words, the Navarre plan of active regroupment of forces had in fact been turned into a forced dispersal of these same forces. The much-vaunted "Navarre mobile corps" in the delta had been reduced from forty-four to twenty battalions. It was the beginning of the end of the Navarre plan.

For us, the first phase of the winter-spring campaign was a series of offensives launched simultaneously on various important sectors where the enemy was relatively exposed, in which we annihilated part of the enemy's forces and liberated occupied areas, at the same time compelling the enemy to scatter his forces in many directions. We continually kept the initiative of the operations and drove the enemy on to the defensive. Also in this period, on the main battlefront, we pinned down the enemy at Dien Bien Phu, thus creating favorable conditions for our troops on other battlefields. In the national theater of operations, there was large-scale coordination between the main battlefields and the theaters of operation in the enemy's rear. In each theater, there was also close coordination between the main battlefield and the fronts in the enemy's rear. On the Indochinese battlefront, Dien Bien Phu became the strongest base of regroupment of the enemy forces and therefore the most important battlefield. As Dien Bien Phu had been encircled for a long time, there were new favorable conditions for the great intensification of guerrilla activities and the winning of major successes in the Red River delta, in the southern part of Trung Bo as well as in Nam Bo. The enemy lacked the forces to launch mopping-up operations on any considerable scale. During this time, our free zones were no longer threatened. Moreover, our compatriots in the free zones could go to work even in the daytime without being molested by enemy aircraft.

It was also in the course of the first phase of the winter-spring campaign that we completed our preparations for the assault on Dien Bien Phu. During this period, the dispositions of the fortified entrenched camp had also undergone great changes. On the one hand, the enemy's forces had been increased and their defense strengthened; on the other hand, after the successive liberation of Lai Chau, Phong Saly, and the Nam Ou River valley, Dien Bien Phu was completely isolated, some hundreds of miles from its nearest supply bases, Hanoi and the Plaine des Jarres.

From March 13, 1954, there began the second period of the winter-spring campaign. We launched the big offensive on the Dien Bien Phu fortified entrenched camp. This was a new step in the progress of the hostilities. Sticking firmly to our strategic principles—dynamism, initiative, mobility, and rapidity of decision in face of new situations—and having the conditions for victory well in hand, we directed our main attack on the most powerful entrenched camp of the enemy. The task of our regular forces on the main battlefield was no longer to encircle and immobilize the enemy in their barracks, but to go over to the attack and to concentrate forces to annihilate the Dien Bien Phu fortified entrenched camp. The task of the other battlefronts in North, Central, and South Vietnam was to intensify activities continuously in coordination with Dien Bien Phu, in order to annihilate more enemy manpower, scatter and pin down enemy forces, hampering the enemy in his efforts to reinforce Dien Bien Phu. On the Dien Bien Phu battlefield, our combatants fought with remarkable heroism and stubbornness. On all the coordinated battlefronts our troops did their utmost to overcome very great difficulties. They reorganized their forces while fighting and carried out the order of coordination with admirable determination and heroism.

Such was the essence of the strategic direction of the Dien Bien Phu campaign and of the winter-spring campaign as a whole. This direction drew its inspiration from the principles of dynamism, initiative, mobility, and rapidity of decision in face of new situations. Its main object was the destruction of enemy manpower. It took full advantage of the contradictions in which the enemy was involved and developed to the utmost the spirit of active offensive of the revolutionary army. This correct, clear-sighted, and bold strategy enabled us to deprive the enemy of any possibility of retrieving the initiative and to create favorable conditions for us to fight a decisive battle on a battlefield chosen and prepared for by us. *This strategic direction insured the success of the whole winter-spring campaign which was crowned by the great victory of Dien Bien Phu.*

The Direction of Operations at Dien Bien Phu

We have expounded the essence of the strategic direction of the 1953–1954 winter-spring campaign. The spirit and guiding principles of this strategic direction posed two problems to be solved for the direction of operations on the Dien Bien Phu battlefield:

1. *To attack or not to attack Dien Bien Phu?*
2. *If we attack, how should we go about it?*

The parachuting of enemy troops into Dien Bien Phu was not necessarily to be followed by an attack on the fortified camp. As Dien Bien Phu was a very strongly fortified entrenched camp of the enemy, we could not decide to attack it without first weighing the pros and cons very carefully. The fortified entrenched camp was a new form of defense of the enemy developed in face of the growth in the strength and size of our army. At Hoa Binh and at Na San, the enemy had already entrenched his forces in fortified camps. In the winter-spring campaign new fortified entrenched camps appeared not only at Dien Bien Phu but also at Seno, Muong Sai, and Luang Prabang in the Laotian theater of operations, and at Pleiku, on the Western Highlands front.

With the enemy's new form of defense, should we attack the fortified entrenched camp or should we not? While our forces were still obviously weaker than the enemy's, we always stuck to the principle of concentration of forces to attack the points where the enemy was relatively weak to annihilate his manpower. *Our plan was, time and again, to pin down the enemy's main forces in the fortified camps, while choosing more favorable directions for our attack.* In spring 1952, when the enemy erected the fortified camps at Hoa Binh, we struck hard and scored many victories along the Da River and in the enemy's rear in North Vietnam. In spring 1953, when the enemy fortified Na San, we did not attack his position but intensified our activities in the delta and launched an offensive in the west. During the last months of 1953 and at the beginning of 1954, when the enemy set up fortified camps in various places, our troops launched many successful offensives on sectors where the enemy was relatively weak, and at the same time stepped up guerrilla warfare behind the enemy's lines.

These tactics of attacking positions other than the fortified entrenched camps had recorded many successes. But these were not the only tactics. We could also *directly attack the fortified entrenched camp to annihilate the enemy's manpower in the heart of his new form of defense.* Only when we had wiped out the fortified entrenched camp, could we open up a new situation, paving the way for new victories for our army and people.

That was why, on the Dien Bien Phu battlefield, the problem of whether to attack or not had been posed, especially as Dien Bien Phu was the enemy's strongest fortified entrenched camp in the whole Indochina war theater, while our troops had, up to that time, attacked only fortresses defended by one or two companies, or one battalion at most.

Dien Bien Phu was the keystone of the Navarre plan, and we considered that it should be wiped out if the Franco-American imperialist plot of protracting and expanding the war was to be smashed. However, the importance of Dien Bien Phu could not be regarded as a decisive factor in our decision to attack it. In the relation of forces at that time, could we destroy the fortified entrenched camp of Dien Bien Phu? Could we be certain of victory in attacking it? Our decision had to depend on this consideration alone.

Dien Bien Phu was a very strongly fortified entrenched camp. But on the other hand, it was set up in a mountainous region, on ground which was advantageous to us, and decidedly disadvantageous to the enemy. Dien Bien Phu was, moreover, a completely isolated position, far away from all the enemy's bases. The only means of supplying Dien Bien Phu was by air. These circumstances could easily deprive the enemy of all initiative and force him onto the defensive if attacked.

On our side, we had picked units of the regular army which we could concentrate to achieve supremacy in power. We could overcome all difficulties in solving the necessary tactical problems; we had, in addition, an immense rear, and the problem of supplying the front with food and ammunition, though very difficult, was not insoluble. Thus we had conditions for retaining the initiative in the operations.

It was on the basis of this analysis of the enemy's and our own strong and weak points that we solved the question as to whether we should attack Dien Bien Phu or not. *We decided to wipe out at all costs the whole enemy force at Dien Bien Phu,* after having created favorable conditions for this battle by launching numerous offensives on various battlefields and by intensifying preparations on the Dien Bien Phu battlefield. This important decision was a new proof of the dynamism, initiative, mobility, and rapidity of decision in face of new situations displayed in the conduct of the war by the Party's Central Committee. Our plan foresaw the launching of many offensives on the points where the enemy was relatively weak, availing ourselves of every opportunity to wipe out the enemy's manpower in mobile warfare. But whenever it was possible and success was certain, we were resolved not to let slip an opportunity to launch powerful attacks on strong points to annihilate the more concentrated enemy forces. Our decision to make the assault on the Dien Bien Phu fortified camp clearly marked a new step forward in the development of the winter-spring campaign, in the annals of our army's battles and in the history of our people's resistance war.

We had pledged to wipe out the whole enemy force at Dien Bien Phu, but we still had to solve this problem: how should we do it? *Strike swiftly and win swiftly, or strike surely and advance surely! This was the problem of the direction of operations in the campaign.*

In the early stage, when we began the encirclement of Dien Bien Phu, and the enemy, having been newly parachuted into the area, had not yet had time to complete his fortifications and increase his forces, the question of striking swiftly and winning swiftly had been posed. By concentrating superior forces, we could push simultaneously from many directions deep into enemy positions, cut the fortified entrenched camp into many separate parts, then swiftly annihilate the entire enemy manpower. There were many obvious advantages if we could strike swiftly to win swiftly: by launching a big offensive with fresh troops, we could shorten the duration of the campaign and avoid the wear and fatigue of a long operation. As the campaign would not last long, the supplying of the battlefront could be ensured without difficulty. However, on further examining the question, we saw that these tactics had a very great, a basic, disadvantage: our troops lacked experience in attacking fortified entrenched camps. If we wanted to win swiftly, success could not be ensured. For that reason, in the process of making preparations, we continued to follow the enemy's situation and checked and rechecked our potentialities again. And we came to the conclusion that we could not secure success if we struck swiftly. In consequence, *we resolutely chose the other tactic: to strike surely and advance surely.* In taking this correct decision, *we strictly followed this fundamental principle of the conduct of a revolutionary war: strike to win, strike only when success is certain, if it is not, then don't strike.*

In the Dien Bien Phu campaign, the adoption of these tactics demanded of us firmness and a spirit of resolution. Since we wanted to strike surely and advance surely, preparations would take a longer time and the campaign would drag out. And the longer the campaign went on, the more new and greater difficulties would crop up. Difficulties in supply would increase enormously. The danger increased of our troops being worn out while the enemy consolidated defenses and lined up his forces. Above all, the longer the campaign lasted, the nearer came the rainy season with all its disastrous consequences for operations carried out on the mountains and in forests. As a result, not everybody was immediately convinced of the correctness of these tactics. We patiently educated our men, pointed out that there were real difficulties, but that our task was to overcome them to create good conditions for the great victory we sought.

It was from these guiding principles that we developed our plan of progressive attack, in which the Dien Bien Phu campaign was regarded not as a *large-scale attack on fortresses carried out over a short period, but as a large-scale campaign carried out over a fairly long period, through a series of successive attacks on fortified positions until the enemy was destroyed.* In the campaign as a whole, we already had numerical superiority over the enemy. But in each attack or each wave of attacks, we had the possibility of achieving absolute supremacy and ensuring the success of each operation and consequently total victory in the campaign. Such a plan was in full keeping with the tactical and technical level of our troops, creating conditions for them to accumulate experience in fighting and to insure the annihilation of the enemy at Dien Bien Phu.

We strictly followed these guiding principles throughout the campaign. We encircled the enemy and carried out our preparations thoroughly over a period of three months. Then, after opening the offensive, our troops fought relentlessly for fifty-five days and nights. Careful preparation and relentless fighting led our Dien Bien Phu campaign to resounding victory.

Some Questions of Tactics

Dien Bien Phu was a fortified entrenched camp defended by fairly strong forces: seventeen battalions of infantry, three battalions of artillery, without counting tank-engineer units, air and transport units, and so on, most of them picked elements of the French Expeditionary Corps in Indochina. The fortified camp was made up of forty-nine strongposts, organized into fortified resistance centers and grouped into three sectors capable of supporting each other. In the middle of the central sector, which was effectively guarded by the resistance centers on the hilltops in the east, were mobile forces, artillery positions, and tank units, as well as the enemy headquarters. The airfield of Dien Bien Phu was near here. This whole vast defense system lay within strong underground fortifications and trenches.

The French and American military authorities believed that the fortified entrenched camp of Dien Bien Phu was impregnable. They were certain that an offensive against Dien Bien Phu would be suicidal, that failure was inevitable. Therefore, during the first weeks of the campaign, the French High Command firmly believed that there was little possibility of an offensive against Dien Bien Phu by our army. Until the last minute, the offensive launched by our men was unexpected by the enemy.

General Navarre had overestimated the Dien Bien Phu defenses. He believed that we would be unable to crush even one center of resistance. Because, unlike the simple strongposts at Na San or Hoa Binh, these were centers of resistance forming a much more complex and strongly fortified defense system.

The destruction of the fortified entrenched camp as a whole was, to Navarre's mind, still less feasible. In his opinion, his artillery and air forces were powerful enough to wipe out all forces coming from outside before these could be deployed in the valley and approach the fortifications. He was not in the least worried about our artillery, which he thought weak and not transportable to the approaches of Dien Bien Phu. Nor was he anxious about his own supplies, because both airfields, surrounded by the defense sectors, could not be in danger. Never did it enter his head that the whole fortified camp could be annihilated by our troops.

The enemy's estimates were obviously wishful thinking, but they were not totally without foundation. In fact, the Dien Bien Phu fortified entrenched camp had many strongpoints which had given our army new problems of tactics to solve before we could annihilate the enemy.

The fortified entrenched camp was a defense system manned by big forces. The centers of resistance, which were closely connected to one another, were effectively supported by artillery, tank units, and aircraft, and could easily be reinforced by mobile forces. This was a strong point for the enemy and for us, a difficulty. *We overcame this difficulty by applying the tactics of progressive attack,* by regrouping our forces to have a great local superiority, by striving to neutralize as much as possible the enemy artillery fire and mobile forces, bringing everything into play to wipe out the centers of resistance one by one, or a group of centers at one time in a wave of attacks. By concentrating forces to achieve absolute superiority at one point, we were certain to crush the enemy, especially in the first days of the campaign, when we attacked the enemy outposts.

The fortified entrenched camp had quite powerful artillery fire, tank, and air forces. This was another strong point of the enemy, a very great difficulty of ours, especially since we had only very limited artillery fire and no mechanized or air forces. *We overcame this difficulty by digging a whole network of trenches that encircled and strangled the entrenched camp,* thus creating conditions for our men to deploy and move under enemy fire. Our fighters dug hundreds of miles of trenches. These wonderful trenches enabled our forces to deploy and move in open country under the rain of enemy napalm bombs and artillery shells. But to reduce the effect of enemy fire was not enough: *we still had to strengthen our own firepower.* Our troops cut through mountains and hacked away jungles to build roads and haul our artillery pieces to the approaches of Dien Bien Phu. Where roads could not be built, artillery pieces were moved by nothing but the sweat and muscle of our soldiers. Our artillery was set up in strongly fortified firing positions, to the great surprise of the enemy. Our light artillery played a great part in the Dien Bien Phu battle.

While neutralizing the enemy's strong points, we had to make the most of his weak points. His greatest weakness lay in his supply, which depended entirely on his air forces. Our tactics were from the very beginning to use our artillery fire to destroy the airstrips, and our antiaircraft guns to cope with the activities of enemy planes. Later, with the development of the waves of attacks, everything was brought into play to hinder enemy supply and gradually to stop it altogether.

These are a few of the problems of tactics we solved in the Dien

Bien Phu campaign. They were solved on the basis of our analysis of the enemy's strong and weak points, combining technique with the heroism and hard working and fighting of a people's army.

To sum up, our plan of operations based upon these tactical considerations consisted in setting up a whole system of lines of attack and encirclement, permitting our forces to launch successive attacks to annihilate the enemy. This network of innumerable trenches with firing positions and command posts encircled and strangled the enemy. It was progressively extended with our victories. From the surrounding mountains and forests, it moved down into the valley. Each enemy position, once wiped out, was immediately turned into our own. As we encircled the enemy-fortified entrenched camp, a real fortified camp of our own, very mobile, gradually took shape, and kept closing in, while the enemy camp was constantly narrowed down.

In the first phase of the campaign, from our newly built network of attack and encirclement positions, we annihilated the Him Lam and Doc Lap centers of resistance, and the whole northern sector. The enemy made desperate efforts to destroy our firing positions. Their planes poured napalm bombs on the mountains around Dien Bien Phu. Their artillery concentrated powerful fire on our firing positions. But we held on.

In the second phase, the "axis" communication trenches, with their innumerable ramifications, starting from our bases, extended down into the valley and isolated the central sector from the southern sector. The fierce and successful assault on the eastern hilltops enabled our belt of artillery fire to close in. From the captured positions, our guns of all calibers could exert pressure on the enemy. The airstrips were completely controlled by our fire.

The enemy became increasingly active, bringing reinforcements for his mobile forces, launching counterattacks and furiously bombing our lines in an attempt to save the situation. It was a desperate positional battle. Many hilltops were captured and recaptured many times. Some were occupied half by our troops and half by the enemy.

Our tactics were to encroach, harass, and wrest every inch of ground from the enemy, destroy his airstrips, and narrow down his free airspace.

The third phase was that of general offensive. The enemy had been driven into an area of about one square mile. His forces suffered heavy losses. Once Hill A-1 had been completely occupied by our troops, all hope of continued resistance vanished, and the enemy's morale sank extremely low. On May 7, our troops launched an offensive from all directions, occupied the enemy headquarters, and captured the whole enemy staff. That night, the southern sector was also wiped out.

The Dien Bien Phu campaign ended in a great victory.

Our Army's Determination to Fight and to Win

The great task assigned to the whole army and people by the Party's Central Committee and the government was: *to concentrate forces, to be thoroughly imbued with determination, "to actively develop the spirit of heroic fighting and endurance to bring the campaign to complete victory."* For the Dien Bien Phu campaign, as has been pointed out by President Ho Chi Minh and the Political Bureau of the Central Committee of the Vietnam Lao Dong Party, was a historic campaign of exceptional importance to the military and political situation in our country and to the full growth of our army, as well as to the struggle for the defense of peace in Southeast Asia.

Our troops fought to carry out this great task with unshakable determination. Our combatants' will to fight and to defeat the enemy was one of the decisive factors which brought the Dien Bien Phu campaign and the winter-spring campaign in general such brilliant victories on all battlefronts.

Throughout the history of the armed struggle of our people, never had our army been entrusted with so great and heavy a task as in winter 1953–spring 1954. The enemy to be annihilated was rather a strong one. Our forces thrown into the battle were very large. The theater of operations was extensive, and the operations lasted half a year. On the Dien Bien Phu battlefield, as on all other coordinated battlefields, our combatants, with a spirit of heroism and endurance, surmounted countless difficulties and overcame many great obstacles to annihilate the enemy and fulfill their task. The heroism and endurance were tempered and enhanced by the long years of resistance. Particularly in winter 1953–spring 1954, the revolutionary enthusiasm of our combatants increased greatly after their study of the policy for the mobilization of the masses for land reform. Here, stress should be laid on the considerable contribution made by the land-reform policy to the victories of the winter–spring campaign, particularly on the Dien Bien Phu battlefield.

On the Dien Bien Phu battlefront, in the period of preparation, our armymen opened up the supply line from Tuan Giao to Dien Bien Phu; built through mountains and forests roads practicable for trucks to move artillery pieces into position; built artillery emplacements; dug trenches from the mountains to the valley; changed the terrain; overcame enormous obstacles; and in all ways created favorable conditions for the annihilation of the enemy. Neither difficulties, fatigue, nor enemy bombing and artillery fire could shake the iron will of our men.

From the first shot touching off the offensive against Dien Bien Phu, and throughout the battle, our combatants fought with extraordinary heroism. Under the deluge of bombs from the enemy air force, and under the enemy's cross fire, our fighters valiantly stormed and captured Him Lam and Doc Lap hills, put the enemy troops entrenched on the eastern hills out of action, expanded our bases, cut off the airfields, repulsed counterattacks, and kept tightening our encirclement. During all this time, the enemy's napalm bombs burned down the undergrowth on the hills surrounding Dien Bien Phu, and enemy bombs and shells plowed deep into the fields in our zones of operations. But our combatants kept moving forward to carry out their tasks. One fell, but many others rushed forward like a sweeping, rising tide that no force on earth could hold back. *We witnessed a phenomenon of collective heroism in which the most admirable deeds were performed by To Vinh Dien, who threw himself under the wheel of an artillery piece to prevent it from slipping back; Phan Dinh Giot, who silenced an enemy gun nest with his own body; the shock troops who planted the banner of "determination to fight and to win" on Him Lam hill, and the shock troops who captured the enemy headquarters.*

The spirit of heroism and endurance of our fighters on coordinated battlefields should also be mentioned. On the Western Highlands, great successes were scored at Kontum and An Khe. In the Red River delta, our troops destroyed seventy-eight planes on Cat Bi and Gia Lam airfields, wiped out several enemy fortified positions and cut off Road No. 5, the enemy's main supply line. In South Vietnam, more than one thousand enemy posts were annihilated or evacuated, many stocks of bombs destroyed, and ships sunk. On the battlefields of our two neighboring countries, our people's volunteers, together with the army and the people of these friendly countries, wiped out the invaders and scored many great victories.

Never had our army fought with such endurance for so long a time as in winter 1953–spring 1954. There were units which marched and pursued the enemy for more than eighteen hundred miles. There were others which moved secretly for more than five hundred miles on the Truong Son* mountain range to take part in fighting on a far-off battlefield. The units on Dien Bien Phu battlefield moved from the delta to the mountains and at once set passionately to work, at the same time fighting to protect their preparatory labor. Then came the battle, and our troops lived and fought for two months in trenches after having spent three months of hardship in the jungle. While the battle was going on, certain units rushed to places one or two hundred miles away to launch surprise attacks on the enemy,

---

* Range of mountains running from the north to the south of Central Vietnam, along the Vietnam-Laos border.

then came back to take part in the annihilation of the enemy at Dien Bien Phu. The spirit of cooperation between the various units and various arms was enhanced during the battle, and there was close coordination between the various battlefields.

Our combatants' *determination to fight and to win as described above came from the revolutionary nature of our army and the painstaking education of the Party. It had been enhanced in battle and in the ideological remolding classes.* This does not mean that, even when the Dien Bien Phu battle was at its height, negative factors never appeared. *To maintain and develop this determination to fight and to win was a whole process of unremitting and patient political and ideological education and struggle,* tireless and patient efforts in political work on the front line. This was a great achievement of the Party's organizations and branches and of its cadres. After a series of resounding victories, we found in our ranks signs of underestimation of the enemy. By criticism, we rectified this state of mind in good time. In the long period of preparation, particularly after the second phase of the campaign, when attack and defense were equally fierce, negative rightist thoughts cropped up again to the detriment of the carrying-out of the task. In accordance with the instructions of the Political Bureau, we opened in the heart of the battlefield an intensive and extensive struggle against *rightist passivity,* and for the heightening of revolutionary enthusiasm and the spirit of strict discipline, with a view to ensuring the total victory of the campaign. This ideological struggle was very successful. This was one of the greatest achievements in political work in our army's history. It led the Dien Bien Phu campaign to complete victory.

The determination to fight and to win of our army on the Dien Bien Phu and other coordinated battlefields was a distinctly marked manifestation of the boundless loyalty of our People's Army to the revolutionary struggle of the people and the Party. It was a collective manifestation of proletarian ideology, of the class-stand of the officers and men and Party members in the army. It maintained the

Vietnam People's Army tradition of heroic fighting, endurance, and determination in the fulfillment of duty. It made of the soldier of the People's Army an iron fighter. Dien Bien Phu will forever symbolize the traditions of fighting and winning victory of our army and people. Our military banner is the banner of "Determination to win."

The People's Devotion to Serving the Front

The Party's Central Committee and the government decided that the whole people and Party should concentrate all their forces for the service of the front in order to ensure the victory of the Dien Bien Phu campaign. During this campaign, and generally speaking, during the whole winter-spring campaign, our whole people—workers, peasants, youth, intellectuals—every Vietnamese patriot answered the appeal for national liberation and did his utmost to achieve the slogan "All for the front, all for victory" with an ardent and unprecedented enthusiasm, at the cost of superhuman efforts.

Throughout the long years of the resistance war, our people never made so great a contribution as in the winter 1953–spring 1954 campaign, in supplying the army for the fight against the enemy. On the main Dien Bien Phu front, our people had to ensure the supply of food and munitions to a big army, operating three to four hundred miles from the rear, and in very difficult conditions. The roads were bad, the means of transport insufficient, and the supply lines relentlessly attacked by the enemy. There was, in addition, the menace of heavy rains that could create more obstacles than bombing.

On the Dien Bien Phu front, the supply of food and munitions was a factor as important as the problem of tactics; logistics constantly posed problems as urgent as those posed by the armed struggle. These were precisely the difficulties that the enemy thought insuperable for us. The imperialists and traitors could never appreciate the strength of a nation, of a people. This strength is immense. It can overcome any difficulty, defeat any enemy.

The Vietnamese people, under the direct leadership of the committees of supply for the front, gave proof of great heroism and endurance in serving the front.

Truck convoys valiantly crossed streams, mountains, and forests; drivers spent scores of sleepless nights, in defiance of difficulties and dangers, to bring food and ammunition to the front, to permit the army to annihilate the enemy.

Thousands of bicycles from the towns also carried food and munitions to the front.

Hundreds of sampans of all sizes, hundreds of thousands of bamboo rafts crossed rapids and cascades to supply the front.

Convoys of pack horses from the Meo Highlands or the provinces headed for the front.

Day and night, hundreds of thousands of porters and young volunteers crossed passes and forded rivers in spite of enemy planes and delayed-action bombs.

Near the firing line, supply operations had to be carried out uninterruptedly and in the shortest possible time. Cooking, medical work, transport, and so on, was carried on right in the trenches, under enemy bombing and cross fire.

Such was the situation at Dien Bien Phu, but on the coordinated fronts, big armed forces were also active, especially on the Western Highlands and in other remote theaters of operation. On these fronts, as at Dien Bien Phu, our people fulfilled their tasks. They admirably solved the problems of supply to enable the army to defeat the enemy, always to win new victories.

Never had so large a number of Vietnamese gone to the front. Never had so many young Vietnamese traveled so far and become acquainted with so many distant regions of their country. From the plains to the mountains, on roads and paths, on rivers and streams, everywhere, there was the same animation: the rear sent its men and wealth to the front in order to annihilate the enemy and, together with the army, to liberate the country.

The rear brought to the fighter at the front its will to annihilate the enemy, its strong unity in the resistance and the revolutionary enthusiasm of the land reform. Each day, thousands of letters and telegrams from all over the country came to the Dien Bien Phu front. Never had Vietnam been so anxious about her fighting sons, never had the relations between the rear and the front been so intimate as in this winter-spring campaign.

Indeed, a strong rear is always the decisive factor for victory in a revolutionary war. In the Dien Bien Phu campaign and, generally speaking, the whole winter-spring campaign, our people made a worthy contribution to the victory of the nation.

We cannot forget the sympathy and hearty support of the brother peoples, of the progressive peoples all over the world, including the French people. Every day, from all corners of the earth, from the Soviet Union, China, North Korea, and the German Democratic Republic, Algeria, India, Burma, Indonesia, and other countries, news reached the front through broadcasts, bringing the expression of the boundless support of progressive mankind for the just struggle of the Vietnamese people and army. This was a very great encouragement for the combatants of the Vietnam People's Army at Dien Bien Phu, as on all other fronts.

The War in the South

The Political and Military Line of Our Party

Armed Struggle Is the Prolongation of Political Struggle

The military line of our Party derives from and always follows its political line; it endeavors to achieve the political aims of the revolution through armed struggle or political struggle combined with armed struggle. Our revolution must go through the stage of national people's democratic revolution and advance toward the socialist revolution, bypassing the stage of capitalist development. Our military line is based on the line of a thoroughly national people's democratic revolution; it is the *line of the people's revolutionary war,* the war of a people made up mainly of peasants, which is aimed at overthrowing imperialism and feudalism, reconquering independence for the nation and giving land back to the tillers. It is the line of thorough war of national liberation, a just war to counter the unjust war of aggression waged by the enemy.

The two revolutionary tasks, the national and the democratic, are closely linked with each other. That is why, in order to give a strong impulse to the people's revolutionary war and bring it to a victorious conclusion, it is indispensable to mobilize and organize the entire people, particularly to mobilize and organize the large mass of peasants under the leadership of the working class, and to solve a whole series of questions relating to the democratic revolution, especially the agrarian question.

To wage a revolutionary war thoroughly victoriously, it is indis-

---

This is a slightly edited version of the text which appeared under the same title in *Vietnamese Studies,* n. 7 (Hanoi, n.d.), pp. 123–152. It was originally published in *Nhan Dan,* the organ of the Central Committee of the Lao Dong, on December 22, 1964, the twentieth anniversary of the founding of the Vietnam People's Army.

pensable to strengthen the leadership of the vanguard Party of the working class. It is this leadership which has created all the conditions and provided all the guarantees to insure the transition from the national people's democratic revolution to the socialist revolution through a continuous revolutionary process. On this road, the people's armed forces, which are in fact those of the laboring people —workers and peasants—are constantly directed and educated by the Party. They are constantly animated with a highly combative and consequently revolutionary spirit and have all the necessary conditions to go forward and fulfill their task in the new stage, which is to become a *sure instrument in the service of the state of proletarian dictatorship.*

On the other hand, our country was a colonial and semifeudal country with a territory which was not very vast, a population which was not very large, and an economy which was essentially agrarian and backward. Our enemies—Japanese fascists or French colonialists —were much stronger than we materially, having a developed capitalist economy and powerful regular armies. At present in the South, United States imperialism, served by its lackeys, is also an economically and militarily strong enemy.

In these conditions, our military line is that followed *by a small nation struggling against a much stronger enemy*. This strategy has been successful in solving, creatively and adequately, a fundamental problem: relying on our absolute political superiority, on the righteousness of our cause, and on our people's unity in struggle, it is possible *to use what is weak to fight what is strong, to defeat the most modern weapons with a revolutionary spirit.* Consequently, a small nation is quite capable of defeating the professional army of the imperialist aggressors.

The success of our Party's military line is *typical of the creative application, in our concrete conditions, of the universal principles of Marxism-Leninism on revolutionary war, on the building up of revolutionary armed forces, and of revolutionary bases,* and so forth. Its content reflects the character and the universal laws of revolu-

The Political and Military Line of Our Party 165

tionary war in general and the character and the particular laws of revolutionary war in our country. Its content is particularly rich and creative in the combination of political struggle with military struggle, the combination of the entire people's political struggle with the entire people's uprising, with the people's war, in order to win the greatest victories for the revolutionary cause.

This military line *regards the leading role of our Party as most important,* as a sure guarantee of final victory. The reason is that our Party is the vanguard Party of the working class, the most intransigent representative of the interests of the class, the people, and the nation. Our Party is not only determined to carry out a most thorough revolutionary struggle, it is also imbued with the principles of Marxism-Leninism which is the most progressive science. Thus, it is capable of determining the most correct strategy and tactics to ensure victory.

On the one hand, our people's revolutionary struggle in the present period applies the precious experience of fraternal countries in revolutionary struggle; on the other hand, it continues and develops to a high degree our people's *traditions of indomitable struggle against foreign aggression* and the spirit of resolute and heroic struggle of our peasants' uprisings in the past. Marxism-Leninism never disowns the history and the great constituent virtues of a nation; on the contrary, it raises these virtues to new heights in the new historical conditions. During the many thousand years of their history, our people repeatedly rose up to struggle heroically against foreign aggression and reconquer national independence. In those armed struggles, our people made creative contributions to military art; they relied on justice and humanity to defeat a powerful enemy, used what was weak to fight what was strong, won victories with forces of small size in large-scale wars; sometimes they attracted the enemy far into our own territory to annihilate them; sometimes they temporarily withdrew troops from the capital, seeking favorable occasions and places gradually to drive the enemy to defeat and liberate the country; sometimes they built up revolutionary armed forces in regions of mountains and forests, creating bases for a protracted struggle until the enemy was completely defeated; sometimes they mobilized the peasants' combative spirit, created a large and mighty army, and wiped out the enemy's main forces by unexpected and bold maneuvers. The indomitable spirit of our people and the military experience bequeathed by our forefathers have both contributed to the elaboration of the military line and military theory of our Party in the present conditions.

From Revolutionary Violence to the Uprising of the Entire People and the People's War

People's war is the basic conception in our Party's military line; it constantly affirms the revolutionary character, the just character, of people's war, the decisive role of the masses, the leading role of our Party. It is the expression of our Party's class viewpoint, of its reliance on the masses.

Our Party's conception of people's war is a new *development of the conception of revolutionary violence* in the revolutionary context of our country.

The Marxist-Leninist doctrine on class struggle and the dictatorship of the proletariat affirms the role of violence in revolution, makes a distinction between unjust, counter-revolutionary violence and just, revolutionary violence, between the violence of the exploiting classes and that of the masses.

Loyal to the Marxist-Leninist doctrine on class struggle and on the dictatorship of the proletariat, our Party has always been imbued with this *conception of revolutionary violence;* it has correctly appraised, on the one hand, the extremely reactionary and cruel nature of the enemy and, on the other hand, the force of unity and struggle of our people—in the first place, the laboring people, the masses of workers and peasants—and consequently it has clearly shown that *revolutionary violence is the only correct way* to overcome the enemy and win political power for the people, win victory for the revolu-

The Political and Military Line of Our Party 167

tion. Our Party holds that the contradictions between imperialism and our people, as well as the contradictions between our people, between the peasantry and the feudal landowners' class, are antagonistic ones, which can be radically solved only by revolutionary violence. In particular, the present revolution for national liberation, the people's national democratic revolution in our country, is under the leadership of the working class; it belongs to the category of proletarian revolutions, and so its character of class struggle is all the more acute and violent. Violence is the universal objective law of all thorough national liberation revolutions, of all revolutions which are truly popular in character. As to the forms of violence, they may be political or military or political combined with military struggle, but whatever form it may take, it must depend on the strength of the politically conscious popular masses. As Engels said, "All revolution, whatever form it may take, is a form of violence."

Since its foundation, in the circumstances of a stubborn struggle against the terror of the imperialists and their agents who tried to drown the revolutionary movement in blood, our Party, on the one hand, mobilized the strength of the masses for the political struggle and, on the other hand, made preparations for an armed uprising. It organized self-defense groups for the protection of the masses. After World War II broke out, national liberation became an urgent task; during this period, on the basis of a powerful upsurge of the internal and external conditions which were coming to maturity, our Party gave a further impulse to the preparations for an armed insurrection, and launched a guerrilla war against the Japanese imperialists.

The general insurrection of August 1945 was an uprising of the entire people. Our entire people, united in a broad national front, with their armed and semiarmed forces, unanimously rose up everywhere, in the countryside and in the cities, and conquered political power at a favorable political conjuncture, when the Japanese imperialists had lost the war, their army was in a process of disintegration, and their lackeys were demoralized and powerless. This victorious uprising chiefly relied on the political violence of the masses supported by armed violence. *The uprising of the entire people in our country was a new development of revolutionary struggle: combining political and armed violence, and carried out simultaneously in the countryside and the cities, the principal means being the political strength of the masses; this strength, organized into a broad united front based on the alliance of the working class with the peasantry,* was mobilized, organized and led by the party of the working class. Thus, we can clearly see that the practice of the August 1945 general insurrection had a highly creative content. In a former colonial and semifeudal country like ours, the revolution of national liberation does not necessarily take the form of a protracted struggle, or that of an armed uprising in the cities, but it is quite possible for it to combine, in a creative manner, these two forms of struggle.

Our nationwide resistance war, which was a people's war, was a new development; it was a *true revolutionary war, a war by the entire people, a total war.* A revolutionary war, because it was carried out on the basis of the mobilization and organization of the masses, with the aim of achieving a national democratic revolution. A war by the entire people, because it was a war in which a whole nation struggled in unity, each citizen becoming a combatant, a war in which our Party's correct revolutionary line succeeded in grouping all patriotic strata of the population in a broad front based on a strong worker-peasant alliance, and mobilizing them for the struggle. A total war, because armed struggle was frequently combined with political struggle, because at the same time as we engaged in a military struggle, we carried out reduction of land rent, land reform, political struggle in urban centers and enemy-occupied areas, and struggle in the economic and cultural fields.

It should be stressed that during the resistance, we used *armed struggle as an essential form of struggle,* with the countryside as a base. The enemy we faced was the expeditionary corps of French colonialism, an old-type colonialism. It was only through armed

Portrait. (1956)

General Giap with the founding members of the Armed Propaganda Detachment. (December 22, 1944)

General Giap and his staff at his secret headquarters near Dienbienphu. (c. 1953)

General Giap and President Ho participating in a division maneuver at the military institute in Son Tay province. (1957)

Truong Chinh, Phan Ke Toai, President Ho, Hoang Quoc Viet, Pham Van Dong, and General Giap. (Recent)

General Giap with President Ho. (Recent)

General Giap with members of his staff. (Recent)

struggle that it was possible, in such circumstances, to decimate and annihilate the enemy, and win victory for the resistance.

In the South of our country, in the conditions of struggle against neo-colonialism and the "special war" of United States imperialism, historical conditions present some aspects which are similar to those of the resistance against French colonialism, but others which are peculiar to the liberation war in South Vietnam. Our people in the South enjoy a clear political superiority over the enemy; they also have traditions of and experience in political struggle and armed struggle and are animated with ardent patriotism and high revolutionary spirit; the enemy are strong materially and technically, but the social bases of the reactionary forces in the service of the United States imperialists being extremely weak, they are in a state of complete political isolation, and their political weakness is irremediable. Because of our country's temporary partition, a phase has appeared of acute political struggle against the war unilaterally started by the enemy, developing afterward into political struggle combined with armed struggle. The war of liberation now being waged by our countrymen in the South is *a revolutionary war, a war by the entire people, a total war* using simultaneously the two forms of struggle, *regarding both as fundamental and decisive*. Armed struggle has developed on the basis of political struggle brought to a higher level; these two forms of struggle develop simultaneously in a vigorous manner and stimulate each other. Armed struggle which becomes more and more vigorous does not make political struggle decrease in intensity but, on the contrary, gives it a stronger impulse; together they pursue the aim of annihilating and dislocating enemy armed forces, striking vigorously where the enemy is basically weak, on the political ground. The people's war in the South applies at the same time the laws governing revolutionary armed struggle during our nationwide resistance and the laws governing this struggle during the August 1945 general uprising, which makes its content infinitely rich and creative.

The practice of revolutionary struggle in our country in new historical conditions has made an original contribution to Marxist-Leninist theory on revolutionary armed struggle, according to which revolutionary struggle is a dialectic combination of political struggle and armed struggle, sometimes taking the form of political struggle, sometimes the form of a long revolutionary war, sometimes the form of an entire people's uprising, and sometimes combining all the above forms. This is what we mean when we say that the people's uprising and the people's war in our country are new developments in the conception of revolutionary violence.

From the Revolutionary People to the Revolutionary Armed Forces

The Marxist-Leninist doctrine holds that revolutionary struggle in general and armed struggle in particular must be the work of the masses who, once they are conscious of the political aims of the revolution, are ready to be organized and resolute in rising up to fight, so that they become capable of defeating the most wicked enemy. As Lenin said, "The masses who shed their blood on the battlefield are the factor which brings victory in a war."

In order to carry out a people's war, the entire people must be mobilized and armed. Our Party's fundamental concept in this matter is that of the *people's armed forces*. This concept is indicative of the revolutionary character, the popular and class character of the armed forces; it is indicative of the Party's absolute leadership of the armed forces.

Because armed struggle is the continuation of political struggle, no powerful armed forces could be built without the people's mighty political strength. Looking back at our people's long and arduous revolutionary struggle, we can clearly see that the years of bitter political struggle after our Party was founded, to enlighten and organize the masses, to build the worker-peasant alliance, to create a People's United Front, to affirm the leading role of the Party, were the years of preparation of forces for the subsequent armed struggle. After our Party had decided to prepare for an armed uprising and later, to wage a long resistance war, it continued to attach much importance to propaganda, to mobilization work among the masses, to stimulating the patriotism of various strata of the people and their hatred of the enemy, organizing the people, especially the workers and peasants, into a strong basis for the great union of the entire people for the resistance. The political force of the masses, of the people, is the strongest possible base on which to develop the armed forces. Furthermore, even in the circumstances of revolutionary war, this political force continues its direct support for the front and participates in the struggle against the enemy, assuming a most important role in the war.

In the first days, when our Party decided to make preparations for an armed uprising, it relied only on the force of the politically conscious masses, having then not even the smallest armed force. In the first days, when our Party called on the entire people to rise up and take part in the resistance war for national salvation, the principal force opposing the aggressors was the united force of the entire people, while the people's armed forces were still weak in numbers, equipment, and experience. In recent years, our countrymen in the South at first also relied basically on their political force when they heroically rose up to fight against a wicked enemy. Their innumerable heroic deeds are further proof that the source of strength of the armed forces in a revolutionary war is the strength of the united struggle of the entire people; that once patriotism and revolutionary ideas have penetrated deep into the people, they become an invincible force.

The people's armed forces are born of the revolutionary people. The worker-peasant self-defense units in the days of the Nghetinh soviets,* the small semiarmed and armed forces in the period preceding the general uprising, the National Salvation units,† the Propa-

---
* Peasant Soviets of 1930–1931.
† Created in 1943–1944.

ganda Groups for the Liberation of Vietnam, the Ba To guerrillas,* the thousands of self-defense and self-defense fighting groups throughout the country, were built up on the basis of consolidating and developing the political organizations of the masses. During the resistance, the recruiting of cadres and combatants for main-force units and local units, militia and guerrilla groups relied chiefly on that inexhaustible source of supply: the revolutionary people, the best elements in the mass organizations led and educated by the Party. Today, when in the completely liberated North, we have powerful armed forces, we still keep very close relations with the organizations of the masses led by the Party. Born of the people, the people's armed forces can grow in strength only thanks to their unreserved support and by continuously learning from their revolutionary spirit and rich experience in revolutionary struggle. To consolidate and continuously develop blood relations with the people, our armed forces have not only to fight, but also to work and produce, remaining always close to the political movement of the masses.

The people's armed forces are the revolutionary armed forces of the laboring people, of the workers and peasants; they fight to defend the interests of the people, the class, and the nation. These armed forces must be placed under the leadership of the vanguard party if they are to have a revolutionary character and an increasingly high combative spirit. That the armed forces should have a revolutionary character, a class character, is the essential point in our Party's theory on the building of the armed forces. That is the reason why our Party attaches great importance to the role of political work, regarding it as vital to the armed forces. To make unceasing efforts to enhance the class consciousness and patriotism of cadres and combatants, to ensure the absolute loyalty of cadres and combatants to the Party, the people, the fatherland, and their readiness to sacrifice

---

* Giap is referring to the southern insurrection at Ba To in 1945.

everything for the revolutionary cause—these tasks must be fulfilled to make the armed forces a reliable instrument of the Party and the people in the national democratic revolution and in the socialist revolution. Our People's Army is a heroic army, firstly because it is an army born of the people, fighting to defend the people's interests; because it is determined to carry out a thorough revolution, determined to fight and to win, and has a tradition of heroic fighting, hard work, endurance, determination to overcome difficulties, to fulfill all duties. To firmly maintain and consolidate the absolute leadership of the Party in the armed forces, to intensify the education of cadres and combatants in proletarian ideology and in the Party's line and revolutionary tasks, to realize unity within the army, unity between the army and the people, international unity, to provoke the disintegration of enemy forces, to realize broad inner democracy and at the same time strict self-imposed discipline—these are *the fundamental principles to follow in the building of the people's armed forces in the political aspect,* and the factors which will preserve their class character and ensure their constant growth and victory.

In order to carry out a people's war, the armed forces must have adequate forms of organization comprising *main-force troops, regional troops, militia,* and *self-defense units.* The main-force troops are mobile units which may be used in fighting in any part of the country. Regional troops are the mainstay of armed struggle in a region. Militia and self-defense groups are extensive semiarmed forces of the laboring people who, while continuing their production work, are the main instrument of the people's power at the base.

The practice of revolutionary armed struggle by our people has proved that the three above-mentioned forms of organization of the armed forces are wholly adequate for the tasks of promoting a people's war, for mobilizing and arming the entire people for the war. We have to look back at our people's struggle through successive periods to grasp fully the importance and strategic role of those three categories of armed forces. If we had not organized secret self-defense units during the preinsurrection period, the powerful armed forces such as we had later on would never have come into being; if during the resistance we had not organized an extensive network of self-defense groups and strong regional units, guerrilla warfare could not have developed to a high degree, and still less could we have built a powerful main force. On the other hand, if we had not had a large mobile main force when the armed struggle was at a victorious stage, there would have been no great battles to annihilate enemy forces, no victorious campaigns, and the glorious Dien Bien Phu battle would not have taken place. Today in the South of our country, in the main the armed forces are developing according to the same laws as those discussed above. The extensive semiarmed organizations efficaciously supported the movement of the masses in the countryside, when the people were rising up to free themselves from the enemy's grip, undertake partial uprisings at the base, and promote guerrilla warfare. It was while these political and armed struggles were raging that the three categories of armed forces were formed and developed. The South Vietnam Liberation Army has been growing rapidly and unceasingly. We can say that the above three forms of organization have extremely close, organic relations, which ensure an inexhaustible source of strength from the masses of the people for the people's armed forces, and make it possible for them not only to carry out their task of annihilating enemy forces but also to protect our political and economic bases and preserve the potential of the liberation war.

Our country has no vast territory, no large population; numerically, our armed forces cannot compare with those of large countries. For this very reason, to defend our country efficaciously, to defeat an enemy who is stronger than we materially and technically, we have to apply those three forms of armed forces strictly. Extensively and strongly organized militia and self-defense groups, strong regional troops, powerful and highly mobile main-force troops: that is a sine qua non condition for developing our fighting power and raising our national defense capacity to a high degree, even in the present conditions, when our People's Army is being built into a modern regular army.

From Correct Revolutionary Strategy and Tactics to Military Art in a People's War

To insure the success of a revolutionary war, it is necessary to have both correct strategy and correct tactics, which constitute the *military art of people's war*.

This military art must originate from the Party's revolutionary strategy and tactics. From the strategic objective, the objective of operations, to the principles guiding military strategy, and the like, all these fundamental questions are determined by the general strategy and tactics of the revolution. Military art must originate from the revolutionary character, the just character of the people's war, and also from the particular conditions of the enemy, our own and those of the theater of operations, if it is to solve in a correct and creative manner the problems relating to the direction of strategy, operations, and tactics, with a view to winning victory.

Our Party's military art is imbued with the popular character of revolutionary armed struggle; it regards the masses', the workers' and the laboring people's determination to carry out a thorough revolution, and the determination of the armed forces to fight and to win as the most basic and decisive factor in bringing about victory. That is also the *revolutionary character,* the *class character,* and the *Party character* of our military art.

Our military art is that of a small nation, whose armed force is still weak in equipment and technique but which rises up to fight against an enemy who is materially much stronger. This is a military art, whose characteristic is to *defeat material force with moral force, defeat what is strong with what is weak, defeat what is modern with* what is primitive, defeat the modern armies of the aggressive imperialists with the people's patriotism and determination to carry out a thorough revolution.

Our military art has successfully solved a number of questions relating to strategy, operations, and tactics, with a view to defeating a strong enemy; it has correctly determined *the relations between man and weapons, politics and technique,* regarding the human factor, the political factor, as the decisive factor, while considering weapons and technique also important. Now that the people's armed forces have the possibility of having better equipment, of being strengthened materially and technically, our military art is still firmly maintaining the above guiding principles, combining politics and technique on the basis that politics and fighting spirit are the essential factor, which enhances to the highest degree the fighting power of the armed forces.

Our military art thoroughly grasps the dialectical process of revolutionary violence evolving into an entire people's uprising or developing into a people's war; that is why it not only stresses that armed struggle is the continuation of political struggle, but attaches great importance to the political force of the masses while building the armed forces, as it considers the *combination of political struggle and armed struggle* as a problem of strategic direction, and a most important factor to ensure victory.

The people's war generally takes place in conditions when our side enjoys absolute political superiority over an enemy materially stronger than we are. Considering the revolutionary character of the war and the balance of concrete forces, our military art has determined the following strategic orientation: *to promote a war by the entire people, a total and protracted war.* We have to wage a long war in which our political superiority will prevail, and we can gradually increase our strength, pass from a position of weakness to a position of strength, change the balance of forces between us and the enemy, and ensure victory for our side. Looking back at our people's revolutionary struggle over past periods, we can see that we have, as a rule, resorted to the strategy of long struggle, and this strategy led the previous sacred resistance war to a glorious victory. But this does not mean that in certain concrete historical conditions, when on account of the political superiority we always have, or some other reason, the balance of forces changes rapidly to our advantage, we do not avail ourselves of the opportunity to give a strong impulse to the people's revolutionary struggle and promptly win a decisive victory. This is what happened in the glorious days of August 1945. Our entire people, responding to the Party's appeal, moved from a political struggle and local guerrilla warfare directly to a general uprising and won a glorious victory.

According to our military theory, in order to ensure victory for the people's war when we are stronger than the enemy politically and the enemy is stronger than we materially, it is necessary to promote an extensive *guerrilla war* which will develop gradually into a *regular war* combined with a guerrilla war. Regular war and guerrilla war are closely combined, stimulate each other, deplete and annihilate enemy forces, and bring final victory. Looking back at our people's armed struggle through successive periods, we can fully realize the strategic role of guerrilla war combined with regular war. Without the guerrilla war in the early days, there would have been no August general uprising, no victorious regular war during the resistance. Today on the South Vietnam battlefields, guerrilla war in the form of partial uprisings in the countryside has attained an extremely important strategic role and is developing to an increasingly high degree. On the other hand, if guerrilla war had not been combined with regular war, our people could not have won a decisive victory in the previous sacred resistance war. Guerrilla war and regular war are indispensable forms of war in a people's war, but this does not mean that in all circumstances a people's war must necessarily begin as a guerrilla war, and develop afterward into a regular war. Should the enemy now launch an aggressive war against the North of our country, on account of the concrete conditions on our side and theirs, regular war and guerrilla war would be waged simultaneously.

In all wars, the activities of the armed forces are either offensive or defensive. A revolutionary war also uses both these forms but regards offensive activities as the most essential. As a result of concrete practice of revolutionary armed struggle, our military art has created original forms of struggle: *guerrilla warfare, mobile warfare,* and *positional warfare.* All these forms, in offensive and defensive operations, can raise to the highest degree the determination of the people's armed forces to wipe out the enemy, to defeat what is strong with what is weak, that is, their determination to carry out a thorough revolution.

Our military art has also established correct principles of operational direction to guide all war activities by our armed forces. These principles have gradually taken shape in the course of our people's armed struggle, they have also been developed and brought to a higher level. These principles are indicative of our determination to carry out a thorough revolution; they attach the greatest importance to the determination to wipe out enemy manpower and preserve and strengthen our forces; they are, at the same time, penetrated with the thought that everything should be done to gain initiative in offensive operations, achieve great mobility, develop political superiority and heroism in fighting, in order to defeat an enemy stronger than we in equipment and technique, keeping in mind that victory must be won for each battle, that our armed forces must grow in strength with each battle, and win victory in the war.

Our military art must develop continuously if it is to meet the requirements of revolutionary tasks and *the requirements of a people's war in the present conditions.* A war may take place in circumstances when the enemy has modern equipment and weapons, while our side has inferior equipment and weapons, as on the South Vietnam battlefield at present. Our countrymen in the South have enhanced their fighting tradition and applied in a creative manner the experience gained during the resistance in order to defeat the enemy. A war may also take place in circumstances where the enemy has modern equipment and weapons while our equipment and weapons, though still inferior to those of the enemy, are becoming relatively modern. In these circumstances, our military art is still based on the popular character of the war, on politics and heroic fighting spirit, and on this basis, the efficaciousness of equipment and weapons will be increased, the organization and direction of operations will be brought to a higher level, and our armed forces will have an increasingly greater fighting power.

From Political Bases Among the Masses to a Popular National Defense

A strongly organized rear is always a factor of success because it is a source of political and moral stimulation and mobilization to the front, a source of supply of manpower, materials, and money for the war. As the war grows in scale, the role of the rear becomes increasingly important.

We attach the greatest importance to the role of the rear in a war. As soon as the question of armed struggle was posed, another question was also posed—that of having places where our people's armed forces could be hidden, trained, supplied, strengthened, and could rest. While revolutionary struggle was developing, we created a rear where there had been none, developed it, beginning with political bases among the masses, and now have a relatively complete system of popular national defense. We can say that in the early days when our Party made the decision to prepare for an armed struggle, we did not have a single inch of free territory; at that time, the only rear we had was our secret political bases, and the complete loyalty of the people who had become conscious of their revolutionary cause. It was from these secret political bases that our Party— our first guerrilla units were then concentrating on armed propaganda, political activities being regarded as more important than military activities—endeavored to build up secret bases for the armed struggle, and gradually came to wage partial guerrilla war and to create a free zone. Afterward, during the precious long resistance war, we had vast free zones as a strongly organized rear for the armed struggle, besides the guerrilla bases and guerrilla zones in the enemy's rear. Our rear, which was increasingly strengthened in every aspect, was the starting point from which our concentrated main-force units launched offensive operations on battlegrounds favorable to us; this rear made it possible to prepare and supply efficaciously the armed forces, in increasingly great counteroffensive campaigns. In the enemy-occupied areas, the rear was at first places where the politically conscious people hid cadres and guerrilla fighters in underground caches, sometimes for several months at a time; these places developed into guerrilla bases and guerrilla zones. In the liberation war now waged by our countrymen in the South, as a result of the political struggle of the masses combined with vigorous and extensive guerrilla warfare, liberated zones have come into being and are expanding, playing an increasingly important role in bringing about victory.

Looking back at our people's armed struggle through successive periods, we can fully grasp the strategic significance of the rear in relation to the war and draw this conclusion: from the viewpoint of the people's war, *the building-up and consolidation of the rear must be carried out in every aspect;* the political, economic, and military aspects are equally important, but most important is the political factor, the "people" factor. That is why in the last war, with the support of the people, we succeeded in building up relatively safe bases, not only in inaccessible mountainous regions, but also in the midst of the vast, open delta region, crisscrossed with rivers and studded with enemy posts.

At present, the liberated North, engaged in successful socialist construction, is our vast and strong rear; it is the base for the entire Vietnamese people's struggle for their revolutionary cause. In order *to consolidate national defense in every aspect,* greatly increase the defense capabilities of the country, we have not only to endeavor to build up powerful people's armed forces but also make great efforts to consolidate our rear in every aspect. The most fundamental question is to enhance the people's patriotism, socialist consciousness, awareness of being masters of their own country, and revolutionary vigilance, and on this basis, *to mobilize the entire people for increasing production and building socialism, while being always ready to fight for the defense of the North.* It is necessary continuously to consolidate the state of dictatorship of the proletariat, broaden democracy for the laboring people, resolutely repress the counter-revolutionaries. When internal order and security are ensured, no foreign aggressors are to be feared. A powerful people's national defense must have its material and technical bases; therefore, the building of socialist industry and agriculture, development of means of communication and transportation, and so forth, have a great importance for the consolidation of national defense in the North. While building up the economy, it is necessary *to coordinate better the economic construction with national defense, peacetime needs with wartime needs.* Only in this way can we fulfill our revolutionary tasks in the present situation, increase the national defense potential of our country and ensure successful completion of all tasks by our armed forces, foil all enemy maneuvers of provocation and aggression.

The Present Tasks

In this new phase of the revolution, the people's armed forces, which were the instrument of the state of worker-peasant dictatorship, have become the instrument of the state of dictatorship of the proletariat; such a development requires a deeper ideological transformation, as the socialist revolution is the deepest and most thorough revolution in history. Consequently, the task of heightening the cadres' and combatants' class consciousness, educating them in Marxist-Leninist ideology, becomes all the more urgent. At present, when the economy in the North is developing gradually and surely, we have new capabilities to improve our military equipment and strengthen the material and technical bases of the armed forces. And thus, thorough studies to grasp modern military technique and science, with a view to raising the level of organization and command, are becoming an important political task; but the Party leadership must continue to give the foremost place to the preservation and strengthening of the revolutionary character, the class character, of the people's armed forces.

In order to grasp fully the military line of our Party, we should also be imbued with our viewpoint on practice, because this military line results from an ingenious application of the universal principles of Marxism-Leninism on war and the armed forces to the concrete conditions of our country. War is a social phenomenon and develops according to definite laws. The revolutionary war in Vietnam is subject to the general laws of revolutionary war, but, at the same time, it has its specific laws. Our Party has successfully led the war because it has grasped the above general and specific laws and has based itself on the concrete conditions of our country in order to solve all the fundamental military questions. Thus, to be imbued with the military line of the Party also means to endeavor to study and gain a thorough knowledge of the enemy we must defeat, of the situation and characteristics of the people's armed forces, the situation and capabilities of our national economy, the question of coordination between economic activities and national defense, the characteristics of the battleground, and so forth, in order correctly to solve the questions of building up the armed forces and directing operations. We should fight against thoughts and acts which are mechanical, stereotyped, divorced from realities, in organization and equipment as well as in tactical training and ideological education.

To grasp fully the military line of the Party, we should also clearly see *the role of the fighting tradition and experience* of the people and the people's armed forces. Through the practice of an extremely heroic, rich, and creative revolutionary struggle, our people and our people's armed forces have built up a glorious fighting tradition and gained most precious and rich experience. In the conditions of modern warfare in the future, this tradition and this experience will still have a high value and a great role. Therefore, we must endeavor to preserve and develop the great traditions of our people and army; we must highly value their fighting experience, endeavor to make a synthesis of it, develop and use it in the new conditions.

We should also *emulate the spirit of resolute struggle, the determination to carry out a thorough revolution of our southern compatriots and the heroic South Vietnam Liberation Army.* The South Vietnam people and Liberation Army, with their ardent patriotism and deep hatred of the enemy, have gained extremely rich fighting experience, defeated all modern tactics and weapons of the United States imperialists and their agents, and driven them to severe, humiliating defeats in their "special war."

Magnificent heroism, military struggle combined with political struggle, annihilation of enemy troops by hundreds of thousands, including over three thousand United States aggressors, persuasion of over one hundred and fifty thousand enemy troops to return to the side of the fatherland, defeats inflicted on the "heliborne" and "armor-borne" tactics, basic destruction of the system of "strategic hamlets" set up by the enemy and the building of thousands of our own fighting villages and hamlets, over a hundred million participations in direct political struggle against the enemy, liberation of three-fourths of the territory with over eight million inhabitants—all these glorious deeds make up the experience that our countrymen in the "Bronze Citadel of the Fatherland" * and the heroic Liberation Army have gained at the price of great sacrifices, in their liberation war which is extremely arduous and fierce, but rich in brilliant victories. This has raised our people's experience of armed struggle to a new level, both in revolutionary content and

---

* South Vietnam has been called the "Bronze Citadel of the Fatherland" by Ho Chi Minh.

method of struggle; this is a very important contribution to our people's theory of revolutionary struggle and revolutionary military art.

We must also carefully study *the advanced experience of the armies of fraternal countries,* which has made a great contribution to our people's armed struggle. But in this study, we should be careful to make a correct choice and analysis, keep in mind the realities of our country and our army, our tradition of armed struggle and our fighting experience, and apply what we have learned in a creative manner, guarding ourselves from mechanical imitation and dogmatism.

In the leadership of our people's struggle for their revolutionary cause, our Party has thoroughly grasped the question of revolutionary armed struggle. Applying Marxist-Leninist principles, it has creatively elaborated a correct military line and led our people's revolutionary armed struggle to glorious victories.

By its character and its peculiarities, the military line of our Party has achieved an increasingly great international significance; it is a great contribution to the national liberation movement now rising indomitably in all the countries of Asia, Africa, and Latin America.

At present, our countrymen in South Vietnam are winning increasingly important victories in their liberation war, the United States imperialists and their lackeys are in an extremely severe political and military crisis. In an attempt to save the situation, they are now endeavoring to intensify their "special war" in the South, at the same time increasing their activities of sabotage and provocation against the North, and seeking to expand the war to the North. Now more than ever, our entire people in the North, while exerting the greatest efforts to construct a socialist economy, must endeavor to consolidate national defense, build up powerful people's armed forces, stand ready to take part in the struggle to safeguard peace, defend the socialist North, and actively support the heroic struggle of our countrymen in the South.

The South Vietnamese People Will Win

Ten years ago, on July 20, 1954, following the great victory of our army and people on the Dien Bien Phu battlefield, the Geneva agreements were signed, restoring peace in Indochina, on the basis of respect for the sovereignty, independence, unity, and territorial integrity of our country, Vietnam, and of two friendly countries, Cambodia and Laos.

As laid down in the agreements, free general elections would be held throughout Vietnam two years after the armistice for the peaceful reunification of our country. To create every favorable condition for this work, the belligerent armies were provisionally regrouped respectively north and south of the seventeenth parallel, and the administration of each zone undertook to insure all democratic liberties for the people, and at the same time determined not to accept weapons and military personnel from any country nor to join any military alliance.

Ten years have elapsed since the Geneva agreements were signed. During these ten years our people have successfully carried out socialist revolution and construction in the completely liberated North. However, throughout these ten years, the United States imperialists and their henchmen have done their utmost to sabotage the Geneva agreements and have unleashed a war to invade and sell out the South of our country. Thus, after fighting valiantly for ten years, making a great contribution to the victory of the first sacred

---

This is an edited condensation of General Giap's article entitled "The Liberation War of the South Vietnam People Against the U.S. Imperialists and Their Henchmen Will Certainly Win," published originally in *Nhan Dan* on July 19, 1964 (the tenth anniversary of the signing of the Geneva accords). It was published as a pamphlet by the Foreign Languages Publishing House, Hanoi, in 1965.

resistance, our fourteen million southern compatriots had again to rise up and wage a second sacred resistance against the United States imperialists and their stooges, for independence, democracy, peace, neutrality, for the implementation of the Geneva agreements, and then for the reunification of the fatherland.

I

The Geneva agreements were a great victory for our people, the fruit of ten years of long and hard resistance, of nearly one hundred years of national liberation struggle. This victory has safeguarded the gains of the August revolution in the North of our country. It has helped the Vietnamese revolution in the North to attain the socialist stage and the Democratic Republic of Vietnam to become the first socialist country in Southeast Asia.

For French and American imperialism, the Geneva agreements were a most pitiful setback. They have put an end to the domination of the French colonialists in Indochina. They have foiled the scheme of the United States imperialists to prolong and extend the war and turn the Indochinese countries into new United States colonies and military bases. They were the bitterest defeat of the United States imperialists in Southeast Asia after their disaster in the Chinese mainland and in Korea.

While the Indochinese countries scored a great victory in their valiant and hard resistance and the French Expeditionary Corps faced grave danger, United States imperialism made strenuous efforts to salvage the situation, but in the end it, together with its defeated ally, was forced to sit for negotiation to end the war. This came as no surprise to us, and historical facts have given added proof that even when negotiating to reach an agreement, United States imperialism already schemed to sabotage it with a view to impairing the victories of the Indochinese peoples and restricting its defeats to the utmost.

No sooner had the ink of the signatures on the Geneva agreements

The South Vietnamese People Will Win   187

dried than the United States imperialists set up the aggressive Southeast Asia military bloc* and brazenly put South Vietnam, Cambodia, and Laos under its protection. They schemed to consolidate further their strategic position in Southeast Asia while using this new aggressive bloc as a tool to carry on their war policy and curb the development of the national liberation movement. *At utter variance with the provisions of the Geneva agreements, they plotted to continue their aggressive policy under the form of neo-colonialism with a view to turning South Vietnam, Cambodia, and Laos into their new-type colonies and military bases.* This dark and perfidious scheme came out clearly in the statements of the United States government that the security of the United States was decided along the seventeenth parallel and the Vietnam-Laos border.

In the new strategic plan of the United States imperialists, South Vietnam holds a position of utmost importance. This is precisely why soon after the armistice the United States stopped all military aid to the French in Indochina, ousted the latter from the South, and rigged up the Ngo Dinh Diem administration so that it would be entirely at its beck and call, hoping to use this subservient clique *to suppress our compatriots' patriotic struggle in the South, rapidly turn the South into a new-type United States colony and military base, and permanently partition our country.*

The United States imperialists have trampled upon all the provisions of the Geneva agreements, overtly introduced weapons, munitions, and war matériel into the South at an accelerated tempo, and increased their military personnel from two hundred at the end of the war to thirty-five hundred in 1961. They have frenziedly stepped up their intervention in every field, feverishly built up a regular and modern army for the puppet administration, and strengthened such other antirevolutionary armed forces as the civil guard, People's Militia, police, and public security. They have frantically built up and

---

* Giap refers to the Southeast Asia Treaty Organization (SEATO), established in the autumn of 1954.

extended military bases in the South and have constructed a complete system of strategic roads so big and perfect that they can be used not only to carry out the aggressive war in South Vietnam but also to meet the greater requirements of the U.S. Army in Southeast Asia.

With the help of the United States imperialists and in furtherance of their neo-colonialist policy, the supporters of Ngo Dinh Diem dethroned Bao Dai, a puppet of the French colonialists, illegally founded in the South the so-called Republic of Vietnam, and resorted to oppression and flattery to carry out separatist general elections. Meanwhile, they sealed off the provisional military demarcation line and turned down every proposal to re-establish normal relations and convene a consultative conference with the North.

Despite its signboard of "independence" and "democracy" and its other deceptive policies such as "land reform" and "rehabilitation of the national economy," since its very inception the Ngo Dinh Diem administration revealed itself as a traitorous clique and came up against powerful opposition from all our compatriots in the South. It carried out a fascist dictatorial policy of utmost barbarity, launched hundreds of mopping-up campaigns with its regular army, perpetrated countless crimes, and set up prisons everywhere to jail and torture patriots. It implemented a state policy of "indictment of communists" and "extermination of communists" to repress the former resistance members, the parents of those regrouped in the North, those who stood for independence, freedom, peaceful national reunification, and the implementation of the Geneva agreements. It exterminated Buddhist, Cao Dai, and Hoa Hao believers,*

---

* The Cao Dai religion is a synthesis of many faiths, both traditional and modern, while the Hoa Hao is a reformed Buddhist sect. Each has had as many as a million adherents in South Vietnam. For decades they have had their own military forces and strong political hold over large regions. Diem's attack on the sects in the early years of his rule touched off the first armed resistance to his regime.

The South Vietnamese People Will Win 189

and even terrorized those who had closely cooperated with it once they did not submit unconditionally.

This unilateral war started in 1954 and became most atrocious in 1957–1959 after the United States–Diem clique had provisionally consolidated their administrative and military machine. The Phu Loi massacre* and the law 10/1959 † were typical of this most savage policy of terror. With their special military courts, prisons, guillotines, and wartime repressive measures, they hoped to drown in blood the patriotic movement of our southern compatriots in a short period, consolidate their selfish privileges and interests, and realize their dream of "pacifying the South, filling up the Ben Hai River and marching to the North."

However, far from yielding the expected results, the United States–Diem policy of war and terrorism roused high indignation among all strata of our compatriots in the South. *Our fellow countrymen held aloft the banner of peace, independence, reunification, democracy, and waged a persistent and valiant political struggle against the enemy, relying on the just cause and legality of the Geneva agreements.*

When the United States–Diem clique treacherously sabotaged the Geneva agreements, everywhere meetings and demonstrations broke out, slogans appeared demanding an end to terror and reprisals, the re-establishment of North-South relations, a consultative conference for general elections, and the peaceful reunification of the country.

---

* In his letter of January 26, 1961, to H. E. Ambassador M. Gopala Menon, Chairman of the International Control Commission set up at Geneva, Giap reported the food poisoning of over six thousand detainees in the Phu Loi camp in early 1959. Philippe Devillers (in Honey, ed., *North Vietnam Today*, p. 37) records the death of some twenty detainees there in December 1959.

† Promulgated on May 6, 1959, this statute reshaped the entire judiciary system of South Vietnam, establishing special military courts under the direct authority of the Defense Ministry throughout the country. Rights of defense counsel and appeal were removed. The tribunals could only pass sentences of death (carried out on the spot) or hard labor for life.

The political struggle grew all the more powerful when the United States–Diem clique resorted to such machinations to sabotage further independence and national reunification as referendum and separatist general elections. It became fierce and bloody in the waves of struggle against the policy of "indictment of communists," the mopping-up operations, and the massacres of the population. This unyielding political struggle, often waged in front of the muzzles of enemy guns, succeeded in checking and foiling part of their Machiavellian schemes; it highlighted our compatriots' indomitable spirit, and frustrated the enemy's policy of "indictment and extermination of communists" which it has raised to the level of "state policy" in order to divide the southern people, liquidate patriots, and quench the revolutionary movement. With various forms of struggle, relying on arguments, the legality of the Geneva agreements, and the pressure of the masses, our compatriots showed their patriotism and solidarity in struggle, exposed the dictatorial and traitorous Ngo Dinh Diem administration, drove it into ever growing isolation, and pilloried it.

Throughout five years of arduous and fierce political struggle with their bare hands against the violence of the enemy, our southern compatriots experienced countless sufferings and losses, but they carried the day.

Thousands of villages were burned by the enemy, and hundreds of thousands of people were jailed, tortured, and killed in prisons and concentration camps. But sufferings and losses could not dampen our people's combativeness and patriotism. On the contrary, through their fierce political struggle, our compatriots were tempered and became aware of the ferocity of the United States–Diem clique— and of its irremediable fundamental weakness—for it is the enemy of the people and of the fatherland, for it represents violence and injustice.

Through their fierce political struggle, our compatriots clearly realized that *to overthrow the enemy, attain the fundamental aspira-*

The South Vietnamese People Will Win 191

tions of the broad masses of the people, there was no other way than to wage a revolutionary struggle. Far from quenching our compatriots' revolutionary spirit, United States–Diem guns, bullets, prisons, re-education centers, and fascist laws exacerbated it all the more. For five years on end, the United States–Diem clique waged a real war against the people, but the latter's revolutionary spirit held out and in many vast areas the revolutionary forces were still kept intact.

The end of 1959 and beginning of 1960 marked a new development in the southern revolutionary movement. *The persistent political struggle in the past years now bolstered by an armed struggle for self-defense, grew all the more powerful and sweeping.* The revolutionary mettle of the masses in the Mekong Delta as well as in the immense Western Highlands rose as an overflowing tide. The enemy's grip was broken over vast areas. In some places the enemy grass-roots administration was broken up and the cruel devils isolated or punished; in some, the prosperity zones were destroyed and nearly 80 percent of their inhabitants were liberated. *The political situation of the United States–Diem administration underwent a serious and endless crisis.* In face of the people's new revolutionary high tide, they realized that their scheme to "pacify" the South rapidly and use it as a base to attack the North was obviously a fiasco; they had to devote all their efforts to deal with the new developments of the movement.

The United States imperialists openly stepped up their armed intervention in the South of our country. In May 1961 the *bilateral military agreement* between United States Vice President Johnson and Ngo Dinh Diem was signed; then came into being the Staley-Taylor plan* and the setting-up of the U.S. Military Command in

---

* Economist Eugene Staley and General Maxwell Taylor were influential in establishing the broad contours of policy in the beginning of the Kennedy administration. Strategy then called for regroupment of the population into "strategic hamlets," pacification, and economic development.

Saigon under Gen. Paul Harkins.* *The United States imperialists and their henchmen decided to launch an "undeclared war" in the South, to use this area as a testing ground for their so-called "special war" aimed at repressing the national liberation movement.*

In brief, the plan of this "special war," the Staley-Taylor plan, envisaged three stages: first to "pacify" the South and establish a network of spy-commando centers in the North; then to rehabilitate the economy and increase the puppet military forces in the South while stepping up sabotage work in the North; lastly to develop the southern economy and to attack the North.

To carry out the first stage (regarded as most important), they worked out a series of new measures, including the increase of the army's effectiveness, the improvement of equipment, and the raising of the fighting capacities of the puppet armed forces as well as the enforcement of the "state policy" of "strategic hamlets" aimed at gradually concentrating and controlling the bulk of the population. The United States imperialists stepped up their multiform aid to the Ngo Dinh Diem administration; first of all, the military aid. They reckoned that within eighteen months, namely, by the end of 1962, the superincreased reactionary military forces would certainly smash the people's political and military revolutionary forces: meanwhile, most of the fourteen million of our compatriots in the South would be herded into "strategic hamlets," kept under close watch, and severed from all connections with the guerrilla groups; the whole of South Vietnam would then be "pacified"; their first stage would be brought to completion.

At the outset, the enemy's perfidious scheme did cause new difficulties for our compatriots in the South. However, inspired with an unshakable determination to struggle and with a dogged will to overthrow the enemy of the nation, our compatriots have carried on

---

* Head of the U.S. Military Mission to South Vietnam during the Kennedy administration.

their valiant struggle in order to frustrate the United States imperialists' new plan of armed intervention. *To oppose the United States–Diem "special war," the southern people have launched a sweeping and powerful guerrilla war, an all-out and protracted people's resistance.* At the beginning, our compatriots in the South had only their bare hands, while the enemy had a marked superiority in material forces. Our people in the South had to put up an extremely hard and fierce struggle, opposing justice to aggression, weakness to strength, heroism to modern weapons. Capturing enemy weapons to equip themselves, our army and people in the South have overcome all difficulties and trials, developed their forces rapidly, scored success after success, and will win ever greater victories.

The United States–Diem clique regarded military measures as most efficient to crush our armed forces and political bases. Throughout 1962 and 1963 our army and people inflicted upon them many military setbacks. Unable to bring out the expected results, the "helicopter tactics," modern weapons, chemical poisons, and the like, could not even save their initiators from bitter failures. Most of the raids upon the villages, big and small, were repelled or smashed. The southern army and people annihilated many enemy posts, stormed many enemy garrisons, and attacked reinforcements or convoys on road and on water. Early in 1963 the resounding Ap Bac victory of the Liberation Army and My Tho guerrillas highlighted our fighters' boundless heroism and inspired the patriotic armed forces in the South to win battles and destroy the enemy. According to the figures released by the Liberation News Agency, in three years of guerrilla warfare (1961–1963) our southern army and people destroyed and put out of action more than 250,000 enemy troops, among them nearly 1,500 Americans, shot down and damaged hundreds of enemy planes, captured over 30,000 weapons of all kinds.

The stated policy of strategic hamlets is the backbone of the "special war"; the United States–Diem clique pinned all their hopes on this policy and mustered manpower and wealth to enforce it at any cost. They reckoned that in a short time they could build seventeen thousand "strategic hamlets," turning the South into a huge system of prisons. However, at the very start, their plan met with our compatriots' fierce opposition. The herding of people was not as easy as they expected; the tempo of building "strategic hamlets" was slowed down as time passed. A number of "strategic hamlets" were destroyed either immediately after their establishment or so many times that the enemy could not consolidate them. Others, once destroyed, were turned into fighting villages, solid strongholds for guerrilla warfare. No more than six or seven thousand hamlets were set up, according to the statistics of the Ngo Dinh Diem administration.

Together and in coordination with the military struggle and destruction of "strategic hamlets," there developed a sweeping and powerful political struggle involving all strata of the people. Many a time the political force of the masses crushed enemy mopping-up operations and successfully protected our compatriots' lives and property. It is this same force that destroyed the rural administration block by block, liberated many vast areas in the countryside, and called upon tens of thousands of enemy troops and officials to cross over to the people's side. In 1962–1963 alone, more than fifty million individual participations in political struggles under various forms and sizes were recorded. The seething struggle during the second half of 1963 put up by Buddhist believers, youths, students, intellectuals, and laboring people in the towns, big and small, especially in Hue and Saigon-Cholon, plunged the United States–Diem clique into an ever deepening crisis.

After two years of large-scale "special war," the United States imperialists and their henchmen faced many difficulties and setbacks both in the military and political fields. The time limit of eighteen months having elapsed, *their strategy of rapid "pacification" of the South once again floundered. The Staley-Taylor plan turned out to be a fiasco* in the face of the boundless heroism of our army and people in the South.

The South Vietnamese People Will Win 195

Owing to the repeated defeats of the "special war," the internal contradictions between the United States imperialists and their henchmen grew so sharp that late in 1963 and early in 1964, the United States imperialists had to stage two coups d'état aimed at swapping horses midstream and salvaging the situation. Ngo Dinh Diem and Ngo Dinh Nhu were overthrown and assassinated; soon after that, the Duong Van Minh clique was also replaced by new henchmen.

Throughout nine years, the Diem-Nhu brothers efficiently served the United States imperialists, sold out their country and their compatriots, and were praised by the Americans as the "number one anti-communist fighters" in Southeast Asia and as "great men" of the "free world." Now, forced to overthrow Diem-Nhu and ready to kill their faithful servants, the United States imperialists admitted the shameful failure of their new-type colony, the fiasco of their so-called "special war." The pitiful collapse of Diem-Nhu led to consternation in the ranks of the puppet administration and army, rousing bewilderment and weariness among them. It could not solve the ever sharper contradictions between the United States imperialists and their henchmen and instead rendered them more acute and complicated. It could not bolster the sagging morale of the puppet troops and officials, shattering it instead.

Late in 1963 and particularly early in 1964, our people in the South made the best use of the enemy's weak points and difficulties, stepped up their activities in every field, and scored great victories. According to the preliminary statistics of the Liberation News Agency, in the first six months of this year the southern army and people fought nearly 14,000 battles; razed to the ground 400 enemy posts; smashed and forced the enemy to withdraw from over 550 other posts; annihilated and captured 42,000 enemy troops, among them more than 500 Americans; put out of action nearly 30,000 of them; seized 5,000 weapons of all kinds, as well as millions of bullets and hand grenades; and shot down 170 planes of various types, damaging over 320 others. Our people from the Nam Bo Delta and the Western

Highlands to the Fifth Zone coastal areas rose up and demolished nearly 2,000 "strategic hamlets," extending the liberated zone in many regions. The above figures prove *the southern resistance is entering a new stage, and the balance of forces is continuously tipping in our favor.*

Of course, in face of this situation, with their extremely reactionary and cruel nature, the United States imperialists did not admit themselves beaten but frenziedly stepped up their aggressive war. Now they have to envisage a protracted war in the South. They have worked out a new strategic plan, the Johnson-McNamara plan, aimed at "pacifying" the South during 1964–1965. This new plan does not basically differ from the bankrupt Staley-Taylor plan. What is new is that the United States imperialists make greater efforts to increase their war means in the hope of securing better results for their special war. The puppet armed forces are increased to 350,000 regular troops, apart from 200,000 civil guards and reactionary fighting youths; the number of United States advisers and servicemen now reaches 25,000; aircraft of all types amounts to over 700; all other weapons are also increased. The military aid for 1964 goes up from $500 to $625 million. This is a fairly great war effort by the United States imperialists aimed at salvaging the desperate situation of the puppet army, mustering forces to "pacify" the areas controlled by the guerrillas according to plan, first of all again to tighten their grip on the eight provinces in the Mekong Delta and a number of regions in south Central Vietnam.

To carry out this new plan, the United States imperialists sent General Taylor, chairman of the U.S. Joint Chiefs of Staff, as ambassador to the South. This appointment of Taylor shows that the United States imperialists are most obdurate and cling to their "big-stick foreign policy" which has met with failure these past ten years in the South. Taylor is the very man who advocated the theory of "special war" which has been tested for the first time in the South and which has obviously gone bankrupt. Taylor is also the exponent of the theory of pacification of the South within eighteen months;

however, twice eighteen months have elapsed, and this plan has not yet been initially carried out and has been replaced by a new one. The appointment of Taylor to South Vietnam reminds us of that of such top French generals as De Tassigny and Navarre to Indochina every time the French Expeditionary Corps was in serious difficulty. Our compatriots in the South and the heroic southern liberation troops, though having to fight a protracted and hard war, will certainly reserve for Taylor or any United States aggressive general the fate our people reserved for the former defeated French generals.

II

Throughout the French rule, South Vietnamese society, like the rest of our country, was a *colonial and semifeudal* one. After the successful August revolution, the Democratic Republic of Vietnam made its appearance. With the reconquest by the French colonialists' troops, part of our country *bore the character of a people's democracy while part of it remained a colonial and semifeudal country.* Our entire people's great resistance war ended with the historic Dien Bien Phu victory. On the basis of the Geneva agreements, and owing to the United States imperialists' intervention in South Vietnam, our country has been temporarily divided into two zones with differing politico-social systems. The North, completely liberated, has been successfully building socialism; the South, becoming a new-type United States colony, has borne the character of a colonial and semifeudal society. After ten years of revolutionary struggle, new changes in line with the upward trend of history have taken place. Today, part of South Vietnam *remains colonial and semifeudal, while part of it, namely, the ever enlarged free zone, bears a new character:* there, our compatriots enjoy independence, democracy, and freedom.

The very nature of such a society has shown that at present in South Vietnam there exist *two fundamental contradictions: one* between our southern people and the aggressive imperialists, first of all the United States imperialists and their henchmen; *the other* is the contradiction between the southern people, first of all the peasants, and feudal landlordism. These contradictions have defined: (1) the character of the revolution in the South which is a *national democratic revolution;* (2) its strategic task which is the overthrow of imperialism, the completion of national independence in combination with the overthrow of feudal landlordism, and the completion of people's democracy.

Owing to the collusion between United States imperialism and the local reactionary forces, South Vietnamese society contains a basic contradiction, between our southern people on the one hand and aggressive imperialism and its lackeys representative of the most reactionary pro-American feudal landlords and comprador bourgeois on the other. This main contradiction defines the *concrete object and immediate task of the revolution* in South Vietnam, as well as the organization of forces for the completion of this revolutionary task.

Soon after the restoration of peace in Indochina, the object of the revolution in South Vietnam began to change. American imperialism had kicked out defeated French colonialism, seized South Vietnam, and established the pro-American Ngo Dinh Diem administration. United States imperialism has neither established a ruling machinery nor utilized occupation troops in the South as French old colonialism did; but through interventionist policies and military and economic aid, it has controlled the South in all fields.

Neo-colonialism, which is being practiced by American imperialism in South Vietnam, is a product of imperialism in modern times. Owing to the growing influence of the world socialist system and to the national liberation movement which is storming in many countries of Asia, Africa, and Latin America, the imperialists can no longer rule over their colonies with old methods; the native reactionary forces also are frightened and anxious for their privileges. *Neo-colonialism is precisely the collusion and compromise between foreign imperialists and a section of native comprador bourgeois and reactionary feudal landlords to maintain the colonial rule under new forms and methods, while checking and opposing the movement of the broad masses.*

Neo-colonialism is by nature a concentrated expression of the basic tendency of capitalism: the enslavement of weak and small nations, the search for and struggle over markets and raw materials, and the utter oppression and exploitation of the people of these nations. Its main practice is reliance on violence. It differs from old colonialism in the fact that *it carries out its policy of enslavement and uses violence not directly, but indirectly* through the medium of a puppet administration and an army vested with sham independence and democracy, and in the form of "aid" or "alliance" in all respects. Neo-colonialism masks its aggressive and exploiting nature in many cloaks; therefore, it is all the more cunning and wicked and easily induces the people to relax their vigilance. In the South, after the defeat of French imperialism, old colonialism was completely doomed and was buried together with the images of its cruel or crafty governors general and high commissioners and its ruthless expeditionary corps against the will of United States imperialism which, unable to revive that decaying corpse, is compelled to act under the cloak of neo-colonialism.

Neo-colonialism relies on its quislings as a tool to carry out its policy. Its strength is drawn partly from the vast economic and military possibilities—which are many—of the metropolis, but which, on the other hand, are directly determined by whether or not the native reactionary forces are strong economically and politically. In South Vietnam, the United States-sponsored puppet administration was set up at a time when our people were gaining successes and imperialism meeting with failure. Therefore, right from its inception, it lacked vitality and was fraught with the inherent causes of inner contradictions, crises, and wars. Its social basis is next to nil: feudalism, landlordism, and comprador bourgeoisie, which had not been very strong under the French rule, were weakened and differentiated during the years of resistance war. After the restoration of peace, they were again divided due to the opposing viewpoints between the

United States and France. On the other hand, the revolutionary people have reached a very high degree of political consciousness and are strongly united.

In these conditions, the United States-backed puppet administration cannot stand firm on its feet without closely clinging to its bosses and making themselves docile lackeys at the beck and call of United States imperialism in all affairs, big or small. In face of the people's revolutionary high tide, it is compelled to embark rapidly on dictatorship and fascism, feverishly carrying out the United States policy of military intensification and war preparation. For its own existence, it is forced to declare bluntly its opposition to the Geneva agreements and the cherished aspirations of our people: peace, independence, democracy, and national reunification. That is why, despite the United States–Diem slogans of "overthrowing colonialism," "boycotting feudalism," and "extermination of communists," and despite their boastful claim of liquidating social evils or carrying out a number of demagogic reforms, the large masses of people have immediately made out behind the mended cloak the real face of the international gendarme, which is the face of United States imperialism and that of the Ngo family, which for many generations have served as running dogs, and the people are all the more resolute in their struggle against them. For many years, the United States-backed puppet administration has had to resort to a policy of violence in order to repress the movement, using privileges and interests as lures to create a new generation of traitors; it has had to strive to put under its close control the army, the police, and the administration at various levels in an attempt to enlarge its social bases. But the rising tide of the ever sweeping and powerful struggle of our people, coupled with the coup d'état overthrowing the rule of the Ngo family, has inflicted heavy losses upon United States imperialism; the ranks of its quislings cannot be consolidated, let alone enlarged.

The policy of United States imperialism and its henchmen is one of invasion and betrayal of South Vietnam. In consequence, both the unilateral war they started in 1954 and the "special war" they have kindled recently are only aimed at repressing the people's revolutionary movement, dominating and enslaving South Vietnam, and transforming it into a United States neo-colony and military base. This is clearly *an unjust war, an aggressive war*. Therefore, in consideration of its political goal and nature, the war carried out by United States imperialism and its henchmen is by no means different from the aggressive war kindled by French colonialism in former times to enslave our people.

In the United States imperialists' strategy of "flexible response," "special war" ranks third, coming after world nuclear war and limited war. Considering that the balance of world forces is tipping unfavorably for them, and the immediate difficulties met in the kindling of a large-scale war, the United States imperialists hope to win successes in "limited war" with conventional weapons, especially in the "special wars" aimed at repressing the liberation movement of the weak and small nations. The United States brass have made a thoroughgoing study of the characteristics of this kind of war, the aim of which, in their opinion, is to oppose guerrilla war, that is, the people's war. Therefore, special warfare takes place within the limits of a country with no fixed frontline and rare mobilization of large units; on the other hand, there must be an all-around combination of military, political, psychological, and economic activities. The foregoing features regarding the limit, scale, or real characteristics of special war by no means change its nature: *special war is aggressive war*.

United States imperialism, the sworn enemy of the southern people and of our entire nation, possessed of a capitalist economy with most developed modern industry, is the most barbarous imperialist chieftain, the main force of war and aggression, the bulwark of the world counter-revolutionary forces. Economically and militarily it is a strong enemy.

Compared with French imperialism in former times, it has greater possibilities in all respects—in money and in modern weapons which are stockpiled in great quantities. But the assessment we make of the enemy forces must be factual. We must view them not only on the basis of the balance of world forces in general but also within the limit of a given area, within the real limit of the southern part of our country. Today in the world, the United States military and economic forces are still strong, but, compared with the revolutionary forces which are developing throughout the world, they are in a weaker position than before. Moreover, United States imperialism is being attacked on all sides and has to scatter its forces in many places.

It suffered heavy defeats in China, Korea, and Cuba, is being beaten in Laos and South Vietnam, and is meeting with difficulties in many other places.

Today in South Vietnam the United States imperialists and their lackeys are ever more isolated politically. Militarily speaking, their army is superior to ours in effectiveness, modern weapons, and mobility. All their temporarily strong points must be studied carefully, especially when solving questions regarding operations and campaigns. However, it is certain that all these strong points cannot make up for their most basic weak points in morale and politics, which are inherent in an enemy of the people, in a counter-revolutionary army. But in the South of our country, these weak points are all the more serious owing to the weakness of the southern reactionary forces and to the peculiar form of the aggressive war which is taking place there.

1. Whether in the unilateral war in former times or in the "special war" at present, the United States imperialists and their lackeys have been conducting an unjust war, that of aggressors and traitors trampling under foot the most elementary rights of our people and the dearest aspirations of our nation. Therefore, they are meeting with the fierce resistance of our fourteen million southern compatriots. They are fighting a whole nation.

2. In this "special war," their military forces are mainly the puppet army. But the absolute majority of their men, being sons of the toiling people, cannot find it in their hearts to go on serving as cannon fodder to defend the interests of the enemy. In the face of the

fierce struggle and successes of the people and Liberation Army, a hatred for war will certainly develop among the reactionary troops. An ever growing number of soldiers, stirred by patriotism, will certainly turn their guns against the enemy and side with the people. Moreover, owing to the weakening of the social basis of the reactionary forces as a result of their inner contradictions, which have grown acute and intricate, the enemy has less and less basis for consolidating his army and administration; the morale of the officials in the puppet administration and of the men among the puppet army is flagging markedly with every passing day.

3. To consolidate the reactionary army, the United States imperialists bring in more advisers, military personnel, and even several task forces. The introduction of greater United States military forces into South Vietnam is immediately effective in controlling the reactionary military forces of their henchmen more closely. But we must clearly realize that, for the United States, the introduction of more military forces into South Vietnam is politically a most passive action. The increase of American military forces will diminish the "special" character of the war. The new face of colonialism has become more ineffective. Our people's hatred will increase and the contradiction between the United States advisers and the puppet officers and men will be sharpened, not to mention the weakness of the GI's in a war against the guerrillas in a tropical battlefield such as South Vietnam. Even the United States brass has to recognize that these weak points have greatly curtailed the effectiveness of their activities.

The South, like the rest of Vietnam, was a colonial and semifeudal country with an extremely backward economy which was, moreover, ruined by war for many years. After the restoration of peace, it had not yet had time to bring its production to normal when it again fell victim to another aggressive war. Our southern people have had to endure privations and misery caused by a war dragging on for decades. With the successful August revolution, the people's power was established. This power was afterward maintained and consolidated in the free zones, guerrilla zones, and guerrilla bases throughout the years of nationwide resistance; however, implementing the Geneva agreements, our power gradually gave place to that of the reactionaries, henchmen of the United States imperialists.

For the same reason our people's armed forces in South Vietnam, which had matured in the Fifth Zone* and Mekong Delta battlefields during the years of resistance against the French, regrouped to the North, provisionally leaving behind their beloved native land which they had protected at the cost of their blood, while, for their part, tens of thousands of enemy troops withdrew from the Bac Bo Delta. Not only did our guerrilla bases and guerrilla zones cease to exist, but even our immense free zones were temporarily put under the control of the opponents. Availing themselves of these conditions, the United States imperialists and the Ngo Dinh Diem administration started a unilateral war to extinguish the patriotic movement with a view to transforming South Vietnam into an American new-type colony and military base. They pinned their hope on our ruined economy and on the very difficult conditions created by the absence of a people's power and army to protect them. And they thought that our southern people had no other way than letting themselves be subjugated by their bayonets and guillotines.

But our southern compatriots are really a heroic people. *They are possessed of an invincible potential power* and a political strength which the United States imperialists and their quislings are incapable of understanding. They have coped with a people having a very high revolutionary spirit and very great political superiority. Revolutionary theory is translated into invincible strength once it has gripped the masses. In a revolutionary war, the people's political superiority will be translated into a material force capable of turning the tables on the enemy, overcoming all difficulties and hardships to defeat in the end an enemy who at first was several times stronger. The southern people are indeed outstanding sons of the Vietnamese people, a people having the tradition of struggling to the bitter end

---

* The northernmost region of South Vietnam.

against foreign invasion, "rather to sacrifice their lives than be enslaved." Our southern people made the Nam Ky and Ba To insurrections;* in the historic days of August they rose up to take the revolution to victory and establish the people's power; they enjoyed the political and economic rights brought to them by the revolution; and they fought heroically, making an important contribution to the victory of the great resistance war of the nation. After a long revolutionary struggle, the southern people reached a high political and organizational level, gaining many experiences from their political and their armed struggles. For this reason, in the face of a most barbarous enemy, the revolutionary movement in the South has been maintained and developed every day.

The southern people, armed with a revolutionary spirit and the experiences gained in their revolutionary struggle, are, moreover, encouraged by the strength of a just cause and closely sealed into a very strong and firm bloc by *lofty revolutionary goals:* national independence, land to the tillers, basic freedoms, peace, and national reunification. After a national democratic revolutionary struggle fraught with sacrifice and hardships, and a great patriotic resistance war, the lofty national democratic ideals broadly disseminated by the Party since 1930 have taken deep root into the heart and mind of the masses of people. We cannot give up fighting so long as we have not wrested back independence, land, and the basic rights to life. The national resistance war ended successfully, the Geneva agreements recognized Vietnam's sovereignty, independence, unity, and territorial integrity; the battle cannot come to an end so long as these clauses of the agreements are not implemented. The southern people are determined to hold firm the national and democratic banner and raise it aloft till victory.

In the former resistance years, President Ho Chi Minh used to say: "Unity, unity, and broad unity; victory, victory, and great victory." The southern people clearly realize that unity is strength, unity is

---

* 1940 and 1945.

the main factor of victory. Though the enemy is materially strong, he is constantly divided by inner contradictions, while the southern people on the contrary enjoy *a tradition of broad unity* established throughout the first sacred resistance war. In the first years following the restoration of peace, the struggle was fraught with difficulties and hardships, and the southern patriots, though at times severed from one another organizationally, were closely bound to one another morally. The love for one's own fellow countrymen, the national pride and solidarity, and the pursuit of common revolutionary goals are sources of strength encouraging our compatriots firmly to maintain and actively to broaden unity. If the South Vietnam National Liberation Front has grown rapidly and enjoyed such a great prestige among the people, it is mainly due to the experiences gained in the past, to the traditions of national unity, and to the development and application of these experiences to the new historical conditions.

Moreover, the southern people are encouraged to organize themselves along a *correct political line and in adequate forms of struggle.* For this reason, however atrocious the enemy, and however difficult and dangerous the conditions of struggle may be, the political and armed forces of the people are growing stronger and stronger. The process of revolutionary struggle of the southern people is a development from political struggle to armed struggle, with both of them then being combined with each other and enhancing each other. The southern people have developed their political superiority to a high degree, having worked out a correct principle and a great many forms of struggle. Politically and militarily speaking, the revolutionary struggle in the South has been developing to a fairly high degree thanks to the creative spirit of the masses; it has, therefore, been able to thwart many dangerous policies and maneuvers of the enemy, frustrate his modern strategy, and achieve greater and greater successes.

The revolutionary war waged by our compatriots in the South has been carried on when half of our country is liberated and advancing to socialism. *The North is a hope and an encouragement for the southern people,* especially in the years when the enemy carries out most atrocious terrorization and repression. The liberated North is the pride of the entire Vietnamese people, a firm and strong base of the struggle for national reunification. Our southern compatriots feel that their northern fellow countrymen are always close by their side in the struggle against a common enemy, which enhances their confidence and strengthens their determination to overcome all difficulties on their advance to victory.

Over the past years, our southern people have been struggling against a most barbarous enemy. The most reactionary and inhuman nature of the United States imperialists and their puppet administration have wrought havoc with our southern people who become all the more aware of the real face of the enemy of the nation and nurture an ever deeper hatred for him. In war the fighting spirit and hatred are a huge force. This explains why the United States jet helicopters, amphibious cars, ultrarapid submachine guns, flamethrowers, automatic mines, noxious chemicals, unsinkable landing craft, and other modern weapons cannot save the puppet army from repeated failures.

On the contrary, the southern liberation forces are armed only with rudimentary weapons, but their very high fighting spirit have helped them score success after success.

At present, the revolutionary war in the South is still facing many difficulties and hardships. However, with their heroic fighting spirit, our southern compatriots and Liberation Army have scored great successes and created stable factors of strategic significance. The people's political forces and revolutionary armed forces have grown stronger and stronger, the liberated area wider. Our southern people are turning the table on the enemy, and the successful development of the liberation war in South Vietnam has eloquently testified that in a revolutionary struggle and in war, the decisive factor is, in the last analysis, man and political lines, and that the decisive strength is that of the masses of people.

III

As has been said above, during the last ten years in South Vietnam, the revolutionary struggle of our people has shifted from the political form to the form of political and armed struggle and has now become a national liberation war waged by the entire people against the "special war" unleased by the United States imperialists and their lackeys.

Basing ourselves on the characteristics stated in Section II, we can draw the conclusion that: *the war for liberation waged by the South Vietnamese people at present is a nationwide, all-sided, self-supporting, long-term, and arduous war which in the end will certainly be victorious.* Besides this fundamental political content, similar to that of the former patriotic war against the French colonialists and American interventionists, the present war for liberation of our people in the South has its own peculiarities in that our enemy is not the old colonialism of the French imperialists but the neo-colonialism of the United States imperialists; our southern compatriots have now made great progress in ideology and organization; the international situation is more favorable; and also the form of warfare used by the enemy is the aggressive war of a special type, not a classical one.

It is clear that this is a *war waged by the entire people*. For the sake of safeguarding the vital interests of the nation, in face of the danger that their country will be subjugated, their homes destroyed, their lives threatened, and their property trampled under foot, fourteen million of our compatriots in the South, regardless of age, sex, nationality, creed, and political affiliation, are resolved not to be enslaved and have risen together against the United States imperialists and their henchmen.

The war has been waged by the entire people because *the political goals of the war for liberation* are just and very lofty, the South Vietnam National Liberation Front has a correct political line which can mobilize and organize the entire people. The platform of the Front—"To struggle for peace, neutrality, independence, and democracy and for the future reunification of the country"—has reflected the primary and urgent requirements and the most profound aspirations of the South Vietnamese people. It has satisfied the immediate revolutionary task created by the social condition of South Vietnam.

The United States imperialists have done their best to practice neo-colonialism, to set up the "Republic of Vietnam" having its "independence" and "sovereignty," because they want to overshadow the fundamental contradictions between our people and the aggressive imperialists and to create conditions for the maintenance of the puppet administration, which hides behind the false images of nation and sovereignty to deceive the masses and win them over. However, the Ngo Dinh Diem administration, owing to the conditions which originated it and to the policies it was compelled to follow from its inception, did not succeed in its deceit and laid bare its face of traitor to the country.

In face of the perfidious scheme of neo-colonialism and the puppet administration, we must raise all the higher the banner of *national independence*. That is why the slogan "National independence and the urgent clauses for national salvation" put forth by the South Vietnam National Liberation Front has been able to rally broadly all patriotic and democratic forces in a united front against the imperialists and their stooges on the basis of the worker-peasant alliance. Not only the grass-roots worker-peasant masses but all the sections of petty bourgeois intelligentsia, the national bourgeoisie, and patriotic personalities have risen as one man against the common enemy under the banner of national independence. The minority people in the South have set a shining example of indomitable spirit. Most of the religious sects also approve of the Front's platform; even the pro-French elements and the large majority of Catholic refugees from the North have today sympathized with the Front and taken part, to a certain degree, in the struggle for national salvation.

In a revolution to liberate a colonial or semicolonial and semifeudal country the anti-imperialist question cannot be taken apart from the antifeudal question, nor can the national revolution be separated from the democratic revolution, because the substance and content of the national question is the peasant question; without putting forth the democratic question, without rousing the great peasant masses, it is quite impossible to consolidate and strengthen the National United Front and to set up a solid worker-peasant alliance which can serve as a basis to powerfully develop other patriotic forces.

In the specific condition of South Vietnamese society, the democratic problem plays a particularly important role because, with its false agrarian reform policy, the United States imperialists-sponsored puppet administration has done its utmost to grab the land allotted to the peasants during the war of resistance against the French; what this administration called agrarian reform was actually the distribution of a small acreage of land to its faithful lackeys. It is precisely for this reason that the South Vietnam National Liberation Front has raised the slogan: "To carry out land rent reduction and then to solve the land problem for the peasants so that the tillers will have land to till." During the last ten years, the peasants in the South have received in distribution more than 3.5 million acres of land, or nearly three times over the acreage of land allotted during the former resistance war. Most of these lands belonged to the imperialists and reactionary big landlords who had followed the enemy. This distribution of land to the peasants bears a paramount significance because the people's war is a revolutionary war waged by the masses of which the peasants make up over 90 percent. As the peasants in the South have by tradition an indomitable fighting spirit, the fact that they have now received vital interests from the revolution is for them a stimulus and they can organize themselves into a mighty force to wage a long resistance war.

In South Vietnam, not only has the puppet administration grabbed the land of the peasants, but it has daily violated the lives and property of the people, it has sprayed toxic chemicals to destroy the crops, and it has coerced the inhabitants into leaving their homes and villages to be herded into "strategic hamlets." In the town, the economic policy which depends on the United States imperialists has caused the bankruptcy of the native manufacturers and traders and a serious unemployment among the toiling people. That is why the democratic slogan has also another meaning, which is *to improve the people's livelihood* and to demand *the implementation of an independent economic policy*.

Democracy has, furthermore, a political meaning of paramount importance, which is to demand the carrying-out of democratic liberties in opposition to the fascist dictatorial regime. The United States imperialists usually boast that the administrations under their sway have pursued a policy of "freedom," that they have also written down "democratic liberties" in their constitutions. However, in practice, from the very beginning these administrations have become fascist dictatorial powers. That is why the slogans "To institute a broad and progressive democratic regime, to guarantee democratic liberties demanding the implementation of Article 14-C of the Geneva agreements,* to oppose discrimination against former resistance members," and so on, have responded to the urgent requirements of all strata of the population and have effectively urged the broad masses of people to rise against the enemy.

At present our country is temporarily partitioned into two zones, each having a different social regime. The revolutionary task ahead of the South Vietnamese people is to overthrow the United States imperialists and their henchmen and to win independence and democracy. The great majority of grass-roots masses have realized not only the necessity of carrying out this task, they have also aspired to take the revolution to a new height. Meanwhile, the national bourgeoisie and a section of the middle classes on the one hand oppose United States imperialism out of nationalism and, on the other,

---

* Article 14 of the Agreement on the Cessation of Hostilities in Vietnam states: "Each Party undertakes to refrain from any reprisals or discrimination against persons or organizations on account of their activities during the hostilities and to guarantee their democratic liberties."

want to defend the interests of their own classes. In order to rally the largest majority of people, the Front has laid down appropriate home and foreign policies; internally it advocates the *promotion of national industry and trade and development of the national economy;* externally it advocates a diplomatic policy of *peace and neutrality.* The word, "neutrality" has a great echo among the upper classes in South Vietnam and a widespread repercussion among the officers, soldiers, and civil servants of the enemy's administration; it has received the greatest approval and support from abroad. It is necessary to stress the *requirement for peace* and the *step taken to reunify the country* because genuine peace is the aspiration of everyone in the South, the more so since it has experienced twenty years of continual warfare, and because reunification is the profound aspiration of every Vietnamese. Vietnam has ever been one and indivisible.

Because the goal of its struggle is just and conforms to the fundamental aspirations of the people, and is mentioned in its platform, it can be said that at present *the South Vietnam National Liberation Front is able to rally the overwhelming majority of fourteen million people of the South, to mobilize, organize, and lead our compatriots there in the war for national liberation and salvation.* It is obvious that this war, which bears a national character as well as a class character, is mainly a war for national salvation against the United States aggressive imperialists and their myrmidons. This is *a people's war in a new historic condition* in South Vietnam.

The liberation war waged by the South Vietnamese people is *an all-out war.*

In this "special war" the enemy fights us mainly by military means, but he also lays stress on political activities, the *"cong van du* activities," * in order to win over the people and eagerly to penetrate into South Vietnam through economic and cultural media, and the like.

---

* Espionage and intelligence activity carried out by local agents.

The liberation war waged by our people over there covers many fields: military, political, economic, and cultural.

1. Our people cherish peace by tradition. In the early days of the successful August revolution, when the Democratic Republic of Vietnam had just been set up, we did our best to win peace by signing the preliminary agreement with the French government. But historical facts have shown that while we loved peace, the imperialists and colonialists did their utmost to kindle war. In the end, to defend the vital interests of our country, all our people have risen up, using armed violence and revolutionary struggle against counter-revolutionary violence, against the aggressive war of the French colonialists propped up by the United States imperialists. And we have carried the day.

In 1954, after the signing of the Geneva agreements, from North to South, all our people longed for peace; they made every effort to maintain and consolidate it and fought against all acts sabotaging the Geneva agreements in the South. While the United States imperialists and the puppet administration used counter-revolutionary violence to terrorize and massacre them, our people have put up a most valiant political struggle against the enemy for many years. In fact, this struggle has testified once again that *to the counter-revolutionary violence of the enemy, our people must definitely oppose revolutionary violence.*

At the price of their hard-won experiences, our compatriots in the South realized that the fundamental trend of imperialism and its lackeys is violence and war; that is why *the most correct path to be followed by the peoples to liberate themselves is revolutionary violence and revolutionary war.* This path conforms strictly to the ethics and the fundamentals of Marxism-Leninism on class struggle, on the state, and on the revolution. Only by revolutionary violence can the masses defeat aggressive imperialism and its lackeys and overthrow the reactionary administration to take power. When the United States imperialists stepped up armed intervention in the

South, the revolutionary struggle waged by our people turned into a widespread people's war, which has won greater and greater successes with every passing day.

The experiences gained in the revolutionary struggle put up by all our people during the last decades and by our southern compatriots over the past ten years have proved that revolutionary violence and revolutionary war is the correct path followed by the peoples who want to rise up and smash the domination of the colonialist imperialists and their lackeys; in specific conditions they are the real possibilities for these peoples to liberate themselves.

2. Revolutionary violence takes many forms: political violence, armed violence, and armed violence combined with political violence. Basing ourselves on our absolute superiority in the political field, and on the policy of the enemy who uses military as well as political means to quell the revolution, our southern compatriots are now using political violence combined with armed violence against the enemy. They have known how to take advantage of and to develop the valuable experiences gained by all our people in the revolutionary struggles they have waged up to the present time. These various forms of violence have led our people to brilliant victories. We have also known how to apply creatively the experiences gained in the recent revolutionary struggles in the world such as in Cuba and Algeria, where great successes have been achieved as the result of a skillful coordination between armed struggle and political struggle.

It can be said that one of the striking particularities of the revolutionary war in the South, of the comprehensive character of this war, is that it is *developing simultaneously in two forms—political struggle and armed struggle—in a long period.*

Political struggle plays a very fundamental role because our basic strength and the enemy's basic weakness lie in the political field, because the enemy schemes to deceive the people by political means, because the South Vietnamese people are by tradition indomitable in political struggle and have a very high political and organizational spirit. Once the people have a high revolutionary spirit, they are always a huge force, play a decisive role, and are a deciding factor of the revolutionary struggle. However, particularly in the present era, the toiling worker-peasant masses and progressive people of the world have made big strides on the road of revolutionary struggle; particularly in the South our people have been tempered for decades in political and armed struggles; while the administration and army serving the United States imperialists are very weak in the political field, our people have ample possibilities of developing extensively their political strength and of exploiting the great shortcomings of the enemy in order to secure victory for us.

Armed struggle is a high form of revolutionary struggle; *it is playing a very fundamental and important role.* Only with the support of armed struggle can the masses bring into play their political authority. As the enemy is using counter-revolutionary war against the people, to overthrow his domination it is absolutely necessary for the people to annihilate and destroy the puppet army. In the specific situation of South Vietnam, armed struggle should closely combine with political struggle; at the same time, it should abide by the laws on warfare and play its role of annihilating as many enemy forces as possible.

3. In the South, from the two major currents of struggle mentioned above, the masses have formed and built up a very mighty political force and an ever powerful revolutionary armed force.

The *political army of the masses* includes all ages and sexes and has established bases everywhere—in the lowlands and highlands, in town and country. This army has risen up and smashed to pieces the enemy's rural administration, destroyed a great number of strategic hamlets, carried out agitation work among the puppet soldiers, and urged tens of thousands of them to go over to the side of the people; it has fought against conscription and *corvée,* against the spraying of toxic chemicals, repression of religions, arson, and eviction from houses; it has demanded the protection of human lives and property, the improvement of the people's livelihood, the application of democracy, the punishment of Ngo Dinh Diem's henchmen, and the expulsion of the United States imperialists from South Vietnam. This political army has now used a legal form for its struggle, turned what is illegal into legal; it has never threatened by terror and bloodshed; it has advanced bare-handed and used a patriotic language to convince the enemy troops. Nobody can forget the scene in which tens of thousands of peasants broke through the cordon of bayonets, rushed into town, and stirred the streets with shouts of hatred and indignation. Nobody can forget the picture of a mountain girl who threw herself in front of an enemy bulldozer which was destroying her village to build a strategic road; the image of a South Vietnamese girl who, with her body, prevented an enemy cannon from shelling her village.

While workers, pupils, and students have played a worthwhile role in the political struggle in the towns, the women peasants were constantly on the front rank of the struggle in the countryside. When this political army temporarily stops direct struggle, it will engage in the production of foods and weapons, do afforestation work, dig trenches, make spikes, fence their fighting villages, or perform their duty as transporters, scouts, or messengers to help the armymen.

At first, *the revolutionary armed forces* of South Vietnam were the self-defense units and armed propaganda units which saw the light of day in the fire of the movement of political struggles of the people. Then bigger units appeared with the extensive development of the militia and guerrilla units in the course of the war. At present, the armed forces of the South Vietnamese people have grown very swiftly in strength under three forms which coordinate closely with one another in military operations: *the militia and guerrillas, the local troops, and the regular army.* Though still young and fighting in very hard and difficult conditions, the *South Vietnam Liberation Army* has successively defeated the enemy and has now raised the degree of its political consciousness and has increased its equipment, mobility, and fighting strength. In equipment, it mainly relies on the arms and ammunition taken from the enemy and increases its strength in the course of fighting; it is closely linked with the population. Like the Vietnam People's Army, the brother South Vietnam Liberation Army is not only an army which fights heroically but an army which is remarkable in production and excellent in all its work; it can annihilate great numbers of enemy troops at the front and actively make propaganda among the population; it can successfully carry out agitation work among enemy troops; and it can work painstakingly to fend for itself when supply from outside meets with difficulties.

In the face of an enemy equipped with modern arms, one which has great mobility and equipment for its intelligence service, but a very low morale, the South Vietnam Liberation Army has known how to analyze the strong and weak points of the enemy; it has fought unremittingly and got the upper hand of the enemy; together with the inhabitants, it has destroyed strategic hamlets, victoriously resisted small raids and large-scale raids as well; it has laid ambushes, carried out sudden attacks and annihilated whole companies, even whole regiments, stormed small posts, then bigger posts, and even a whole subsector. The Liberation troops have attacked communication lines (roads and waterways) of the enemy, burned oil depots and ammunition dumps, attacked airfields, sunk warships, and killed American advisers in the very center of Saigon. In the recent past, the armed struggle of our people in the South has developed into *a quite extensive guerrilla war of a fairly high level.* It can be said that at present, guerrilla warfare in the South develops at a quicker tempo than during the resistance against the French and faces more difficult fighting conditions. The Liberation troops have performed a great number of heroic deeds. During the arduous and fierce struggle they have waged, there appeared *many examples of immortal sacrifice and great heroism,* which continue the glorious tradition of the nation, the revolution, and the former resistance war—Tru Van Tho plugged a loophole with his body; Mai Van The cut one of his arms to continue the fighting; Nguyen Viet Khai had three helicopters shot down to his credit; Ly Van So damaged three amphibious cars; a group at Ap Bac got its fame; the Long Trung guerrillas persistently resisted a twenty-nine-day raid, and so forth.

The Liberation Army is now heroically annihilating the United States-sponsored puppet army commanded by American advisers. It made its appearance only a few years ago, yet it is the terror of the enemy who has gradually realized that it is not he who in the future will annihilate us, it is the Liberation Army which will defeat him. The heroic South Vietnam Liberation Army deserves the confidence of our southern compatriots and of the fatherland.

4. After the victories of the political struggle and armed struggle, the liberated areas have been broadened, running from the high plateaus of Central Vietnam to the Mekong Delta. The building of these areas in the political, economic, and cultural fields has become an important task and is all the more important for the liberation war in the South. At present, the liberated areas are separated from one another, some are entangled with the enemy-controlled areas, others reach into out-of-the-way places; they cover the provinces of the densely peopled delta and even draw near big and small towns. The liberated areas are not only firm guerrilla bases but are also built to become shining models of a new life, of a new regime in opposition to the gloomy state and stifling atmosphere of the enemy-controlled areas.

Under the direction of the Front, the people of the liberated areas are obviously masters of the land and are doing their best to manage and build their life along progressive lines. Democratic liberties, freedom of belief, freedom of business, and equality among nationalities are respected and widely implemented. Cultural, social, and educational activities as well as the health services are progressing. A healthy patriotic art and literature of a mass character contributes to the mobilization of the people for the struggle.

Here our compatriots are freed from the plunder and exploitation by the enemy; they are enthusiastically tackling production, improving their method of work, raising their livelihood and at the same time actively pooling their efforts to wage the war of resistance. Here the economic, agrarian, and religious policies of the Front, and the policy dealing with the bourgeois and foreign residents, the policy regarding the puppet soldiers and officers who go over to the side of the people are clearly defined and readjusted.

At present, the liberated areas have played their strategic role in the liberation war and have brought great influence to bear on the inhabitants of the enemy-controlled areas, including the towns. The liberated areas are precisely the first pictures of free and independent South Vietnam in the future; they will certainly be expanded and consolidated and will become the regions in which the future regime of the South will be applied after the victory of the liberation war.

IV

Before the danger of a greater failure, the ruling circles in the United States are striving to retrieve their present situation in South Vietnam.

Political circles and influential personalities in the United States have brought forward many opinions and have devised varied military measures not excluding the political ones. This clearly reflects the American embarrassment and deadlock after ten years of intervention and aggression in the South of our country.

After the signing of the Geneva agreements, with the fame and force that the United States had at that time, all American political and military figures were optimistic, thinking that South Vietnam was an easy prey. At the birth of the Staley-Taylor plan, though they were no more optimistic than they had been five or six years before, a great many people from the aggressive circles in the United States were still confident of the "special war" as a means to pacify South Vietnam within eighteen months. But now, after ten years of successive failures, especially the bitter ones over the past three years, their optimism and confidence have vanished; they begin to squabble with one another—and the squabble is growing hotter—about the cause of their defeat and about the measures to restore the situation. During the discussion, they come to agree on one point: their hope of winning swiftly in South Vietnam is lost, but they are still at variance on how to get out of the present tunnel with no end in view.

Owing to its extremely warlike and reactionary nature, the Johnson government is striving to continue the war and is clinging to its aggressive colonial policy in the South. This is easy to understand, if we examine the strategic position of South Vietnam with regard to the whole of the American warlike scheme in Indochina and Southeast Asia, and the important significance of the first experiment of their "special warfare" in the South aimed at repressing the movement for independence of various peoples. Johnson has many a time spoken of the determination of the United States to stay in South Vietnam at all costs. Therefore, it is quite certain that the United States government will *continue to intensify the "special war"* it has kindled and will further speed up every military activity, with a view to boosting the morale and bridging the gap between its lackeys who are wavering and who are at variance with one another, and endeavoring to win some victory before finding another solution.

Simultaneously with the pushing forward of the aggressive war in South Vietnam, the United States imperialists will further *intensify the provocation and sabotage in North Vietnam,* hoping to create more difficulties for our entire people's struggle for national reunification. The fact that the Americans are obliged to increase these acts at present, at this time when they are deeply bogged down in the South, shows that they are in a bitterly passive situation. It is precisely because they are defeated by the southern people that they must take such adventurous measures. It is certain that in intensifying these acts the United States imperialists can threaten no one, but bring upon themselves further shameful failures and hatred of the entire people from North to South. How can these acts prevent the northern people from giving their unshakable support to their southern compatriots' patriotic struggle? How can they lessen the latter's ironlike confidence in and sincere sympathy with the socialist North, the revolutionary base of the whole country?

Owing to their acute crisis in South Vietnam, the United States imperialists have schemed to intensify their armed intervention in the Kingdom of Laos and threaten the neutrality of the Kingdom of Cambodia, with a view to creating tension in Indochina and Southeast Asia. They want to rely upon these provocative acts and this display of force to screen their defeats in South Vietnam, and mislead the world opinion which is severely condemning their aggressive war in the South.

To serve these dark warlike schemes, thousands of United States military personnel, United States weapons, ammunition, and war means have recently been introduced into South Vietnam. At the same time, the United States has carried out the transfer of its army and warships to Southeast Asia.

In the face of the United States policy of adding fuel to the fire, and of intensifying the sabotage of peace in Indochina and Southeast Asia, our people in North Vietnam set themselves extremely heavy responsibilities and tasks: *to strengthen the defense of socialist North Vietnam, to protect our people's peaceful and creative labor; to be determined to support our southern people's patriotic struggle; to push forward the struggle for peaceful reunification of the fatherland; to strengthen the solidarity with and the support to the Laotian and Cambodian peoples in the defense of their independence, sovereignty, and territorial integrity, and in their struggle against the United States intervention and aggression.* This responsibility is very heavy, and this task very high. However, with our thorough revolutionary spirit, profound patriotism, and just international spirit, we will certainly discharge our responsibility before the nation and the world's people.

The resolution of the Third Party National Congress* has stressed: "Vietnam is one, the Vietnamese people is one, our entire people's

---

* September 5, 1960.

will for national reunification is unshakable, the final victory will certainly be ours." In the light of the resolution, we have clearly realized that North Vietnam is building socialism, that South Vietnam is carrying on the liberation war, and that these two tasks have a close relation with each other and help each other. While carrying on the second sacred resistance war to liberate themselves, our southern compatriots also aim at checking and smashing the United States imperialists' scheme of aggression against our whole country. Inversely, to build socialism in North Vietnam peacefully, and to strengthen the force of the North in every respect—political, economic, and national defense—is precisely the most decisive task with regard to the development of the whole Vietnamese revolution, and the struggle for national reunification. Over the past ten years, this ideological trend has unceasingly mobilized sixteen million northern people eagerly to work and record brilliant achievements in the building-up of their country; without halting before any sacrifice, fourteen million southern people are heroically fighting to win back and firmly defend every inch of land of Vietnam. *North and South Vietnam are under the same roof; the South is the front line; the North is the political and moral support of the fatherland.* North Vietnam has the task of building socialism and making it a firm basis for the southern people's patriotic struggle, and the struggle for national reunification. Today in the North the *movement for sworn brotherhood between the northern and southern people,* a lively expression of North and South Vietnam kinship, has gained town and country; the *successive emulation drives for our southern kith and kin and national reunification,* have brought in the highest labor productivity. "Everyone redoubles his efforts to show his gratitude to his southern kith and kin"; this warm appeal from President Ho Chi Minh, the beloved leader of the entire people, is urging every one of us to work.

Facing the United States imperialists' and their lackeys' scheme of intensifying provocative and sabotage acts in the North, our people in North Vietnam must *strive to strengthen and consolidate national defense, defend security, and further raise their revolutionary vigilance and their hatred for the enemy.* We must clearly realize that to build the North and defend it are twin tasks. Each of us in North Vietnam must be aware that the economic building and development of production is the central task; at the same time, he must always pay attention to combining economic building with strengthening national defense, strive to increase the defense work in all respects, be ready to cope with all provocations and sabotages of the enemy, and smash every one of his adventurous acts. All the commandos of the United States imperialists' lackeys in South Vietnam as well as those of Chiang Kai-shek commanded by the United States recently introduced secretly into North Vietnam, were surrounded and completely annihilated by our armymen and people. This shows the high vigilance and sharp readiness for fighting of North Vietnam's armymen and people. We must develop this good point to continue dealing heavier blows at the United States imperialists and their flunkeys if they pursue their aggression against socialist North Vietnam.

The armed forces—the People's Army, the People's Armed Security Forces, the People's Militia, and the People's Self-Defense Units—must clearly realize their heavy responsibility in the present situation of the country. North Vietnam is building in peace; South Vietnam is carrying on the liberation war. Over the past ten years, though being heavily defeated by the southern people, the United States imperialists do not want to draw useful lessons and are pursuing the aggressive war on half of our country. Before the complete victory of our people the extremely hard and complex struggle between our people and the United States imperialists still goes on. Therefore, we must *further raise the tradition of determination to fight and to win, be always vigilant and ready for fighting, heighten the spirit to implement the orders, be united and closely act in unison, boldly wipe out the enemy, and be determined successfully to fulfill every military task entrusted by the Party and government.* We must further develop the spirit of readiness for fighting of a revolutionary army, firmly hold every weapon and instrument of war, and defend the territorial integrity, airspace, and territorial waters of the Democratic Republic of Vietnam. We are certain to defeat every wicked scheme of the United States imperialists.

Recently, simultaneously with the intensification of provocative and sabotage acts in North Vietnam, the strafing and shelling of the Laotian people's liberated zone, and the violation of the Cambodian border, the bellicose Americans have still clamored that they will strafe and shell the territory of the Democratic Republic of Vietnam and extend the war to the North. We warn the United States imperialists: "Should the United States militarists be rash enough to attack the North, the entire people of the country would stand up as one man to smash to smithereens their aggression and completely defeat them all over the country." To attack the North is to attack a socialist country; it is certain that the peoples of the brother socialist countries, of Southeast Asia, and the progressive people the world over will wholeheartedly support us.

The July 15, 1964, statement of our government has said that there is only one issue for the United States imperialists in South Vietnam:

1. The United States government must respect the sovereignty, independence, unity, and territorial integrity of Vietnam and refrain from interfering in her internal affairs.

2. The United States government must put an end to its aggressive war in South Vietnam, withdraw all its troops and weapons from there, and leave the South Vietnamese people to settle their own internal affairs by themselves in accordance with the program of the South Vietnam National Liberation Front.

3. The peaceful reunification of Vietnam is an internal affair of the Vietnamese people; it will be solved in accordance with the spirit of the political program of the Vietnam Fatherland Front and the program of the South Vietnam National Liberation Front.

Except for this, there is no other way out. If the United States imperialists continue their war of aggression against South Vietnam, they will certainly be defeated by the southern people and will finally be doomed to complete failure. If they rashly extend the war to the North, this would be suicide for them.

The successes recorded during ten years of peaceful construction in North Vietnam are filling each of us with enthusiasm. *The socialist building in Vietnam will certainly succeed.*

The successes of the revolution in South Vietnam during the past ten years are powerfully mobilizing every one of us. *The revolutionary work to liberate South Vietnam and peacefully reunify the fatherland will certainly succeed brilliantly.*

Today no reactionary force in the world can prevent thirty million people of our whole country from carrying out their sacred aspiration—*to build a peaceful, unified, independent, democratic, prosperous, and powerful Vietnam.*

The Liberation War in South Vietnam: Its Essential Characteristics

Strength and Weakness of the Enemy

The present war of national liberation in South Vietnam is directed against the neo-colonialism of the United States imperialists and their lackeys, an extremely reactionary and wicked enemy who is materially and technically strong but morally and politically very weak.

In the previous resistance war of national salvation, the revolution in South Vietnam as in the rest of our country was directed against the French colonialists and their lackeys assisted by the United States interventionists. After peace had been restored in Indochina, United States imperialism kicked out defeated French colonialism and set up in South Vietnam the pro-United States Ngo Dinh Diem regime. Unlike old-type French colonialism, United States imperialism did not build up an administrative machine and bring in an expeditionary corps, but nevertheless its control over the South Vietnam regime was complete.

Neo-colonialism is a product of imperialism in the present period. Faced with the powerful influence of the socialist system and the upsurge of the national liberation movements in Asia, Africa, and Latin America, the imperialists can no longer use old methods to impose their rule on their colonies; the local reactionary forces, especially the comprador bourgeoisie and the feudal landlord class, feel great fears for their interests and privileges. Neo-colonialism is the result of the collusion and compromise between the foreign imperialists on the one hand and the local comprador bourgeoisie and

---

This is an edited version of the text which appeared under the title "The Liberation War in South Vietnam: Its Essential Characteristics," in *Vietnamese Studies*, n. 8 (Hanoi, January 1966), pp. 5–36.

feudal landlord class on the other, with a view to maintaining colonial rule under new forms and with new methods, and repressing the revolutionary movement of the mass of the people.

The aims of imperialism remain fundamentally the same; enslavement of the weaker nations, grasping of markets and raw materials, ruthless oppression and exploitation of the subjugated peoples. Its principal method remains violence under various forms. It differs from old-type colonialism in only one aspect: while old-type colonialism directly takes in hand the enslavement of the peoples and uses violence through an administration under its direct control and an army of aggression under its direct command, neo-colonialism carries out enslavement and uses violence in an indirect and more sophisticated manner through a puppet administration and a puppet army camouflaged with the labels of "independence and democracy," and a policy of "aid" or "alliance" in every field. Neo-colonialism, more wily and more dangerous, uses every possible means to conceal its aggressive nature, to blur the contradictions between the enslaved nations and the foreign rulers, thereby paralyzing the people's vigilance and will to wage a revolutionary struggle.

United States neo-colonialism has its own specific characteristics. When United States capitalism reached the stage of imperialism, the great Western powers had already divided among themselves almost all the important markets in the world. At the end of World War II, when the other imperialist powers had been weakened, the United States became the most powerful and the richest imperialist power. Meanwhile, the world situation was no longer the same: the balance of forces between imperialism and the camp of peace, national independence, democracy, and socialism had fundamentally changed; imperialism no longer rules over the world, nor does it play a decisive role in the development of the world situation. In the new historical conditions, United States imperialism, which has a long tradition of expansion through trade—different from the classical policy of aggression through missionaries and gunboats—is all the more compelled to follow the path of neo-colonialism. The countries under its domination enjoy nominal political independence, but in fact are dependent on the United States in the fields of economics, finance, national defense, and foreign relations.

At the end of World War II, United States imperialism already cast covetous eyes on Vietnam and the other Indochinese countries. In the early 1950's, as the situation of the French colonialists was becoming more and more desperate, the United States imperialists gradually increased their "aid" and intervention in the dirty Indochina war. When the war ended with the defeat of the French Expeditionary Corps, they thought that the opportunity had come for them to take the place of the French colonialists. The images of former colonial rule—perfidious and cruel governors general and high commissioners, the ferocious Expeditionary Corps—now belonged to the past. The United States imperialists could not, even if they wanted to, bring to life the decaying corpse of old colonialism. In 1954, when the defeat of the French colonialists was imminent, the United States imperialists envisaged the use of "national forces," made up of reactionary forces in the country, in an attempt to give more "dynamism" to the war. And they began to prepare their "special war" against the South Vietnamese people.

United States neo-colonialism uses its lackeys in South Vietnam as its main tool to carry out its policy of aggression. Neo-colonialism derives its strength on the one hand from the economic and military potential of the metropolitan country, and, on the other hand, from the social, economic, and political bases of the native reactionary forces. In the South of our country, the puppet regime was set up by the United States imperialists at a moment when our people had just won a brilliant victory against imperialism. That is why, since coming into being, it has never shown any vitality and has borne the seeds of internal contradictions, crisis, and war. Its social bases are extremely weak. The feudal landlord class and the comprador bourgeoisie, which had never been very strong under French rule, had become even weaker and more divided in the course of the revolution and the resistance. After peace was restored, they became still more divided, as a result of United States–French contradictions. These reactionary classes have long since shown themselves to be traitors to their fatherland and are hated and opposed by the people. The defeat of the French Expeditionary Corps was a severe blow to their morale.

Under those circumstances, United States imperialism used every possible means to set up a relatively stable administration, camouflaged with the labels of "independence" and "democracy," in an attempt to rally the reactionary forces and at the same time to win over and deceive other strata of the population. With this aim in view, they staged the farce of founding the "Republic of Vietnam" in order to perpetuate the partition of our country. Their puppets, claiming to have regained "independence" from the French colonialists, proclaimed a "constitution" with provisions on "freedom" and "democracy" and put forth slogans of anticommunism, ordered an "agrarian reform," and noisily publicized a program for the "elimination of vices" and the "protection of good traditions," and the like.

However, the puppet regime could not remain in power if they did not cling to their masters and obey the latter's orders. Outwardly, the "Republic of Vietnam" has all the usual government organs of internal and external affairs, defense, economy, and culture, but all these organs, from the central to the local level, are controlled by United States "advisers." The latter, who enjoy diplomatic privileges, are not under the jurisdiction of the puppet administration, whose civil and penal codes cannot be applied to them. They are directly under the United States ambassador's control. It is United States imperialism which determines the fundamental line and policies of the South Vietnam regime. Ngo Dinh Diem, fostered by United States imperialism, was "pulled out of Dulles' sleeve" after Dien Bien Phu. The Diem regime, far from springing, as it claimed, from a movement of "national revolution," was only the result of the replacement of French masters by United States masters.

Faced with a popular revolutionary upsurge, the puppet regime soon took the road of fascism and frantically pursued a policy of militarization and war preparation. To gain a reason for existence, it had bluntly to oppose the Geneva agreements and the deepest aspirations of our people; namely those for peace, independence, democracy, and national reunification. It trampled on the people's most elementary rights and resorted to a most barbarous policy of terror and repression. For these reasons, despite the labels of "independence and democracy" and certain reforms of a demagogic character, the popular masses immediately saw behind the puppet regime the hideous face of United States imperialism, that self-styled international gendarme, and that of the inveterate traitor Ngo Dinh Diem. And resolutely the masses rose up against them.

The United States imperialists also hurriedly built up and trained an army of mercenaries to be used as a tool for the repression of the revolutionary movement, carrying out their perfidious policy of pitting Asians against Asians, Vietnamese against Vietnamese.

With this army of native mercenaries, dubbed "national army," the imperialists hope to camouflage their aggression and save American lives. United States experts have calculated that expenses for an Asian mercenary soldier are twenty-four times less than those required for an American soldier.

The South Vietnam "national army" is staffed by puppet officers from the rank of general downward, but this is coupled with a system of military "advisers" controlling the puppet national defense ministry and extending down to battalion and company level, in the militia as well as in the regular forces. United States advisers in the puppet army supervise organization, equipment, training, and operations. The United States imperialists try to camouflage under the labels of "mutual assistance" and "self-defense" the participation of their troops in fighting. With a view to turning South Vietnam into a United States military base, they have put under their effective control a large number of strategic points, all the main airfields and military ports.

Economic "aid" is used by the imperialists as a principal means to control South Vietnam's economy. This "aid" is essentially a way of exporting surplus goods and capital to serve their policy of expansion and war preparation. Three-fourths of the amount of yearly "aid" derives from the sale of imported goods. The United States aid organs completely ignore both the requests of the puppet regime and the needs of the country and dump into South Vietnam market-surplus farm products, luxury goods, and also consumer goods that could have been produced locally. Furthermore, this aid clearly has a military character. It turns South Vietnam's economy into a war economy, 80 percent of the money being used to cover the military expenses of the puppet regime. This "aid" makes this regime totally dependent on the United States imperialists.

At first, the United States imperialists, thinking that they could rapidly consolidate the puppet regime and stabilize the political and economic situation in South Vietnam, had prepared the ground for the signing of unequal treaties to open the way to a large-scale penetration of United States finance capital. But the situation did not develop as they had expected, and so the money they invested in South Vietnam was insignificant, representing hardly 2 percent of the total investments in various branches of the economy. In general, United States money was invested in joint enterprises, in a very wily economic penetration. Although present conditions are not favorable to the development of the United States sector in the South Vietnamese economy, United States "aid" and the creation of counterpart funds have ensured USOM (United States Operations Mission) complete control over the budget, finances, and foreign trade —in fact, over the whole economic structure of South Vietnam.

For many years now, the puppet administration and army have been maintained in existence only thanks to United States aid. They relentlessly pursue a policy of violence and war in order to repress the patriotic movement, while granting many privileges to a handful of traitors. The social basis of this regime is made up of the most reactionary elements in the comprador bourgeoisie and the feudal landlord class.

The comprador bourgeoisie in South Vietnam is economically entirely dependent on the imperialists—the French imperialists in former days and the United States imperialists in the present time. The comprador bourgeoisie and the feudal landlord class, bound together by many ties, are two reactionary social forces colluding with the imperialists whom they efficiently serve. The comprador bourgeoisie lives on United States aid, on trade with imperialist countries, and seeks joint investments with foreign capital. It includes elements from other social classes, such as the big landlords who seek refuge in the larger cities and become bourgeois. Speaking of the comprador bourgeoisie, we should first of all mention the *bureaucratic comprador bourgeoisie,* essentially made up, in former days, of the Ngo Dinh Diem family, and at present, of high-ranking puppet officials and officers who use their power to get rich quick through pillage, extortion, graft, embezzlement, hoarding, and speculation, and to lay hold of key positions in the economy and seize control over all the important branches.

The feudal landlord class, which owned the larger part of cultivable land, had a great economic influence; but after the revolution of August 1945 and in the course of the resistance against the French colonialists, it became much weaker economically and politically. The United States–Diem regime sought by every possible means to restore the position of landlords whom they regarded as their mainstay in the countryside. The most reactionary elements in the landlord class, brazenly offering their service to the enemy, have taken part in repressing the peasant movement and sabotaging the revolution. They include former big landlords and the new "bureaucratic" landlords who have seized control of village administration, and also bandits, hired thugs, criminals, traitors, and landlords coming from the North, who use their power to seize land from the peasants. A number of other landlords want to keep their privileges and oppose national reunification but dare not collaborate with the enemy. There are also landlords who participated in the resistance against the French colonialists or have children or relations re-

The Liberation War in South Vietnam 233

grouped in the North: they more or less oppose the United States imperialists and their lackeys or approve of a policy of peace and neutrality.

The comprador bourgeoisie and the feudal landlord class are divided into different groups with different economic and political interests, connected with either United States imperialists or French imperialists.

In the new historical conditions, on account of their class character and their desperate situation in face of the victorious revolutionary movement, the pro-United States forces in South Vietnam are extremely reactionary; they are traitors to their country and their people and thirst for class revenge. They are also social parasites, divorced from national production and entirely dependent on United States dollars. This causes their ranks to shrink further and further and to become more and more heterogeneous and divided by conflicts of interest into rival groups and cliques tied up with different tendencies in United States political, military, and intelligence circles. Their position, already not very strong in face of the powerful revolutionary upsurge, has been further weakened and their ranks have become still more divided; consequently, coups d'état have succeeded one another and will continue to do so until their final collapse.

Despite its material power, United States imperialism has fundamental weaknesses.

1. Economically and militarily, the United States of America is now the most powerful country in the imperialist camp. But, faced with the socialist countries, the independent nationalist countries, and the revolutionary peoples of the world, its strength is declining further and further. Everywhere now, United States imperialism is reduced to the defensive; its forces scattered all over the world have proved incapable of saving it from disastrous defeats in continental China, Korea, and Cuba. The United States imperialists have suffered many defeats and are meeting with many difficulties in Laos

and other places. In South Vietnam, their situation is becoming more and more critical.

2. In its aggression against South Vietnam, United States imperialism has revealed a fundamental weakness: it has been forced to resort to a neo-colonialist policy when important factors for the success of this policy are lacking.

Firstly, it has to try to deceive our people, posing as a "knight," as defender of the independence, sovereignty, and freedom of the peoples. But the present conjuncture in the world as well as in South Vietnam is not favorable to such a maneuver. Our people, with their high revolutionary consciousness, have long since recognized in United States imperialism the number one enemy of the world's peoples. United States imperialism unmasked itself by supporting the French colonialists during the Indochina war, a war waged with French blood and United States dollars and weapons. It conceived a criminal plan in a vain attempt to save the French Expeditionary Corps from the Dien Bien Phu disaster. Our people did not wait until 1954 to see in United States imperialism an aggressor, and since that date, they have realized even more clearly that it is the number one enemy of the Vietnamese revolution and people.

Secondly, United States imperialism cannot carry out its neo-colonialist policy without a strong support from local reactionary forces, without an outwardly "independent and democratic" native administration and a "national" army. But we can affirm that this extremely important, this crucial condition, which decides the fate of neo-colonialism, does not exist in South Vietnam. The reactionary forces, in the first place the most reactionary and pro-United States elements of the comprador bourgeoisie and the feudal landlord class, have become extremely weak socially and economically, and completely isolated in the political field. Billions of dollars and hundreds of thousands of tons of arms will not fill this political vacuum. United States imperialism will never be capable of creating a stable political regime with even an appearance of independence and democracy. Each puppet administration has proved more impotent than its predecessor. U.S. imperialism is also incapable of building up an army with any fighting spirit; however modern its equipment, the South Vietnam puppet army will never be able to consolidate its sagging morale.

Thirdly, imperialism cannot carry out its neo-colonialist policy without revealing its aggressive nature. Repression of the revolutionary movement must be essentially the work of native reactionary forces, and the war of aggression must be waged mostly with native reactionary armed forces. This is the essence of what is called "special war" by the Pentagon strategists. But a problem arises: what if the puppet forces prove incapable of serving the aims of their masters? The only possible solution is to increase the number of United States "advisers," military personnel, and combat troops and to take part more and more directly in the war of aggression. The United States has been going further and further on this road, which is full of insoluble contradictions. The introduction of United States troops into South Vietnam may have the immediate effect of strengthening the puppet army to some extent and creating some difficulties for the South Vietnamese people, but on the United States side, militarily it constitutes an obviously defensive measure and politically, a severe defeat. The more United States troops are brought in, the more the "special" character of the war diminishes. United States neo-colonialism loses the façade which distinguishes it from classical colonialism, not to speak of the many trials that await United States troops in a counterguerrilla war on a tropical battlefield. United States strategists have admitted that the political, geographic, and climatic conditions in South Vietnam constitute insurmountable difficulties for them.

Thus, it is in the political and moral field that the United States imperialists and their lackeys have proved to be fundamentally weak. The political aim they pursue remains the same, whether in the years of more or less camouflaged intervention or in the present "special war": to conquer South Vietnam, to trample on our people's right to live and their deepest aspirations. They are the enemy of our people and are being resolutely opposed by them. Their fundamental weakness is still aggravated by the shaky position of the local reactionary forces, the special form taken by the war of aggression in South Vietnam, and our people's indomitable spirit and close unity. *This fundamental weakness will certainly lead the United States imperialists to complete defeat.*

On the Side of the Vietnamese People

To the new-type war of aggression waged by the United States imperialists our southern countrymen oppose a patriotic war of liberation with a view to achieving independence, democracy, peace, and neutrality and advancing toward national reunification. *Temporarily much weaker than the enemy materially and technically, the popular forces, on the other hand, enjoy absolute political and moral superiority.*

South Vietnam, like the rest of our country, was a colonial and semifeudal country with a backward agriculture, which, after long years of war, has not yet been restored to its normal production level. The successive wars of aggression during the past decades have caused untold sufferings to the population. The people's power, set up after the revolution of August 1945, maintained and consolidated during the resistance in the free zones with a population of several million, was replaced, in implementation of the 1954 Geneva agreements, by a reactionary regime in the service of the United States imperialists.

The South Vietnam people's armed forces, which had matured considerably in the course of the heroic and victorious fight against the French colonialists, were made up, at the end of the war, of regular troops, regional troops, and people's militia operating on all battlefronts. In implementation of the Geneva agreements, hundreds of thousands of enemy troops evacuated the North to be concentrated in the South, while our troops left the South to be regrouped in the North, evacuating not only the guerrilla zones and bases but also extensive free zones which were temporarily transferred to the control of enemy troops and of the puppet administration. It was in these conditions that United States imperialism and the Ngo Dinh Diem administration carried out their ferocious policy of terror, then started a bloody undeclared war with a view to repressing the patriotic movement and turning South Vietnam into a United States colony and military base. They pinned their hopes on the bad economic situation, on the people's aspirations for peace after long years of war, on the extremely difficult situation in which the people found themselves, deprived as they were of protection from the people's power and army. The United States imperialists and their lackeys felt certain that the South Vietnamese people, faced with their hundreds of thousands of soldiers armed with up-to-date weapons, could not but submit.

But our countrymen in the South, worthy sons of a heroic people, have an *invincible potential force, an immense political power* that the enemy can never fathom. United States imperialism and its lackeys have to deal with a people with an extremely high revolutionary spirit and absolute political superiority. Our countrymen in the South belong to an indomitable people with long-standing traditions of struggle against foreign aggressors, a people who would rather die as free men than live as slaves; they had raised high the banner of resistance right in the first days of French aggression and heroically risen up in the Nam Ky and Ba To insurrections.* During the glorious days of August 1945, they joined hands with the rest of the people to bring about the triumph of the revolution and set up the people's power. During the nine years of resistance, they heroically fought against the French colonialists and the United States interventionists, contributing an important part to the common victory. Through a long revolutionary struggle, the South Vietnamese people have attained a high level of political consciousness and organization and have gained rich experience in political and

---

* 1940 and 1945.

armed struggle. That is why in the face of an extremely ferocious enemy the revolutionary movement has been expanding unceasingly, and the war of liberation has been winning ever greater victories. In South Vietnam, the comprador bourgeoisie and the landlords, lackeys of the United States imperialists, constitute an insignificant minority, while the overwhelming majority of the people belong to the revolutionary and patriotic classes, united in a common struggle.

The South Vietnamese working class, nearly one million strong, and concentrated in cities and plantations, constitutes the main production force in important economic enterprises. Having to bear the triple yoke of imperialism, the bourgeois class, and the feudal class, it is the most resolute, the most radically revolutionary of all social classes. Under the leadership of our Party, in South Vietnam as in the entire country, the working class has been the vanguard of the nation in the national democratic revolution and recorded many achievements in production and fighting in the years of resistance. In the past years the United States imperialists and their lackeys, using terror and corruption, and through the setting-up of reactionary trade-union organizations, have been endeavoring to control and divide the ranks of the workers and to weaken their class consciousness and national consciousness. However, the working-class movement has been developing gradually and surely, with rich and varied forms of struggle and slogans and increasingly better organization and great solidarity. Fierce struggles regularly broke out in state enterprises under the South Vietnam puppet administration, and in enterprises under United States or joint United States-local comprador-bourgeois management. The worker movement has been growing in intensity, going from small-scale actions to partial and general strikes, from economic claims in the interests of the workers to demands in favor of other sections of the population (such as distribution of land to the peasants and pay increases for the soldiers) and to political slogans condemning the policy of terror and repression, denouncing the puppet administration and demanding the withdrawal of United States imperialism from South Vietnam.

In recent years, the growing strength of the worker movement has resulted in the weakening of the enemy's most vital positions. It has given a strong impulse to the struggle of the laboring masses, particularly to the poorer sections of the urban population and to the students in the cities. Born (for the majority) of families of ruined peasants, the workers, as a class, have many ties with the mass of peasants, and this has greatly facilitated the forming of the worker-peasant alliance—basis of the National Democratic Front— and political work among those of the puppet troops who evince some degree of patriotism, most of them being sprung from the laboring peasantry. In short, the working class, by its traditions of struggle and its combative spirit, has always been the symbol of our southern countrymen's revolutionary determination.

The South Vietnamese peasantry, more than ten million strong, is the largest revolutionary force, and with the working class constitutes the main forces of the revolution. Mostly made up of landless peasants working in hard conditions and living in misery, it has long since evinced a high revolutionary spirit, especially since it was placed under the leadership of the vanguard Party of the working class. Together with the latter, it rose up to attain power, and in the ensuing years it has fought against the enemy to defend the people's power and the tillers' right to land ownership brought about by the revolution. The peasantry has gained rich experience in political and armed struggle, guerrilla warfare, organization of armed forces, and the building of resistance villages.

When peace was restored, the United States–Diem clique, through a so-called agrarian reform, heavy taxation, and "agricultural credit," robbed the South Vietnamese peasantry of two-thirds of the land it had been given during the resistance. The policies of "agricultural settlements," "prosperity zones," and "strategic hamlets," and the permanent terror directly and seriously threatened the peasants' lives and property. As a result, until 1959 in the South Vietnam countryside the peasantry was rapidly undergoing a process of differentiation which continues up to the present time in the zones still occupied by the enemy. For the majority of peasants, life has been seriously disrupted; working and living conditions have become unbearable, not only for land-poor and landless peasants, but also for middle peasants, and even for the majority of rich peasants. The number of totally or partially unemployed persons in the countryside has been rising rapidly. A large number of peasants have been press-ganged into the puppet army or herded into "agricultural settlements" for forced labor; others have had to leave for the towns to look for work.

Faced with the grave danger threatening his fatherland and his own family, the peasant has resolutely taken part in political actions against the enemy and, in recent years, has risen up in a fierce, large-scale revolutionary struggle which has shaken to its foundation and broken up the puppet administration in the countryside. *This revolutionary upsurge is in essence an insurrectionary movement of the mass of peasants, in which they carry out successive uprisings,* to take power at the base and regain the right to land ownership. A guerrilla war has been started in the rural areas, which has gradually spread to every part of the country, in opposition to the counter-revolutionary war waged by the enemy.

The petty bourgeoisie comprises the mass of small merchants and manufacturers, handicraftsmen, members of the liberal professions, civil servants, intellectuals, college students, and schoolchildren. All these strata of the small bourgeoisie are oppressed and exploited by imperialism, the bureaucratic comprador bourgeoisie and the feudal forces. Their living conditions have been worsening. Animated with fairly strong patriotism, they sympathize with the revolution. They constitute the majority of the population of South Vietnam's towns and cities, totaling nearly four million.

The small bourgeoisie's patriotism and political consciousness were heightened by the revolution of August 1945 and the resistance against the French colonialists. With the northern half of the country completely liberated, the yoke imposed on the South by United States imperialism and its lackeys only stimulates their patriotism and exacerbates their hatred of the invader. For this reason, the small bourgeoisie constitutes one of the motive forces of the revolution and *a sure ally of the working class,* which is the only leading force capable of helping them advance steadily on the road of the revolution.

In the atmosphere of terror and demagogy created by the United States imperialists and their lackeys in South Vietnam, a number of persons belonging to the small bourgeoisie, especially its upper strata, have fallen under the influence of reactionary forces and played into the hands of reactionary parties. Others are passive, indifferent, or vacillating.

However, in the face of the aggressive policy of the United States imperialists and the traitorous behavior of their lackeys, in face of the enemy's repeated defeats and the people's revolutionary upsurge, an increasingly large section of the small bourgeoisie in the cities has shown a growing revolutionary militancy. In many urban centers, the struggle movement of college students and school pupils, in coordination with that of the workers and the other poorer sections of the population, is growing in intensity and, on several occasions, had a direct aggravating effect on the crisis suffered by the puppet regime in the cities. This movement will certainly play a more and more important role.

The intellectuals, college students, and schoolchildren, though belonging to different social strata, are in general animated with ardent patriotism; only a handful has become lackeys of the enemy or fallen under their influence. They hate the United States imperialists, hate and despise the traitors. During the patriotic war against the French colonialists, they sympathized with the resistance, supported it, or joined it. At present, they approve of the political program of the National Liberation Front, and large numbers of them are actively taking part in the struggle of the masses in the cities.

The national bourgeoisie, in the South as in the rest of the country, is economically weak, although economic enterprises in South Vietnam are generally more important than in other parts of the country. According to figures which have yet to be verified, in 1956, the national bourgeoisie comprised about fifteen thousand persons. Many have gone bankrupt since, and in 1963, only half of the above number were still in business, running a number of precarious enterprises. Oppressed by the imperialists and the feudal class, the national bourgeoisie to some degree evinces an anti-imperialist and antifeudal spirit.

Following the return of peace, the South Vietnamese national bourgeoisie had expected it would get something from the policy of "national economic rehabilitation" announced by the United States–Diem clique. But United States economic and military "aid" has only aggravated the situation of the South Vietnamese economy, and the national bourgeoisie has found it more and more difficult to engage in industry and commerce. A number of national bourgeois joined the ranks of the compradors. As the United States imperialists expand their war of aggression in an attempt to enslave our country and impose their control over all branches of the economy, the contradictions between the national bourgeoisie, on the one hand, and the United States imperialists and their lackeys, on the other, have become more acute. The national bourgeoisie is increasingly opposed to United States imperialism and its puppets and more and more favorable to a policy of independence, peace, and neutrality. A number of national bourgeois even approve of a gradual advance toward national reunification according to the program of the NLF. However, on account of its economic and political weakness and the fact that it has not completely severed its ties with the imperialists and their lackeys, the national bourgeoisie is not determined to take the road of the revolution.

The national minorities in South Vietnam are more than twenty in number and total over a million persons living in strategically important mountainous regions which constitute two-thirds of the land. In these regions, imperialism pursues a "divide-and-rule" policy, pitting the national minorities against one another and against the Kinh.* But the national minorities in South Vietnam as in the rest of the country have long since become conscious of their interests and have foiled the perfidious maneuvers of the imperialists. Heirs to the national traditions of heroic struggle against foreign invaders, the minority people in South Vietnam contributed greatly to the triumph of the revolution of August 1945 and actively took part in the resistance against the French colonialists. At present, only a handful in the upper strata has been bought over by the enemy; the majority of the people believe in the victory of the revolution and are resolutely fighting against the United States imperialists and their lackeys.

The religions in South Vietnam comprise Buddhism, Christianity, Cao Dai, Hoa Hao, and others. Buddhism, practiced for many centuries, has no deep influence but has a relatively large number of believers. Christianity is practiced by about a million persons. The Cao Dai religion, a synthesized religion based on Buddhism, has over a million believers, mostly poor peasants. Hoa Hao, which is related to Buddhism, once had nearly a million believers. The religious sects were born and developed at a time when the people's revolutionary struggle was growing in intensity and scope. They have been used to some extent by the French colonialists, then by the United States imperialists to further their political aims. But these sects have also suffered from division, restrictions, coercion, and repression, and they are more or less opposed to imperialism and its lackeys in matters of national, religious, and class interests. Under Ngo Dinh Diem's rule, even among the Catholics, there were, besides those who supported the puppet administration, those who were against it. The religious sects are in general heterogeneous in their political tendencies, but, as the majority of believers are laboring people, as the United States imperialist aggressors and the

---

* The majority population.

traitors have shown their true colors, and as the revolutionary tide has been surging irresistibly, new tendencies have appeared in their ranks. The progressive tendency has been gaining ground, which more or less approves of a policy of peace, neutrality, and struggle against imperialism.

The puppet army now constitutes the enemy's main tool to carry out their policy of terror and repression. For over ten years now the United States imperialists and their lackeys have made great efforts, spent much money, and resorted to most perfidious means to corrupt the puppet soldiers and turn them into criminals. They use terror and harsh discipline to coerce, and especially "psychowar" techniques to deceive the troops, inculcate in them an "anticommunist ideal," a hostility against North Vietnam, and a servile admiration for the United States imperialists. But the majority of the soldiers and noncommissioned officers of the puppet army are sprung from the laboring masses, chiefly the laboring peasantry; so their basic interests are in contradiction with the policies of the United States imperialist aggressors and their lackeys. They more and more clearly realize that to fight against the United States imperialists to save the fatherland is the only way to fulfill their deepest aspirations: land and peace. The internal contradictions of the puppet army merely reflect the class and national contradictions in South Vietnamese society.

To build and enlarge the puppet army, the Saigon administration has had to institute compulsory military service and resort to press-ganging. Owing to the development of the revolutionary war and the repeated victories of the liberation forces, opposition to war is growing in the puppet army. United States imperialism is meeting with growing difficulties in the use of this puppet army against the people. Political work among the soldiers of this army enjoys more and more favorable conditions for the eventual building of a united front of workers, peasants and soldiers to fight against the United States imperialists and save the country.

The "refugees" from the North are mostly Catholics deceived by the mendacious propaganda of reactionary priests, or working people trying to make a living in the South. Forced to move South for some reason or other, they more and more see through the demagogic tricks of the United States imperialists and their lackeys. Herded into "agricultural settlements" or victims of the plan for "slum clearance in the capital," many of them are jobless, live in miserable conditions, and are even subjected to repression. For this reason, more and more of them long for peace and neutrality. Many dream of returning to the North to start a new life.

The patriotic classes and strata of South Vietnamese society, with long traditions of and rich experience in revolutionary struggle, are united in a solid front on a just cause. In its long liberation struggle against the colonialist aggressors to reconquer national independence, give land to the tillers, defend the fundamental rights of man, realize peace and national reunification, our entire people, in the South as in the North, have risen up and fought with great heroism and perseverance. The noble ideals of serving the interests of the nation and of the oppressed classes have been propagated by our Party since 1930. Through many years of revolutionary struggle full of hardships and sacrifices and the glorious resistance war against the French colonialists, these ideals have been anchored fast in the minds and hearts of the masses. Our people are determined to carry on their struggle, as long as they have not reconquered national independence, the right to live, and land for the tillers. They will never give up their struggle as long as they have not achieved sovereignty, independence, unity, and territorial integrity for the fatherland, which were recognized by the 1954 Geneva agreements.

During the years of revolution and of resistance, our people in the South and the North were bound into a broad and strong union represented by the National United Front based on the worker-peasant alliance. It is this union which has led our people to great victories. The enemy remains temporarily strong, materially speaking, but has always been politically isolated, and torn by internal contradictions. On the other hand, the higher the South Vietnamese people raise the banner of their just cause, the more they develop their traditions of broad and strong union. In the first years following the restoration of peace, when the situation was very difficult, the patriots of South Vietnam could not yet organize themselves but had remained closely bound to one another, politically and morally. Patriotism, national pride, class solidarity among the laboring masses, reciprocal love and mutual aid, the will to fight to the end for the triumph of the noble ideals of the revolution—all this constitutes the force which had helped our southern compatriots overcome all difficulties and stand firm in face of the enemy until their ranks could be consolidated and broadened. The National Liberation Front's strength and prestige are due to the fact that it has brought into play our people's traditions of national union in the new historical conditions.

During the past years, the South Vietnamese people have been struggling against an *extremely barbarous and ferocious* enemy. They have met with difficulties and suffered losses, but, on the other hand, they have seen even more clearly the cruel nature of the enemy, felt ever deeper hatred for him, and, with an iron will, they will fight to the end, until final victory.

The patriotic forces in South Vietnam, with a highly combative spirit and long traditions of revolutionary struggle, have furthermore been mobilized and organized *according to a correct political line and adopted appropriate forms of struggle*. For this reason, faced with a wicked enemy and in difficult circumstances, the people's political and military forces have been growing steadily.

The revolutionary movement has passed from the stage of political struggle to the stage of armed struggle; it closely coordinates the two forms of struggle, which stimulate each other. The South Vietnamese people have developed to a high degree their political superiority, charted a correct orientation, and devised extremely varied forms of organization and struggle. The inventiveness of the masses has foiled many enemy policies and maneuvers and their most modern tactics. Revolutionary thinking, a revolutionary political and military line, once it has penetrated into the masses, becomes an invincible force. Our people's political superiority has become a material force which helps them create means they did not have, pass from a position of weakness to a position of strength, overcome all difficulties, and win final victory over an enemy who was at first much stronger than they were.

The liberation war in the South takes place at a time when one half of our country, liberated from colonialism, is building socialism. *The North has been for our southern countrymen a source of hope and encouragement,* especially during the dark years of terror and repression. The liberated North is the pride of the Vietnamese nation; it constitutes a strong base for the struggle for national reunification, and the bastion of the nationwide revolution. Facing the enemy, our southern countrymen certainly feel the presence by their side of their brothers in the North; this will give them more confidence to overcome all difficulties and strengthen their determination to advance on the road of struggle and victory. Since the United States imperialists started their war of destruction against the North, the entire country has risen up to take part directly in the fighting, and the effect of the North on the liberation war in the South has become ever more important.

The liberation war of our countrymen in the South will have to face still many difficulties and hardships, but our southern countrymen and the Liberation Army, with unequaled heroism, have won brilliant successes and created factors of strategic significance to bring about final victory. With *the growth of the people's political power and that of the revolutionary armed forces,* the liberated zones are continually expanding. The development of the situation in South Vietnam eloquently proves that in a revolutionary struggle, in a revolutionary war, the decisive factor remains the human factor, the political factor, and the decisive force, the force of the popular masses. *Final victory will inevitably come to the South Vietnamese patriotic forces, the South Vietnamese people, the Vietnamese nation.*

The Trend of the World Situation

The South Vietnamese revolution is an integral part of the world revolution. Each great event in the world has a bearing on our people's struggle; on the other hand, the influence of this struggle on the revolutionary movement in other countries is by no means insignificant. Especially at the present time, the South Vietnamese revolution in particular and the Vietnamese revolution in general are more than ever closely bound to the world situation. All the fundamental contradictions in our time have appeared in Vietnam.

The "special war" of the United States imperialists and their lackeys and the liberation war of our people take place in *circumstances which are favorable to the Vietnamese side and unfavorable to the enemy side.*

Since the end of World War II, *the balance of forces between revolution and counter-revolution in the world has undergone great changes.* The revolutionary upsurge in the world has been battering the bastions of imperialism and winning repeated victories. The founding of the People's Republic of China was a historic event of great importance. For more than ten years after the severe defeat of the United States imperialists and their satellites in Korea and that of the French colonialists and United States interventionists in Indochina, great revolutionary changes have occurred in the world, to the advantage of the struggle for peace, national independence, democracy, and socialism.

A world socialist system has come into being and is developing, comprising thirteen countries with a population of over a billion, covering a quarter of the world's area. The socialist system accounts for 38 percent of the world's industrial output, has powerful defense forces, and occupies first place in many essential branches of technology. Despite internal difficulties resulting from rapid growth, the socialist system, on account of the excellence of the socialist regime, the great vitality of Marxism-Leninism, has been growing in strength, continuously and in every aspect; it is the bastion of world revolution, the mainstay of the national liberation movement and of the movement for the defense of world peace. Its birth and development have changed the balance of forces in the world, and it has become the decisive factor in the development of human history. The socialist countries are unanimous in supporting our people in the two zones. The considerable aid they have given us constitutes an extremely important factor for the triumph of our people's revolutionary struggle.

The national liberation movement is seething on the Asian, African, and Latin American continents, dealing heavy blows to imperialism headed by United States imperialism, causing the old colonial system to collapse in big chunks. During the past twenty years, over fifty countries with a population of a billion have attained political independence in different degrees. Many countries are in full revolution. National, regional, and international anti-imperialist fronts have come into being and are being consolidated, with extremely rich and varied forms of struggle.

Africa, only yesterday "the dark continent," has become the hotbed of anti-imperialist revolution, where many countries are actively struggling against colonialism and neo-colonialism, some of them carrying out an armed struggle.

In the twenty countries of Latin America, this "back yard" of United States imperialism, the national liberation movement is developing powerfully. The scope of the peasant movement in many Latin American countries has led a United States journal to the conclusion that *the chance of an explosion in that part of the world is not a possibility but a reality.*

In Asia, the national liberation movement is mounting in a powerful upsurge, especially in Southeast Asia.

The revolutionary struggle for national liberation is directly altering the balance of forces between the socialist and the imperialist camps. It is shaking the rear of imperialism; it is a great support for the construction of socialism in the socialist countries and an active contribution to world peace. It forces imperialism (headed by United States imperialism) to scatter its forces, thus creating weak links in the imperialist chain where revolutionary situations appear which may lead the liberation struggle toward victory. This is an important aid and encouragement to the revolution in the South of our country. To cope with an uprising of the Dominican people alone, the United States imperialists had to send tens of thousands of troops. What would they do when faced with other Santo Domingos?

In this third stage of the general crisis of imperialism, the contradictions among the imperialist countries are becoming ever more acute, as a result of their struggle for markets, which is conditioned by the law of unequal development of the imperialist countries and the narrowing down of territories under their control. The powerful economic growth of the capitalist countries of western Europe and Japan in the past years more and more restricts the role of United States capitalism in the world's industrial production and exports. The western European countries now have more important gold reserves than the United States. A number of countries show a tendency to become independent, to free themselves from United States influence. In the face of the increasing development of the world revolutionary movement, the imperialist countries are forced to form alliances, but these alliances by no means exclude competition and contradictions. NATO is deeply divided. SEATO is dangerously cracked, due to the opposition of France and Pakistan. CENTO now has only a symbolic character. With regard to a solution to the Vietnam question, conflicts of interest have caused the imperialist countries to hold different views, and the most visible contradiction is that opposing France to the United States.

In the capitalist countries, while monopoly capitalism is heading toward militarization and fascism, the working-class movement has been given a new impetus. The working class in many countries has succeeded in rallying the large masses and giving a strong impulse to the struggle for democracy, peace, and a policy of independence vis-à-vis the United States. In the Western European countries and in Japan, the great working masses resolutely support the Vietnamese people's just struggle and severely condemn the United States imperialists' war of aggression. These great historical changes have created objective conditions which are extremely favorable to the world revolution and to the South Vietnamese revolution. *The world revolution follows a complex process of development, a zigzag course, but it continually forges ahead.* Recently, in the ranks of the international communist movement, which is the vanguard force in our time, differences have appeared, but they have only a temporary character, and revolutionary practice will certainly iron them out. In the face of imperialism, the common enemy, which more and more clearly reveals its aggressive and bellicose nature, the true communists in the world will close their ranks. The communist parties will come out of this struggle stronger than ever for the defense of Marxism-Leninism against modern revisionism, the principal threat to the international communist movement. The imperialists are seeking to exploit the differences in the socialist camp and the international communist movement. On the Vietnam question, the United States imperialists are also endeavoring to make full use of these differences. But the objective laws of history will necessarily lead toward unity based on true proletarian internationalism and Marxism-Leninism, which are invincible. A front of the world's peoples against imperialism headed by United States imperialism has come into being, which comprises the socialist countries as the main force, and the oppressed peoples, the working class in capitalist countries, and the forces of peace and democracy. This front is developing and being consolidated continuously; it cannot be weakened by any reactionary force.

A survey of the relation of forces in the world today shows that *the revolutionary forces are stronger than the counter-revolutionary forces, and the forces of peace stronger than the forces of war.* We are going upward, and the enemy, downward. The world has changed so much since Lenin forty years ago set forth *the objective conditions for the triumph of national liberation wars over the imperialist powers*, namely:

1. Joint efforts of *large sections of the populations* of the oppressed countries.
2. A *particularly* favorable international situation (resulting from antagonistic contradictions among the imperialist powers).
3. A *simultaneous uprising of the proletariat against the bourgeoisie* in one of the imperialist powers.

In our time it is not merely a few peoples who have risen up separately to conquer independence; billions of persons have joined in multiform struggle against colonialism and neo-colonialism, forming an extensive front against imperialism.

In our time, the proletariat has risen up, not in one, but in many countries, and has successfully carried out the proletarian revolution there. A mighty world socialist system now serves as a nucleus for the international working-class movement and provides support for the national liberation movement. The working-class movement in many capitalist countries has become a political force with a marked mass character.

The position of United States imperialism in the world today is no longer what it was at the end of World War II. Not only has it not succeeded in achieving world hegemony, but *even its supremacy in the capitalist world has been badly shaken*. It no longer holds an atomic monopoly and can no longer blackmail the peoples of the world. Today, the Soviet Union has built up a powerful system of defense and holds a leading position in space research. The People's Republic of China now has its atomic bomb. United States imperialism has been forced to change its military strategy, passing from "massive retaliation" aimed at attacking the socialist camp, to "flexible response" with the immediate aim of suppressing the national liberation movement, while frantically preparing for a new world war. Everywhere, it has been unmasked as an international gendarme, and this has greatly impaired its political prestige and aroused opposition by all the nations in whose affairs it intervenes. *Never has United States imperialism found itself so isolated in the world.* Lately, it has been forced to ask its allies to help it get out of the South Vietnam quagmire. But, besides some important satellites such as South Korea, Thailand, Taiwan, Australia, and New Zealand, most of its friends give only verbal support or stand aloof. The French government has publicly disapproved of United States armed aggression in Indochina and advocates the neutralization of all the countries of Southeast Asia. It has withdrawn its delegation from SEATO. French imperialism is the most important buyer of South Vietnamese goods, and French investments at times represent 50 percent of the total investments in South Vietnam; French property is valued at 2 billion francs; 90 percent of the rubber areas and a large number of light industrial enterprises belong to French capitalists. No wonder that such a situation has led to acute contradictions between France and the United States. The governments of Great Britain and Japan, though lately taken in tow by the United States in political matters, have expressed anxiety about the United States policy of war expansion, which they fear may bring severe defeats to imperialism. Until 1965, the contributions by United States satellites in the war of aggression in South Vietnam represented hardly 3 percent of the total expenses. The contributions in manpower and equipment have somewhat increased but are still very small. Formerly, when the French Expeditionary Corps found itself in difficulties, it could expect assistance from the United States. Today, the United States imperialists, bogged down in South Vietnam, can expect aid from nobody. If in the Korean war, the United States imperialists managed to get the support of the majority of UN member countries, today they cannot even use the flag of this organization. United States allies do not want a second Korea, for they had suffered severe defeats during the Korean war.

Since the United States imperialists extended the war to the North of our country, *they have become still more isolated.* Not only have they been denounced by progressive humanity, but even among their friends and satellites, voices of dissent have been heard. Not only are they opposed by the United States people, but even in the United States Congress, disagreement is becoming acute over the Vietnam question. The people of the United States have held meetings and demonstrations in many large cities to protest against the war of aggression in Vietnam. Heated and lengthy debates and controversies about Johnson's Vietnam policy have taken place in United States universities and in the United States Congress. Lately, the United States people's struggle has reached a new high when mass actions were undertaken to stop trains with troops bound for Vietnam.

On the other hand, *our people's just war of liberation enjoys extensive and increasingly powerful support in the international arena.* We have not only the unreserved support of the peoples of the Soviet Union, China, and the other fraternal countries in the socialist camp but also the sympathy of progressive people in all countries, including the United States. *This political, moral, and material support* has been expressed through extremely varied forms: demonstrations, fund-collecting drives, letters, messages, resolutions, and statements of solidarity and support, violent demonstrations against United States embassies and propaganda organs, refusal to transport United States arms, preparations with a view to sending, if necessary, arms and volunteers to help the South Vietnamese people. Days and Weeks of Solidarity with the South Vietnamese people have been organized in nearly all countries. A Conference of the World's Peoples and two International Trade Union Conferences for Solidarity with the Vietnamese People against the United States Imperialist Aggressors were held in Hanoi. At many other important national conferences, the Vietnamese problem has been a major subject of discussion. The prestige and role of the National Liberation Front, which is regarded as the only authentic representative of the South Vietnamese people, are growing continuously. The NLF maintains official relations with popular organizations, and with governments in forty-four countries, has permanent delegations in eight countries (namely, Cuba, Algeria, China, the Soviet Union, Czechoslovakia, the German Democratic Republic, Indonesia, and Poland), and has a delegation to the Asian and African Peoples' Solidarity Committee in Cairo. The Front's member organizations are members of ten international organizations and members of the bureaus of nine of these organizations.

We can say that never in the history of their revolutionary struggle have our people enjoyed such extensive and powerful international support. Since the United States imperialists introduced combat troops into South Vietnam and carried out air and naval raids against North Vietnam, the movement of the world's peoples in support of Vietnam has been given a strong impetus. All the brotherly countries in the socialist camp are unanimous in supporting the stand and the line of struggle of the government of the Democratic Republic of Vietnam and of the NLF. Providing aid in all fields, they are greatly contributing to our revolutionary struggle. *The eyes of the whole world are turned to Vietnam; the whole world actively and resolutely supports the Vietnamese people against the United States imperialists.*

During the first years of the resistance against the French colonialists, our country was surrounded by hostile neighbors. But the liberation war now being waged by the South Vietnamese people enjoys much more favorable conditions. The South is carrying out its struggle at a time when the other half of the country has been liberated, and the neighboring countries are friendly: Laos is heroically fighting against United States imperialism and its lackeys, and the Kingdom of Cambodia is resolutely defending its active neutrality. Furthermore, Vietnam as a whole is geographically linked with the mighty socialist camp; she is a close neighbor of China and lies in the heart of the zone of revolutionary tempest in Southeast Asia where large masses are rising up in revolutionary struggle and the Marxist-Leninist parties have gained rich experience in revolutionary leadership. *South Vietnam, regarded by United States imperialism as the main link in its Southeast Asia strategy, is now on the front line of the national liberation movement in this part of the world. And our country as a whole is regarded as the center of the peoples' revolutionary struggle against United States imperialism.* Directed against a common enemy, and with a common banner of national independence and democracy, the revolutionary movement now developing in Southeast Asia and other parts of the world constitutes an effective support and a great encouragement for the Vietnamese people.

We attach very great importance to the sympathy and support of the forces of peace, national independence, democracy, and socialism in the world, and consider it an *extremely important factor* for our people's final victory. While the peoples of the world deem it their international duty to support us, our people's *glorious international duty* is to fight resolutely against United States imperialism until final victory so as to achieve national independence and reunification and contribute actively to the defense of peace in Indochina, Southeast Asia, and the world.

Once Again We Will Win

United States imperialism is the international gendarme, the leading imperialism, having the most powerful economic and military potential in the imperialist camp. In taking a direct part in the aggressive war it hopes it can rely on its material strength to overcome all difficulties in manpower and in political matters, thereby salvaging the situation in the South. With a sizable expeditionary force which is to be eventually increased, it hopes to gain some advantage in the theater of operations: first, to strengthen its military force in general and its strategic mobile force in particular, thus to tilt the balance of forces in its favor; second, to control important strategic areas and set up firm bases as springboards to launch mopping-up operations or attacks against the liberated areas; third, to strengthen its air force, to develop its ability to thin out our forces and to strike deep into the liberated areas.

The American imperialists' scheme is to prevent the collapse of the puppet army and administration, to launch offensives aimed at wiping out the revolutionary forces in the South, especially the Liberation Armed Forces, to strive to consolidate the areas still under their control and gradually to carry out pacification by priority sectors, to attack the liberated zones and to wrest back some of the lost areas, to seek every means *to encircle and isolate the southern theater.* At the same time, they intend *to intensify sabotage warfare* against the

---

This essay was first published in the January 1966 issue of *Hoc Tap* (Studies), the theoretical review of the Lao Dong Party. An abridged version appeared in English in the January 27, 1966, issue of *Vietnam Courier* (n. 44). A full translation was published later that year by the Foreign Languages Publishing House, Hanoi. The article was originally published under the title "Let the Entire People Resolutely and Unanimously Step Up Their Great Patriotic War to Defeat the U.S. Aggressors." This is an edited condensation.

North *and carry on deceptive "peace offensives."* Banking upon a force of over seven hundred thousand men, to be increased eventually, they hope to realize the above-mentioned scheme by means of more radical and efficacious measures. They reckon that they can gradually win military and political successes, secure a position of strength to end the war with a solution favorable to them, or if need be, to prolong or expand the aggressive war.

The United States imperialists' design is very ambitious, their scheme most perfidious, and their military and political maneuvers extremely cruel and Machiavellian. However, besides their limited strong points of a material nature they have *most fundamental weak points*, both political and military, in both strategy and tactics.

First of all, the United States imperialists are *the enemy not only of the Vietnamese people but also of progressive people throughout the world.* In the present situation, whereas the socialist camp is growing, the national liberation movement surging, the workers' movement in the capitalist countries and the movement for peace and democracy developing, the forces of imperialism are continually declining. In the over-all relation of forces in the world, the American imperialists are not in a strong but in a weak position and have to scatter their forces to cope with the situation everywhere. That is precisely why they cannot send to South Vietnam whatever number of troops without reckoning with their difficulties in every field in the world, right in the United States, and in the Vietnam theater.

The dispatch of an expeditionary force for the invasion of our country is itself fraught with most fundamental dangers that they cannot overcome.

First, the sending of American troops to invade our country *exposes the United States imperialists still more clearly as aggressors and their lackeys as traitors; thereby the contradictions between the United States imperialists and our people become all the sharper.* Stirred by more hatred for the aggressors, our entire people more broadly and more firmly unite in the National United Front against the United States imperialists and their stooges. All the patriotic forces become more determined to fight for national salvation. Moreover, many Vietnamese in the areas temporarily controlled by the enemy, even in the puppet army and administration, in the parties and organizations under the United States puppets' sway, so far unaware of the real nature and intention of the American imperialists and their minions, now begin to see their true faces and more and more definitely side with the people to oppose them.

Second, the United States imperialists introduce their troops to invade our country at at a time when *their "special warfare" strategy has fundamentally gone bankrupt, whereas our people's patriotic war has powerfully developed,* the Liberation Armed Forces have matured, and the liberated areas have included the majority of the southern population and territory. Precisely this makes it impossible for the aggressors, though they may bring in several hundred thousand men, strategically to avoid losing command of the situation and compels them to scatter their forces defensively as well as offensively. It is not easy for them to wrest back the initiative as they wish. Instead, they will face the eventuality of increasing failures and deeper entanglement.

Third, owing to the loss of political and military initiative mentioned above, *no matter how modern its equipment, the American expeditionary force cannot bring into full play its power* and escape a defeat inevitable for all aggressive armies facing a whole nation resolutely resisting them. Owing to the unjust character of the war, the morale of the United States expeditionary force, which has no ideal to fight for, is low. Moreover, in the South Vietnam theater, it has to cope with a people's war against which the United States strategy and tactics based on bourgeois military conceptions proves powerless. The organization as well as the composition and training of the American army, generally speaking, is more or less unfit to help deal efficiently with our entire people's revolutionary war, not to mention great difficulties due to unaccustomed terrain and climate and to the considerable needs in supply and logistics.

Fourth, the introduction of American troops into the South aims at preventing the collapse of the puppet army and administration and at creating favorable conditions to consolidate and strengthen the puppet forces. But the United States imperialists openly invade the South of our country at a moment when the puppet army and administration are seriously weakening. At this point, *the more open is the United States aggression, the more isolated and differentiated the puppet army and administration, and the sharper the contradictions between the United States imperialists and their placemen.* Those people in the puppet army and administration who still have some national feeling will become more conscious of the real situation, and the number of those who cross over to the people's side will increase. Consequently, the introduction of more United States troops, far from retrieving the predicament of the puppet army and administration, aggravates the mercenary army's destruction and disintegration, and the puppet administration's collapse in the face of our people's resistance. When the American imperialists' crack troops are defeated by our people, the disintegration and collapse of the puppet army and administration will be all the more inevitable.

Fifth, by starting the war in South Vietnam the *United States imperialists are more and more sternly condemned by the peace-loving people in the world.* Now that they openly send their troops for a direct aggression against the South and use their air force to strike at the North, an independent and sovereign socialist state, they are meeting with increasingly energetic opposition from the peoples of the socialist countries and the world's progressive people, including the American people.

The strong points of the United States imperialists are limited, whereas their weak points are basic ones. As the aggressive war goes on, the latter will become more visible and more serious and will surely lead the American imperialists to ignominious failure.

Above are the American imperialists' strong and weak points after some hundred thousand enemy troops have been introduced into South Vietnam. On our side, we do not enjoy the advantages attached to a country with a wide territory and a large population, but our people are resolved to carry on their just patriotic war to defend our life and wrest back our independence and freedom. In this fierce and protracted revolutionary war against such a cruel enemy as American imperialism, our force has developed unremittingly and has many a time put him into confusion. Weak in equipment and technique and in economic potential, we have absolute political and moral superiority, a correct leadership, the strength of an entirely united people, the invincible people's war, and the sympathy and strong support of people throughout the world. It is certain that, as we fight, we will score ever greater victories and become stronger. These are the fundamental factors accounting for our people's final victory in the sacred liberation war for national salvation against United States aggression. Whatever the number of expeditionary troops that the aggressors may bring in, they can in no way escape the inevitable: they will be defeated; the ultimate victory will be ours.

First, our Party has a correct revolutionary line. This line is the condensed expression of the clever and creative combination of Marxist-Leninist general principles with the correct practice of our revolution. This is the line of the people's national democratic revolution progressing to socialism in a former colonial and semifeudal country. Our Party's line has been tested in our people's long and heroic revolutionary struggle and has led our revolution from one victory to another. In the light of this line, Vietnam has been the first colony to rise up and defeat the mighty army of an imperialist power— France—to liberate itself; the North of our country is also the first state to take the path of socialism in Southeast Asia. Today our people have the honor to be in the forefront of the fight against the chieftain of imperialism—United States imperialism. This correct line is also that of the revolutionary armed struggle of a small country which rises up to fight and defeat an enemy many times stronger, the line of people's war developed to a high degree with a creative and substantial content. A correct revolutionary line is the surest guarantee of our people's final victory in their just struggle against the American imperialists.

Second, our entire people is united in the fight against the aggressors to save our fatherland. North and South are single-mindedly determined to defeat the American invaders and their lackeys, ready to make every sacrifice rather than lose their independence and be enslaved. This iron will reflects our people's tradition of indomitable resistance against foreign aggression. It has brought our people together; millions, like one, are resolute to fight to defend our country and win back independence, democracy, unity, and peace.

Our compatriots in the South have closed their ranks in the fire of the revolutionary struggle, fighting for twenty years, now overcoming countless difficulties and braving a cruel enemy with a firm resolve to march forward, to fight, and to win. Today our people in the South have the National Liberation Front, a broad organization with a correct line and a program which enjoys great prestige at home and abroad. Starting the fight with spikeboards and mantislike guns, they have built big and heroic Liberation Armed Forces comprising three categories of troops, having high combativeness, skillful strategy and tactics, versed both in guerrilla warfare and large-unit operations and credited with wiping out big units of the puppet and American forces. The heroic Liberation Armed Forces have developed everywhere and have been conducting ever more powerful operations throughout the South Vietnam theater, from the Ben Hai River to Ca Mau Cape, from the Western Plateaus to the delta countryside and even in the vicinity of big towns. At present the liberated zone accounts for the majority of the population and territory of the South; the Front's policies are being gradually applied there, a new life under an independent and democratic regime is being built, and, in fact, the liberated zone has become the image of tomorrow's entirely liberated South Vietnam.

Meanwhile, the people in the North are steadily progressing to socialism with an ardent love for the fatherland and for socialism and with an unprecedented political and moral unity. The North, thanks to its excellent political system and its strong economic and national defense potential, is not only a source of inspiration but also a solid rear for our entire people's struggle for national salvation against the United States imperialists. This is a favorable condition which did not exist in our former resistance against the French colonialists.

Since the extension of the war to the North, the Democratic Republic of Vietnam's army and people have been resolutely fighting and have initially foiled the enemy's sabotage air warfare. In response to the call of the Party Central Committee, the government, and President Ho Chi Minh, our people in the North have launched a strong movement for national salvation, carrying out production and fighting at the same time to defend the North, give wholehearted and all-out support to the liberation revolution in the South, and make a substantial contribution to the common victory of the whole nation.

The Vietnamese people have a tradition of unity and unbending resistance against foreign invasion, but if we look back to its millenary history as well as to the revolutionary struggle of the past many years, we shall realize that never have they united so firmly and so broadly as today, and never has their will to fight off the aggressors and defend the country been promoted to such a degree.

Third, our weapon is the invincible people's war, and we have gained experience in conducting it. If it can be said that nowadays in military affairs there is a greater invention than atomic weapons, that is, people's war, then the Vietnamese people have effectually contributed to the perfecting of this new arm and are keeping it firmly in their hands. It has developed in Vietnam's historical, political, and social conditions and has attained a very high degree with an original and extremely substantial content.

In our country, people's war has developed according to the general laws of all revolutionary wars and also to the specific laws of the Vietnamese society and theater of operations. Hence, it is a revolutionary war waged by a whole people on all planes, a revolutionary war fought by a small nation in a narrow and thinly populated country, having an underdeveloped economy, relying on the strength of an entire people united in the struggle. With it the people will finally beat an enemy originally many times stronger.

Generally speaking, people's war in Vietnam is revolutionary armed struggle developing on the basis of the political struggle of the masses brought to a high level. The boundless strength of the revolutionary masses has pervaded the revolutionary armed forces and has given them an extraordinary capacity to fight and to win. Moreover, the outstanding characteristic of people's war in our country at the present stage is that, in its very process, armed struggle and political struggle are very closely coordinated, supporting and stimulating each other. Therefore, the slogan "Mobilize the entire people, arm the entire people and fight on all fronts" has become a most lively and heroic reality. Armed struggle in South Vietnam has budded forth from political struggle carried to its peak, and in guerrilla warfare or in limited regular warfare, the operations of the armed forces have always been carried out in accordance with the principle of closest coordination with political struggle. This principle was observed in the scattered insurrections in the countryside as later on in the movement to destroy "strategic hamlets," in the uprising of millions of peasants in Nam Bo, as more recently in that of millions of peasants in south Trung Bo. Armed struggle in the South has another characteristic: whether in guerrilla warfare or in limited regular warfare, waged artfully it is fully capable of solving the problem of getting the better of a modern army like the U.S. Army. In the South, not only the regular army but also the regional army and the people's militia and guerrilla force can wipe out American and puppet troops and foil their most modern tactics. This is a new development of the revolutionary military art, the main content of which is to rely chiefly on man, on his patriotism and revolutionary spirit, to bring into full play all weapons and techniques available to defeat an enemy with up-to-date weapons and equipment.

In the North, people's war is also developing in the heroic fight against the United States sabotage warfare, in the movement among the army and people to down American planes and to turn our North into a vast battleground to counter and foil the enemy air strikes and inflict heavy losses upon the modern U.S. Air Force. They may attack more fiercely, but they can by no means cut off our main lines of communication or stop our people's productive activities, let alone shake their determination to oppose the American aggressors, defend the North, and give unqualified assistance to the South.

People's war in Vietnam is the product of our people's resolute and indomitable revolutionary struggle, and also that of the revolutionary struggle of the world's people in our times. People's war has led our nation to splendid victories in the revolutionary struggle against Japanese fascism, in the resistance war against French colonialism, and has brought our people great successes in the past few years both in the South and in the North. The great people's war of the Vietnamese nation will certainly outdo the aggressive war of the American imperialists in the eventuality of their increasing the United States expeditionary force up to several hundred thousand men.

Fourth, we enjoy the warm sympathy and wholehearted support of the people of the fraternal socialist countries, and the progressive people the world over, including the American people. Our people's struggle for national salvation against United States aggression aims not only at liberating half of our country still under domination but also at defending socialist North Vietnam. This grand struggle is the spearhead of all progressive mankind against American imperialism, a great contribution to the world people's revolutionary struggle for peace, national independence, democracy, and socialism. That is why the fraternal socialist countries have given their unreserved support to the stand and line of struggle of our government and the

South Vietnam National Liberation Front, and provide all-out assistance to our people to defeat the United States imperialist aggressors. The working class and the toiling people of the capitalist countries, the people of the newly independent countries, also side with us, expressing their sympathy and giving their support. All great international conferences and quite recently the Tri-Continental Conference held in Havana addressed warm feelings and very encouraging words to the fighting Vietnamese people and sternly condemned the American imperialists' aggression. Even in the United States, the struggle of the American people against the Johnson administration's aggressive policy is involving ever larger strata, taking on bold forms such as self-immolation, the burning of draft cards, and the holding-up of the transport of troops to Vietnam. This movement is gaining momentum everywhere on a scale unprecedented in the history of the United States. Never in the history of their revolutionary struggle have our people enjoyed such widespread and strong world sympathy and support as today.

What is the development of the war on the Vietnamese theater of operations since the United States imperialists introduced their expeditionary force on a large scale into South Vietnam and, at the same time, began to intensify their air attacks on North Vietnam?

Our entire people, like all progressive mankind, have seen that the United States imperialists' open invasion of our country unmasks their true face as invaders, and the aggressive and unjust character of the war they have kindled is laid bare before world public opinion. The justice of our patriotic struggle and the absolute political supremacy of our people become all the more evident. Our enemy himself has realized that in invading our country with his own troops he has suffered a political failure. Nevertheless, he thinks that, with the increase of his armed forces and the superiority of his equipment and technique, he can defy the protest of the world's people and trample underfoot all the elementary principles of international law which demand that the sovereignty and independence of all nations be respected; he thinks that he can overcome all political difficulties to reach his final goal, which is to seize the southern part of our country.

The question is: who will win in the fight between the United States imperialist aggressors, who pursue an unjust cause, and our people, who pursue a just one? Throughout the past eleven years, every time the United States imperialists launched a new aggressive scheme, the same question was raised. The liberation struggle of the heroic South Vietnamese people has supplied an eloquent answer: whatever trick the American imperialists may resort to, they will inevitably fail in the end. And the fundamental law of the great patriotic struggle of our fellow countrymen in the South throughout the various stages is: the further the United States imperialists and their flunkeys engage in their scheme to enslave the South of our country, the deeper they will be bogged down and the greater their defeats, whereas the more determined the Vietnamese people in their struggle, the greater their victories will be.

Today the question as to who will win in South Vietnam is more pressing than ever, for in the present juncture there has emerged a new factor: the introduction by the American imperialists of some hundred thousand troops. Can these massive reinforcements reverse the situation? Can the Vietnamese people, who have recorded many great successes in their just struggle, win new victories in the face of direct aggression by such a modern army as the United States imperialists? Can they defeat the American expeditionary force?

We have analyzed above the strong and weak points of the enemy and ourselves, assessed his and our strength and capabilities, and have drawn the conclusion that the enemy will be defeated in the end and that we will certainly win. This is the theoretical side of the problem. On the other hand, since the introduction of a big United States expeditionary force, the realities of our people's struggle on the South Vietnamese theater have further illuminated the question and are demonstrating that our foregoing theoretical conclusion is entirely correct.

If in the past when the American imperialists brought Ngo Dinh Diem to power and began to tackle the Collins plan* or, later on, when they put forth the Staley-Taylor plan and the Johnson-McNamara plan, they were extremely optimistic and reckoned that their dark design would certainly be achieved, recently, when they started sending a large expeditionary force to South Vietnam, they believed that they could turn the tide. They were confident that within a short time the face of the aggressive war would change, that with their best divisions and brigades and strategic and tactical air force they would be perfectly capable of changing the relation of forces, set up solid defense positions, launch bold offensives, and push ahead their pacification by priority sectors, thereby not only preventing the collapse of the puppet army and administration but also consolidating and strengthening the puppet forces. The Pentagon generals hastily declared that at the very moment when the big United States combat units were introduced into the South and the war was intensified, there were wide prospects for a quick victory. When their initial military operations did not meet with appreciable counterblows, they proved still more optimistic and declared that they had shifted to the offensive and compelled the South Vietnam liberation troops to switch from large-scale actions to small-unit operations. They also made feverish preparations for attacks on all fronts in the dry season in order to wrest back the initiative and hold it more and more firmly, and to drive the South Vietnamese people into an ever more serious defensive position.

However, reality has fallen short of the United States imperialists' expectations and purposes. From the point of view of an over-all

---

* Gen. J. Lawton Collins arrived in South Vietnam as special envoy with the rank of ambassador (replacing Ambassador Donald Heath) in November 1954. He stated on November 18, "I have come to Viet Nam to bring every possible aid to the government of Diem and to his government only. It is the legal government in Viet Nam, and the aid which the United States will lend it ought to permit the government to save the country." (See Ellen Hammer, *The Struggle for Indochina*, pp. 357–358.)

strategy in the southern theater of operations, is the enemy's strategy offensive or defensive? Is he following the strategy of lightning attack and lightning victory or that of protracted war? As regards operations on various battlefields, is he bending his energies in the coastal theater where he can bring into full play the power of his technical weapons, or in the hinterland theater where he most dreads facing defeat? Is he concentrating on the Nam Bo battlefield where lie great political and economic centers or on the high plateaus that he considers an important strategic position? As regards coordination with the puppet troops, is he concentrating on independent or joint operations? These are strategic questions to which the enemy himself cannot give clear-cut answers, for the American expeditionary force is strategically engaged in a "blind tunnel." The most outstanding feature of the military situation over the past several months is that the South Vietnam Liberation Armed Forces have not only kept on stepping up guerrilla warfare but they have also developed large-unit actions. If for the whole year 1965 they wiped out over two hundred thousand enemy troops, including some fifty battalions completely annihilated, in the last five months, since large United States contingents landed in South Vietnam and especially since the beginning of October, enemy casualties ran to more than one hundred thousand men, among them about twenty-five battalions entirely put out of action, including five American infantry battalions and a number of American armored units. This hard fact shows that despite the introduction of several hundred thousand troops the United States imperialists cannot reverse the situation. It shows that, confronted with the widespread and powerful development of the people's war, they have no other alternative than to scatter their forces over all theaters of operations and thus cannot avoid being driven onto the defensive, and they cannot easily wrest back the initiative and bring into full play the combativeness of their troops. The outstanding feature of the military situation in the South Vietnam theater is that the Liberation troops have not only successfully turned to account their offensive position since the Binh Gia victory but, right after the introduction of a big United States expeditionary force, they still hold the initiative and promote their vantage ground on an ever larger scale. No wonder that in the face of the heavy setbacks suffered by the expeditionary force McNamara and the American brass have shown dismay and toned down, declaring that the war in Vietnam would be long or that the United States troops' present attacks are only defensive. We did not yet mention the morale crisis of the American troops, who fear hand-to-hand fighting; leave behind their casualties on the field when hard pressed; throw away their weapons and munitions when withdrawing; are afraid of the jungle sun, wind, malaria, and especially of the Liberation troops and even of the ordinary Vietnamese—including old women and children—so much so that an American general, speaking of the United States expeditionary force, said that "its upkeep was expensive, and its fighting skill poor." We did not yet mention either their great difficulties in logistics and supply, as admitted by the American press: "Once again the United States is fighting a big war on the ground and finding itself far from ready to fight that war; the big bottleneck holding up combat operations in this war is logistical." This growing confusion certainly aggravates the United States' economic and financial difficulties and "gold hemorrhage" and reduces its competitive capacity on the world market.

At present, it is evident that, from the point of view of military strategy, the American imperialists are at sea. And what about their *tactical* position? Though the trial of strength between the United States expeditionary corps and the Liberation Armed Forces has begun recently, the latter have proved perfectly capable of checking all of their enemy's tactics.

The Van Tuong battle can be considered to be another Ap Bac for the American expeditionary force. The United States deployed a far superior force, including crack troops supported by armored units, air force, and navy, to attack a unit of the South Vietnam Liberation Army. The result was that, far from being wiped out, the

Liberation troops fought most valiantly and put out of action many enemy troops. The Van Tuong battle, which the American generals think can be likened to the fiercest hand-to-hand engagements of World War II, was a great victory of the South Vietnamese army and people, foreshadowing the tactical failure of the United States expeditionary force.

After Van Tuong came Chu Lai, Da Nang, Dat Cuoc, Bau Bang, Pleime, Dong Duong, and many other battles in which many American and puppet troops were wiped out.

Those resounding and repeated victories prove that:

1. The most solid United States bases are not immune from attacks.
2. The crack American infantry units, such as those belonging to the First Infantry Division, can be wiped out (and wiped out at the rate of one or several battalions in a single battle).
3. Crack United States air cavalry units, such as those of the First Airmobile Cavalry Division (so much boasted of by the United States defense secretary), can be put out of action.
4. Puppet units, though supported by the United States expeditionary force, continue to be cut to pieces, not by the battalion but by the combat group at Pleime, by whole battalions in a single battle (for example, at Dong Duong), or by the regiment, as at Dautieng.
5. United States troops, whether on the defensive or on the offensive, can be wiped out not only by the Liberation Army, but also by regional troops, militiamen, and guerrillas.

Those splendid exploits are accomplished at a time when the enemy is actively trying to make the best use of his technical weapons, including B-52 strategic planes which have already made more than one hundred sorties, while spraying chemicals to destroy vegetation and crops and savagely resorting to poison gases in a number of operations. They are achieved at the same time as great feats performed by the army and people in North Vietnam deal deadly blows to the modern U.S. Air Force's prestige in their continued efforts to defeat the enemy's sabotage warfare.

The significance of those achievements scored in the annihilation of the American and puppet forces lies in the Liberation Armed Forces and people of heroic South Vietnam being perfectly capable of putting out of action crack units of the United States expeditionary corps, gaining more initiative, stepping up their attacks on all theaters, and winning ever greater victories. In other words, the strategy and tactics of people's war can and will certainly prevail over strategy and tactics based on the outmoded bourgeois military conceptions of the American army; in theory as in practice, people's war will certainly prevail over the United States imperialists' neo-colonialist war of aggression.

The great victories of the army and people in both zones since the American imperialists started a direct aggression against the South of our country greatly encourage our entire people and cause our friends on all continents to rejoice. We definitely guard against subjectivism and never underestimate our opponent, for American imperialism is a cruel and perfidious enemy who, moreover, has considerable military potential, an enemy not only obdurate but also quick in drawing lessons from experience to contrive fiercer and more ruthless fighting methods. However, the lively reality of our struggle for national salvation over the past eleven years has strongly convinced our people and the people's armed forces in both zones that we will certainly defeat the United States aggressors under any circumstances.

The heavy defeats of the expeditionary corps right in its first operations in the Vietnam theater have caused the United States imperialists and their puppets many more difficulties, not only military but also political and economic. Far from being strengthened, the puppet army and administration are deteriorating as they have lost faith in their patron's modern army. The antiwar movement in the United States is developing with every passing day, while the in-

Once Again We Will Win 273

ternal contradictions in the Washington ruling circles are mounting.

In view of this situation, the American imperialists are planning to send more combat units to South Vietnam, increase the United States expeditionary force by 50, 100, or more percent. They are plotting to intensify their sabotage air warfare against the North while threatening to expand the war to Laos and neutral Cambodia. President Johnson has talked about taking "hard steps" in Vietnam. Secretary of State Dean Rusk has also stressed, "We will not withdraw from Vietnam," for the United States must "keep its commitments." The American imperialists' familiar trick is to couple the intensification of their aggressive war with a ballyhoo about their "will for peace." This time, along with preparations for new adventurist military moves, the United States administration opens a fraudulent "peace campaign" on a large scale. The Johnson administration's "peace efforts" are only aimed at placating public opinion at home and abroad which has been energetically protesting against their aggressive policy in Vietnam.

But, whatever honeyed words the American imperialists may use, they cannot deceive the Vietnamese people and peace-loving people throughout the world. There has not been the slightest change in their basic design. They cling to South Vietnam to keep Vietnam permanently partitioned. They do not want to withdraw their troops from the South and to recognize the South Vietnam National Liberation Front as the sole authentic representative of the South Vietnamese people; they cynically arrogate to themselves the right to bomb and strafe the territory of the Democratic Republic of Vietnam, an independent and sovereign socialist state, and go to the length of demanding from the Vietnamese people a compensation for the interruption of their bombing of North Vietnam. The essence of the "unconditional discussions" hoax is to compel our people to accept their terms.

We must heighten our vigilance in the face of the enemy's perfidious scheme. We must step up our entire people's patriotic war, resolutely fight until victory, no matter how many hundred thousand troops the United States imperialists may dispatch to South Vietnam and how far they may escalate their sabotage warfare against North Vietnam. Our people are determined not to shrink from any sacrifice to bring our great struggle against the American aggressors for national salvation to final victory.

The War
of Escalation

The War of Escalation: An Interview

QUESTION: From a military point of view, what is your assessment of the effects of fifteen months of American air attacks and bombing against the Democratic Republic of Vietnam?

ANSWER: As you know, in carrying out attacks and bombing against the Democratic Republic of Vietnam parallel to the intensification of aggression in South Vietnam, the American imperialists seek to shake the morale of our people, to destroy our military and economic potential, and thereby to turn the situation in South Vietnam in their favor.

Since their defeat in Korea, and after the first failures of the GI's in South Vietnam, the American imperialists have had a glimpse of what is involved for them in committing American infantry on the Asian mainland. (They see this, yet they go on; they will pay the price.) Accordingly, a war with their air force against the Democratic Republic of Vietnam seemed to them a fortunate discovery at the beginning. In order to wage it, they mobilized the planes of the Seventh Fleet and simultaneously their squadrons based in South Vietnam and in Thailand. They attacked indiscriminately channels of communication, industrial centers, populous regions in North Vietnam, sparing not even day nurseries, schools, hospitals, pagodas, and churches.

The American imperialists have not, for all that, attained the objectives envisaged. Their overt and cynical aggression against the Democratic Republic of Vietnam, an independent and sovereign country, a country of the socialist camp, only served to sharpen the hatred and strengthen the will to struggle on the part of the Vietnamese people and to provoke a vast protest movement throughout

---

This interview was granted by General Giap to Wilfred Burchett and Roger Pic on April 21, 1966. They furnished us with the French text and authorized its publication.

the world and in the United States of America itself. Even the Pentagon had to recognize that it was dealing with an adversary which showed no signs of weakening.

Our army and our people have inflicted severe losses on the enemy: as of today, 967 enemy planes shot down. And socialist construction continues. This year we have had an excellent harvest. As you can verify, the trains still run, prices do not rise. Our economic and military potential increases instead of diminishing.

And in South Vietnam, how have things gone? Our compatriots in the South have wiped out the best American units in Zone D to the north of Saigon, at Pleime, at Ia Drang, in the plains of Central Vietnam; they have successfully attacked bases which are still solidly defended: Da Nang, Chu Lai, and most recently Tan Son Nhut. The South Vietnamese mercenary army has suffered a series of defeats. As for the Saigon puppet government which President Johnson tried to salvage at Honolulu, what does it govern? The recent political events which now unfold at Hue, Da Nang, Saigon, and in other South Vietnamese cities show that it does not even control the urban centers. On the contrary, the South Vietnamese Liberation Army has proved that it is capable of defeating the American (and other) troops, however well armed they may be. The National Liberation Front of South Vietnam is increasingly confirmed as the sole authentic representative of the people.

Things are clear: the fifteen months of aerial bombardment against the Democratic Republic of Vietnam have cost the American aggressors new and heavy defeats, in the North as well as in the South, and an extremely grave political isolation. More than ever, they are at an impasse.

QUESTION: These last days, the Americans have employed B-52's against the North. They have also bombed Nam Dinh and the suburbs of Hanoi and Haiphong, the three biggest cities in the North. What is your reaction?

ANSWER: The savage bombardment is no surprise to us. It reflects the hysterical reaction of the American imperialists in the face of new military setbacks in South Vietnam. Far from being able to stop the deterioration of their situation in South Vietnam and restore the morale of a handful of agents despised by the people, once again they have only exposed the impudent trickery of the Johnson administration's proposals of so-called unconditional negotiations.

The American government will have to bear all the grave consequences of each new military venture against the Democratic Republic of Vietnam.

QUESTION: What is your opinion about the American theses according to which they can win the war in South Vietnam by paralyzing the port of Haiphong and destroying the economic potential of your country?

ANSWER: It is not "theses" which are lacking in American strategy. There are the theses of which you speak, but there are also other theses, more reasonable ones, which admit that it is in South Vietnam that the outcome of the war will be decided. And the outcome of the war, naturally, does not depend on what the enemy could do to certain of our ports or channels of communication.

The sole correct thesis is this: the war which the United States government now wages in South Vietnam is a war of aggression, a war of neo-colonialist aggression. As for our people in South Vietnam, they pursue a fight of legitimate defense in order to safeguard their national rights and to contribute to the maintenance of peace in Asia and throughout the world. Strong in their own right, united as a single man, knowing how to wield this invincible weapon which is people's war, supported by the socialist countries and by those throughout the world who cherish peace and justice, they have gone from one success to another, even after the unleashing of the air attacks against the Democratic Republic of Vietnam.

Whatever the means which the Americans put to work or could put to work, they do not know how to modify this irreversible truth in the epoch in which we live, the epoch of the triumph of socialism and of the peoples' liberation movements. Our war of liberation is a just war. We shall win.

QUESTION: What are, in your opinion, the repercussions which the Americans could provoke by attacking North and South Vietnam at once?

ANSWER: Vietnam is one; it is indivisible. The Geneva agreements of 1954 have expressly looked forward to its reunification by peaceful means. The intervention, followed by armed aggression, of the American imperialists in the South already constitutes a most grave assault on the sovereignty of our country. By the air raids against the Democratic Republic of Vietnam, they have carried the war in Vietnam to the whole of Vietnam. In such circumstances, to resist the American aggression, arms in hand, for the sake of national salvation, is the most sacred duty of every Vietnamese patriot, of the entire Vietnamese people. Our people are resolved to fight in order to defend the North, liberate the South, and accomplish the peaceful reunification of the fatherland.

QUESTION: How do you see the evolution of the war in the South and in North Vietnam?

ANSWER: The war of neo-colonialist aggression of the American imperialists will evolve as it has evolved up to this day: it will go from setback to setback and end in total defeat. Meanwhile, the war of liberation of our people will go from success to success until final victory.

As everyone knows, the United States experimented with their neo-colonialist policy with the installation of the bloody regime of Ngo Dinh Diem, with the use of one hundred and fifty thousand Diemist troops equipped and supported by Washington. They failed pitiably.

Afterward, there was the famous "special warfare" which Kennedy unleashed, which Johnson pursued with a half-million South Vietnamese mercenaries and some thirty thousand American advisers.

In its turn, "special warfare" failed, while the heroic South Vietnamese people accomplished still greater successes.

And now, there is a new stage. Washington now sends a massive American expeditionary corps composed of elite troops and wages an "escalation" war against North Vietnam. Since then, has the military and political situation of the United States in South Vietnam improved? Absolutely not! On the contrary, it has worsened rapidly. The American imperialists have failed in what they call the "dry-season offensive"; they will fail again. They have failed in their desperate attempt to instill courage in the government of marionettes in Saigon. Meanwhile, the armed forces of liberation and the people of South Vietnam accomplish ever more brilliant victories, and the Democratic Republic of Vietnam still holds firm, stronger than ever.

The American imperialists could still reinforce their expeditionary corps in South Vietnam, intensify the aerial bombardment of North Vietnam, and indeed undertake other adventurous measures. But the more they engage in the extension of the war, the more they expose themselves to heavier defeats.

Our country has known war for more than twenty years. Our country profoundly aspires to peace. But, as our President Ho Chi Minh has said, no true peace without true independence. We shall fight until the final victory against the American aggressors, to safeguard the independence of our country, to realize the profound aspirations of our people to liberty and reunification, to contribute to the maintenance of peace in Asia and throughout the world. We shall win.

American Defeats: An Interview

The year 1966 essentially bore the stamp of defeat . . . a severe defeat for the American expeditionary corps in South Vietnam. In this local war which they are obliged to wage in order to save their neocolonialist venture from debacle, the United States has lost the first round. For the Americans, this has been a real surprise of a strategic order. None of their objectives has been attained.

The Americans intended to break the back of the popular forces; that is to say, to exterminate the bulk of the forces of the National Liberation Front, to reconquer important territory which had escaped their control, to consolidate, to invigorate the sullen Saigon regime and its army. Indeed, none of these objectives, absolutely none, has been attained. On the contrary, the regular forces of the National Liberation Front have been strengthened, the liberated zones have been enlarged, and the crisis of the Saigon regime worsens without respite.

QUESTION: What are the effects of the bombardment against the North?

ANSWER: There, too, complete fiasco. Nothing can shake our determination to combat the aggression and to aid our brothers of the South as effectively as possible. The more the American Air Force increases its raids, the more grave are its losses. At this time [January 13, 1967], more than sixteen hundred Yankee planes have been shot down—and at the same time, our channels of communication

---

This interview was granted on January 13, 1967, by General Giap to Wilfred Burchett and Roger Pic, who have furnished us with the French text and authorized its publication. The text of the interview has already appeared in *Raison Présente*, n. 3.

are not cut off, our defense capacity has not been diminished; quite the contrary.

QUESTION: Do you think that the action of the American troops in the zone around the seventeenth parallel can be a prelude to the invasion of North Vietnam?

ANSWER: This action demonstrates the extent to which American strategy is caught in a position of passivity. American troops went to the rescue of the first puppet division, stationed in the provinces near the seventeenth parallel, and have suffered severe losses. Adventurous plans are conceived by certain American military men to make this operation into a prelude to an invasion of the North and to enlarge the war. I think that they ought to reflect on this. For our part, we are prepared to give them the welcome they deserve. The invader will be annihilated.

QUESTION: The U.S. command wishes to reserve the Saigon soldiers for tasks of pacification, leaving all combat actions to the American troops. What do you think about this?

ANSWER: This will result in the aggravation of American losses without, for all that, saving the puppet troops from certain defeats. What they call pacification is not an easy task. The Saigon army has sought to pacify South Vietnam for the last twelve years without accomplishing this task. Today, demoralized as it is (as you well know), having to confront a population which is completely inured to war, it can only encounter disaster.

QUESTION: What can you say about the American operations in the Mekong Delta?

ANSWER: This exposed one of the most acute contradictions on which American strategy flounders. Is it necessary to disperse their troops in search of an enemy which is everywhere—without finding any part to strike? Is it necessary to regroup their forces, to abandon vast territory to the adversary? When people's war develops, as in present-day South Vietnam, the aggressor's strategy can oscillate from one point to another without finding a correct path. The population of the Mekong Delta has a long experience of armed political struggle. It will certainly deal severe blows to the enemy. Without wishing to play on words, one can foresee that the Americans will be swallowed up in the morass of the Mekong Delta.

QUESTION: What can the military perspectives be for 1967?
ANSWER: Washington will persist in intensifying, enlarging, the war, while at the same time, naturally, speaking of peace. Johnson's recent message proves this. The American generals always think that some supplementary divisions, some supplementary shipments of bombs, of napalm, of toxic gases, can induce the Vietnamese people to capitulate. The bombings, the atrocities, the American crimes multiply. But the defeat of the United States will be so much the more grave as the involvement deepens.

Never have the Vietnamese people, from North to South, been so united, so determined to fight until victory. Never has our defense capacity been so high. Never has the prestige of the National Liberation Front been so great, both within the country and in the international arena. The socialist countries and all of progressive humanity aid us usefully and effectively. American imperialism is more isolated than ever today. We fight for the liberty and independence of our country, for the people's liberation, for socialism and peace. Our cause is just; we shall win.

Great Victory, Great Task

The Defeat of Special Warfare

Between February and June 1965—after the victory at Binh Gia—the southern army and people accelerated the guerrilla war (which was based on a combination of armed struggle and political struggle). At the same time they began making large-scale attacks, bringing the puppet troops to a state of complete collapse as they found themselves unable to resist the Liberation Armed Forces.

During this period, the newly arrived American troops suffered heavy blows at An Tan, Nui Thanh, Pleiku, Da Nang, and especially at Van Tuong. Their bases were tightly encircled by guerrilla belts. Neither the United States forces nor the puppet forces could halt the huge, persistent, and victorious attacks made by the southern army and people. The United States imperialists and their lackeys were increasingly confused.

When the United States imperialists had first used their air force to attack the North (beginning on February 7, 1965), our army and people began to deal resounding blows to the U.S. air force; the imperialists suffered heavy losses and were increasingly on the defensive. Faced with defeat and danger, and confronted, toward the end of 1965, with the fact that the puppet troops were being repeatedly assaulted and demolished, President Johnson forced General Taylor to resign and then decided to send massive United States expeditionary forces to fight in South Vietnam; he thus moved the aggressive war into a new strategic phase, that of "limited war."

By October 1965 there were 180,000 American expeditionary forces in South Vietnam (bringing the total of American and puppet

---

This is an edited and abridged version of a long essay which was serialized in *Nhan Dan,* September 14–16, 1967.

troops to 700,000 men) and the United States imperialists launched their first strategic counteroffensive in the fantastic hope of rapidly destroying the regular units of the southern liberation forces, and thus ending the war in 1966. This strategic counteroffensive consisted of two major, consecutive, operations during the 1965–1966 dry season.

The first operation, begun during the winter of 1965, used a large force of many of the most experienced American armed forces units (the First Airmobile Division, the First Infantry Division, paratroop units, etc.). The attacks were launched in two areas—north of Saigon, and in the high plateaux where the United States imperialists thought the Liberation troops were mainly concentrated. In spite of the wishes of the United States imperialists, both these attacks failed.

Following their heavy losses at Van Tuong, the Americans and their puppets lost many battalions at Bau Bang, Dau Tieng, north of Saigon, Pleime, the high plateaux, and in other areas. The United States troops were thus defeated from the beginning. McNamara was taken aback, and Washington was amazed. The number of American fighting troops was quickly increased and a second wave of attacks began in the spring of 1966.

The number of United States troops had by then reached 250,000. The entire mobile force was sent into a five-pronged attack, aimed at three areas: eastern Nam Bo, the Trung Bo delta, and the high plateaux. The purpose was to annihilate the Liberation Armed Forces, and simultaneously to pacify these areas. Again, these plans failed. The enemy used as many as twenty-seven of their battalions on some occasions in this series of attacks (for instance, at Bong Son and Binh Dinh), but they were unable to destroy any Liberation Army detachment. On the contrary, United States and puppet troops suffered heavy looses—at Cu Chi, Nha Do, Bong Trang, in eastern Nam Bo, at Phu Yen, Quang Ngai, Binh Dinh, in the Trung Bo delta, and in the high plateaux. The first dry-season strategic counteroffensive carried out by the American imperialists ended in tragedy—more than thirty battalions were wiped out (fourteen of these were United States and satellite infantry battalions) and more than 110,000 men were killed or wounded (more than 40,000 of these were United States and satellite troops).

In the 1965–1966 winter-spring period, United States troops were heavily defeated during the initial fighting, and the puppet troops were perpetually on the defensive; the southern army and people maintained and strengthened their forces on the battlefield and stepped up both guerrilla and large-scale attacks. They took the initiative in counterattacking and destroying the enemy during their operations, while at the same time attacking and destroying the enemy deep in their rear—attacking their lairs in Saigon, their barracks and logistic bases across the country, and so on.

The southern army and people defeated the American, puppet, and satellite forces in the very first round of the imperialists' "limited war." Because of the 1965–1966 winter-spring victories, the southern army and people were able to step up both military struggle and political struggle: they attacked the enemy directly, creating an unstable situation in which the puppet authorities and the army faced crises in every area and forcing the United States imperialists into an embarrassing and defensive position. In thirty cities and municipalities throughout the south, urban people rebelled and struggled against the introduction of American aggressor troops and against the Thieu-Ky clique. The political movement which developed during this period was largest and most vigorous in Da Nang and Hue.

Clearly, the conflicts between the United States imperialists and the quislings, and the southern people, were becoming increasingly fierce. Intensive attacks by the southern army and people brought severe military defeat upon the Americans and their puppets, who then faced serious political crises. The result was argument, antagonism, and disharmony among the puppet authorities and the army in the I Corps area. This period of crisis lasted for over two months and led to five changes in command. Six enemy battalions were dispersed because they were shooting at one another.

These setbacks—especially the defeats sustained by the United States troops—accelerated the decline of the puppet troops. In some months there were as many as 20,000 deserters. In addition, military revolts broke out, such as that in the First Regiment at Thu Dau Mot and in other puppet units.

During the summer of 1966—after the defeat of their first dry-season strategic counteroffensive—the American imperialists returned to the defensive in order to avoid the attacks of the Liberation troops, and in order to work at supporting and increasing the number of American expeditionary troops and to prepare a new strategic counteroffensive for the 1966–1967 dry season. During the summer, the American and puppet troops were repeatedly assaulted by the southern army and people on all the important battlefields, from Tri Thien, the high plateaus, and central Trung Bo, to eastern, central, and western Nam Bo.

Once they had strengthened and increased the number of American expeditionary troops to 400,000 men (raising the number of American and puppet troops to more than one million), the American imperialists embarked upon their second strategic counteroffensive. The basic purposes of this major counteroffensive were supposed to be: 1) to carry out a two-pronged strategy of search-and-destroy missions and pacification raids; 2) to learn from the experiences of the defeat in the first counteroffensive and this time to concentrate on accomplishing the main work of the new counteroffensive; 3) to bring about a new division of labor between the two forces, with the United States troops responsible for the search-and-destroy missions and the puppet regulars responsible for pacification.

The United States imperialists launched their counteroffensive with a large military force. The purpose was to destroy areas where they thought resistance organizations were concentrated, in an attempt to destroy the Liberation regulars. They accelerated the pacification campaign in order to win a quick strategic victory and to end the "Vietnamese problem" in a short time. But they again suffered heavy defeats and found themselves in an even more serious defensive position.

On October 17, 1966, the South Vietnam National Liberation Front's Central Committee issued a call to fight resolutely and to defeat the United States aggressors in the winter-spring period; early in the winter of 1966, the southern army and people prepared to counterattack and at the same time began new attacks on every battlefield. At the end of the summer, the southern army and people opened a new front at Tri Thien. They attacked the American and puppet troops forcefully and repeatedly, and made them bring in United States reinforcements from other areas and spread them out to cope with all the different battles on this front.

The United States imperialists were taken by surprise, and were temporarily passive before they began to pour in men for the second dry-season counteroffensive. The Liberation Armed Forces in the high plateaux area lured the United States troops into going to Plei Djereng and then destroyed them in the bloody battles on the banks of the Sa Thay River. The southern army and people created a new offensive situation on the Nam Bo front, particularly in the delta. Liberation Armed Forces victories began with the attack on the bomb depot at Long Binh on October 28 and the shelling of the United States–puppet military parade in the heart of Saigon on November 1. These were serious defeats for the enemy.

Eastern Nam Bo was the main target for United States attacks throughout the 1966–1967 winter-spring period, and they launched many operations there. The most significant were Operation Attleboro, Operation Cedar Falls, and Operation Junction City, all defensive operations designed to deal with the attacks of the southern troops and people. The enemy mobilized more than 30,000 men for Operation Attleboro, but were left with heavy losses in the 196th

Brigade, in units of the Twenty-fifth Division, in the Tropic Lightning, the First Division, the Big Red One, the 173rd Brigade, and in other units.

The Americans poured the largest number of troops into Operation Junction City, which began in February 1967. A large force—45,000 men and a large number of airplanes, artillery, and armored vehicles—was sent onto a battlefield less than 150 miles square in the hope of winning a decisive victory. But the largest operation brought the greatest defeat, and the second dry-season strategic counteroffensive ended in humiliation. The search-and-destroy operations had failed; as one would expect, pacification had brought no results.

The southern army and people continued to fight fiercely, but at the same time increased the coordination of the military and political struggles. The political work of the city people in the south continued to progress, and its anti-American character grew. The liberated areas in the south were enlarged. The failure of pacification brought about the recall of Lodge and Lansdale. Thus, the American imperialists' second strategic counteroffensive was a greater failure than the first. About 175,000 troops were destroyed, and more than 70,000 of these were American. Ninety-nine battalion and battalion-size units, including twenty-eight United States battalions, were taken out of action. Approximately 3,000 aircraft, as well as hundreds of artillery pieces and other matériel were destroyed.

Increasingly, the United States imperialists and their lackeys became bogged down and passive: they could not even destroy one small unit from the Liberation Armed Forces main force, and lost men and matériel in quantity. They were unable to take the offensive and were forced to fight defensively on every front. Their greatest defeats occurred where the bulk of their forces were concentrated. While they had planned to send troops into the Mekong River delta, they were forced to postpone doing this because of the situation on every other front. They were determined to save the puppet troops, but these troops dwindled and lost their ability to fight—or even to carry out pacification work.

This summer, after the failure of the second dry-season strategic counteroffensive, an aura of pessimism has enveloped the United States ruling clique and the Vietnamese quislings in Saigon. The United States aggressors and their lackeys are upset by their growing and insoluble political and military problems, and by the inevitable deadlock that is resulting. They are equally embarrassed by the growing strength of the southern army and people, and by the determination of the Vietnamese people to achieve national salvation. They are faced with the growing opposition of progressive people the world over, even in the United States.

In the White House and the Pentagon, the ruling clique has quarreled fiercely among themselves about the situation in Vietnam. Westmoreland was brought back to the United States to make a speech in which he deceitfully claimed that there was no stalemate, even while at the same time asking Johnson to send more men into the South. Secretary of Defense McNamara—who for the ninth time had rushed to Saigon to study the war at close hand—criticized Westmoreland for wasting manpower and instructed him to use the troops now in Vietnam more efficiently. Then Maxwell Taylor and Clark Clifford toured the United States' Southeast Asian satellites in order to recruit more mercenary troops; in this they failed.

It is obvious that the United States imperialists are stalemated after the second strategic counteroffensive. Their "limited war" has been defeated disastrously. On the other hand, following the 1966-1967 winter-spring victories, the southern army and people have moved ahead and won ever greater victories, helped by the atmosphere of confidence and action which has reigned over every battlefield.

The Liberation Armed Forces have rapidly matured, gained fighting experience, and shown that they are in fine condition. Inspired by their victories, the southern army and people have continued developing their initiative this summer, and have intensified military and political offensives everywhere, dealing the United States, puppet, and satellite troops decisive blows at Gioc Mieu, Con Tien, Gio An, Nong Son, Mo Duc, Tan Uyen, Can, My Tho, and Quoi Son, as well as at such airbases as Da Nang and Chu Lai. This has been the history of the war in the south during the past two years.

At the same time, in the north of the country the United States imperialists have been sending a major portion of their air force, based in the Seventh Fleet in the South and in Thailand, to attack the North. This attempt to extricate themselves from their dilemma in the South, to destroy the morale of the people in both parts of the country, and to hold in check the northern people's support of the liberation struggle in the South represents an important part of the limited-war strategy and is, at the same time, an act of desperation.

They began by attacking the southern areas of the Fourth Zone; gradually they escalated the war into the northern part of North Vietnam. They have temporarily halted the attacks on the North on different occasions in order to deceive their people with their peace tricks and to reorganize their forces; they then continued the escalation of the war above the 17th parallel.

On June 21, 22, and 28, 1966, they began a foolish attack on the capital of the North, Hanoi, which was the most serious escalation of their war of destruction so far. They have also used the ships of the Seventh Fleet and the artillery units stationed south of the DMZ to supplement their air-force attacks against the coastal areas of the DMZ and the southern part of Vinh Linh. Their targets have been communications centers, industrial sites, dams and dikes, cities and other populated areas, schools, hospitals, markets, and so on.

Despite this, the United States war of destruction in the North has been defeated. The imperialists have been faced both with increasing anti-American feeling and with the positive spirit of national salvation of the northern army and people. Almost 2,300 fighter aircraft have been shot down, and thousands of American pilots have been killed or captured in the North. (These figures are as of September 14, 1967.) The prestige of the U.S. Air Force has fallen tremendously.

In the course of the war, the socialist regime in the North has grown stronger, the North has fought well and has also produced well. Good communications and transportation have been maintained, and the economy and culture have been developed steadily. Despite many obstacles created by the enemy, the living conditions of the people are stable. The determination to oppose the Americans and to struggle for national salvation has grown in strength.

In the South, in the spirit of "the North calls, the South answers," the southern army and people have continued to attack the United States, puppet, and satellite troops everywhere, and have tried to attack their air bases and logistical depots, to inflict heavy losses and to force the enemy increasingly on the defensive.

The Limited-War Period: Heavy Defeats for the Imperialists

Following World War II—and especially after their defeats in China, Korea, Indochina, and Cuba—the United States imperialists have begun to sense their inferiority, and that of the imperialist camp, in the global balance of power. The imperialist camp—led by the Americans—has been forced into a passive and defensive position when confronted with the growth of the socialist camp, of the national liberation movements, and of the continuing offensive posture of the worldwide revolutionary movement.

The United States imperialists have been forced to abandon their strategy of massive retaliation in favor of a "flexible" response. They maintain that the strategy of flexible response—which consists of three types of warfare: special, limited, and total—is the strategy most suitable for finding solution to their current defensive situation at a time when they are not in a position to undertake a nuclear war. In addition, they feel it is the best strategy for implementing their aggressive policies and for helping them perform the role of an international police force which copes with the national liberation movements arising the world over, and for preparing for aggression against the socialist countries. They believe these special war and local war tactics are sharp swords which will cut into the national liberation movements and create favorable conditions for a world war.

The United States imperialists attempted the special war strategy in the south of our country and failed. They had to move quickly, while on the defensive, to a strategy of limited war in order to deal with their dangerous military position. This shift not only reflected their failure, but also revealed their unyielding, aggressive, and belligerent nature.

What is the United States imperialists' limited-war strategy? In their own view, limited war in one of the three forms of aggressive war. It is war actually fought by Americans, but limited in size and scope. While special war is fought mainly by local lackey troops, limited war is waged by United States troops themselves.

In general, the aggressive policies of the United States imperialists seek to achieve neo-colonialism. When they fight a limited war to repress a national liberation movement, they must use local troops and puppet authorities openly, as well as American troops. They see the puppet troops and authorities as an important bulwark. In these limited wars, aimed at implementing neo-colonialism, the final goal is the consolidation of the puppet army and government and their transformation into effective tools for the achievement of neo-colonialism. The primarily military aim of the limited-war strategy is to destroy the enemy's military forces; the idea is to attack and attack quickly, in order to end the war quickly.

The restriction of the number of United States troops imposed by a limited war means using only a part of the United States infantry, air force, and navy. The use of their forces must be limited, or their global strategy will run into difficulty and their world influence will be affected. They must limit their forces because otherwise they will

Great Victory, Great Task 295

upset the political, economic, and social life of their own country: a limited war means they can continue economic and social programs at home because their forces will not be fully mobilized. They are willing to limit their war because they are convinced that they can win using only a limited number of troops who participate in a local war aimed at repressing a national liberation movement in any country, in Asia, Africa, or Latin America.

Since they must limit the number of their troops, the American imperialists are particularly careful to use the forces of the local lackeys well. They believe that by using a small number of United States troops as a core for local lackey units—equipped with modern weapons—they can repress their opponents in a country where the economy is backward or newly developing because of their stronger firepower and military force, and that they will therefore be victorious within a short time. Limiting their strategic goals also means limiting their political goals, and, in the military arena, concentrating on destroying the enemy's military forces, particularly the regulars, quickly. This must be done in order to avoid dispersing their troops over different fronts.

They believe that their adversary's backbone is his fighting force, and that if this can be defeated, the war can be ended; they believe that if they fail in this, the war will continue and they will eventually face defeat. They must win in order to create conditions favorable enough for the lackey forces to carry out the political tasks that follow victory, thus allowing the imperialists to bring their troops home while at the same time guaranteeing the political conditions necessary for neo-colonialism will be maintained.

Limiting the scope of the war means fighting only in certain areas, thus preventing the war from spreading to other nations or regions. If the scope of the war is not limited, they believe they will be forced further on the defensive and will face still greater defeats, as larger countries are forced to join in. And as of this moment, they are not ready for a new world war.

Keeping these points about limited war in mind, we see that the limited war that the United States imperialists are now waging in South Vietnam has gone beyond its original limitations. The number of troops has far exceeded the restrictions of a limited war, in which only between three and six divisions should be mobilized: the United States and its satellites now have eleven divisions in South Vietnam, of which nine are American and two are South Korean.

Further, the objectives of the American troops in the South are not restricted to the destruction of the LAF, but include the job of pacification. The United States imperialists have not limited the war to the South, but have used their air force and navy to wage a war of destruction against the North. They continue to intervene with increasing force in the Laotian kingdom, and they continue to provoke the Cambodians; indeed, they have plans to expand the war over the entire Indochinese peninsula in order to extricate themselves from their situation in South Vietnam.

When the United States imperialists shifted to the strategy of limited war in the south of our country, they obviously wanted to establish neo-colonialism. Therefore, even though they have hundreds of thousands of American troops in the South, they have also had to work to keep the puppet army and administration in power as a necessary political and military support for their neo-colonialist war of aggression. They still use the name of the puppet administration and try to hold its army together.

They have frantically carried on the political games of neo-colonialism along with the military games of aggressive war. As a result, the present limited war continues to be an aggressive war aimed at achieving the political objectives of neo-colonialism. The particular strategy of limited war—as well as the general strategy of flexible response—is a product of the bourgeois military thinking of the United States imperialists, thinking which has developed as imperialism has become increasingly depressed, defeated, and on the defensive when confronted with a situation in which the balance of world power is unfavorable.

Great Victory, Great Task

While the United States imperialists have carried on a policy of neo-colonialist aggression, they have also had to send American troops to carry out direct aggression in South Vietnam. This has heightened the contradictions between their political goal of imposing neo-colonialism and the military game of using United States troops to carry on the war. By sending United States troops in to commit direct aggression in the South, the United States imperialists have revealed plainly their brazen, aggressive face, which they cannot conceal. These contradictions have aggravated many of the basic political problems of neo-colonialism, and have led the United States imperialists into many defeats and difficulties.

The United States imperialists' introduction of troops into the South was intended to prevent the fall of the puppet army and administration and to create new conditions for consolidating and strengthening the puppet forces. But the more the war of aggression is Americanized, the more the puppet army and administration in Saigon disintegrates. The treacherous and unpatriotic nature of the leaders of the puppet army administration have been exposed. They have been cursed by all of our people.

In addition, the contradictions inside the puppet army and administration, and the discord between the United States imperialists and the puppet army and administration, have increased. Those in the puppet army and administration who still retain some national spirit have gradually begun to see the light and increasing numbers of them have returned to the people. Confronted with the overwhelming crimes of the United States aggressors and the quislings, the southern people are more filled with hatred, have reinforced their solidarity, and have fought bravely and determinedly for final victory under the anti-American banner of national salvation of the National Liberation Front.

The more they increase the number of troops in the South, and the further they extend the fighting, the deeper the United States imperialists make the contradictions between their limited-war strategy and their global strategy. The more the limited war in the

South is accelerated, the more it will adversely affect other positions the United States imperialists hold around the world—especially since they have had to mobilize forces which far exceeded their estimates for a limited war. As a result, the contradictions between their limited-war strategy and their global strategy have become even more acute.

Revolutionaries throughout the world can make use of this situation to intensify their attacks against the United States imperialists, to turn them back step by step and eliminate their presence bit by bit. The allies of the United States imperialists can also use this situation to press for their own interests and thus create difficulties for the American imperialists.

The American imperialists intended to launch an offensive, but instead they have fallen back into a defensive position. It is very dangerous for an aggressive army to have its forces scattered, and it is even more dangerous to have to remain on the defensive. At the moment, approximately 70 percent of the United States troops perform defensive duties in South Vietnam. According to the Pentagon's calculations, a minimum of 200,000 troops are necessary to defend the United States bases of various sizes in the South. The United States imperialists mobilized one division and deployed it over a fifteen-mile perimeter to defend Da Nang airbase alone. The American imperialists recently estimated that only one U.S. soldier out of eight is engaged in actual combat. McNamara himself admitted that the combat efficiency of United States troops is very low, and he found that only 70,000 of the 500,000 troops in South Vietnam are directly engaged in combat.

All forms of imperialist tactics have proved to be inefficient: search-and-destroy operations, mopping-up operations, pacification measures, and rescue operations, police and security work, firepower attacks, spraying poisonous chemicals, and so on. The battles of Van Tuong, Cu Chi, and Pleime, as well as the search-and-destroy operations carried out during the major campaigns (Five Arrows,

Cedar Falls, Attleboro, Highway 9, Junction City, and others), have shown both the ineffectiveness and the outright failure of these tactics. Modern military bases (such as Da Nang and Chu Lai) and logistic bases (such as Long Binh, Bien Hoa, and others), have been permanently threatened, repeatedly attacked, and have suffered heavy losses.

In addition, the tactics particular to each branch of the United States armed forces have been defeated. The motorized infantry of the First Division, dependent on support from armored vehicles, artillery, and aviation, has been shown to be inefficient. It is weak when opposed by the cleverness of the Liberation troops: it is not free to achieve its plan, but must comply with the conditions and tactics of the enemy. The First Division was defeated bitterly at Bau Bang, Nha Do, Cam Xe, Bong Trang, and in other battles. The massive heliborne-troop tactics of the Air Cavalry Division, intended to stage surprise raids and destroy the enemy quickly, have never been able either to surprise or to destroy any section of the Liberation Armed Forces. The troops of the Air Cavalry Division are even weaker than most of the rest of the United States infantry troops, for they have neither mechanized nor artillery support units. Their units have been battered by the Liberation Armed Forces at Pleime, Binh Dinh, and in other places.

The blocking-defense tactic of the Marines, combined with mopping-up of operations designed to pacify the areas around the military bases, has been shown to be very weak. The Marine bases at Da Nang and Chu Lai stand as isolated islands in the open sea of a people's war. The Marines—the branch of the armed forces which the United States imperialists regard as most seasoned—have frequently and seriously been defeated and are being stretched taught as a bowstring over hundreds of miles in the Tri Thien region and along Highway 9.

Bombing and strafing tactics, aimed at destroying LAF units, resistance bases, and the people, have also proven ineffective because of poor intelligence and the failure to identify targets accurately. United States Air Force bombings and strafings to date, including those of the B-52 strategic bombers, have not wiped out one single LAF unit, and have only shattered trees and destroyed empty tunnels, as the imperialists themselves have admitted.

Why have all these tactics been ineffective? Tactics are not separable from strategy, as everyone knows. If strategy becomes defensive and deadlocked, it will affect tactics sharply and adversely. In addition, the failure and deadlock of the various tactics used by the United States lies in erroneous tactical thinking. The Americans have believed that they could base their operations on the power of weapons, and have assumed that firepower is their soul. When the use of these bases, weapons, and firepower is limited, or fails to become increasingly effective, the tactics become ineffective and themselves fail.

The People Have Won Great Victories

The puppet armed forces depend on the United States forces for their survival and for helping them to consolidate and strengthen their ranks. But they nevertheless play a very important part in aiding the Americans in their neo-colonialist war of aggression. They are useful both as occupation troops and as mobile troops on the battlefield. They are responsible primarily for controlling and oppressing the people, and for simultaneously carrying on pacification work. The fact that they are collapsing and disintegrating will deprive the United States forces of one support for the continuation of their war of neo-colonialist aggression.

The puppet administration is a political framework, an instrument the American imperialists need to effect neo-colonialism. Our people know this and have combined armed struggle with political struggle in order to overthrow the puppet administration, not only at its base—as they have already—but at other levels as well. By seeing their own aims clearly, our people in the South have accurately and successfully defined the tactical and strategic aims of a people's war. They have fought a comprehensive and prolonged resistance war, using all the people, and have always seized the offensive, relied on their own forces (which they considered the principal forces), and have fully appreciated the support of fraternal socialist countries and the progressive people all over the world. Our people's resistance war will be victorious, in spite of sacrifices and hardships.

The primary objectives of the political struggle are to mobilize and organize the people, to guide them in the struggle against the enemy, to maintain close coordination with the military struggle, and to help win the greatest victories for the resistance. The more violent the war becomes, the stronger and more effective the political struggle will be, particularly in the urban centers of South Vietnam, where there are many contradictions between our people and the United States imperialists and their henchmen, and where there are even conflicts among the United States imperialists themselves. As the anti-American resistance struggle for national salvation continues, the political struggle of our urban compatriots in the South will play an increasingly important role and will hit the enemy directly in his deepest lairs.

The military struggle is becoming increasingly important and is playing a decisive role in defeating the enemy on the battlefield. The United States imperialists are concentrating their forces and persevering in a policy of using arms and troops to invade the South and enslave our people. Our people in the South must therefore resort to revolutionary violence in order to oppose this counter-revolutionary violence and they must use the military struggle to oppose the armed aggression of the enemy. The American imperialists have a huge military force to use to carry out their aggression in the South. Our people's military struggle has therefore become increasingly important.

Guerrilla activities and large-scale combat are coordinated, help each other, and encourage each other to grow. They are also coordinated closely with the political struggle in order to win victories in both the military and political fields, and thus lead the resistance to final victory. Prolonged resistance is the essential strategy for a people which lives in a country which is neither large nor populous, one which has a limited economic and military potential but which is determined to defeat an aggressive enemy which has large numbers of well-armed troops.

Our people truly appreciate the struggle being carried on by the American people against the Johnson administration's aggressive war in Vietnam, and we consider it a real sign of sympathy and support for our people's just resistance. Our people are well aware that the decisive factor in the success of the anti-American resistance struggle for national salvation is their attempt to change the balance of power in our favor on the Vietnam battlefield, where there is a struggle between the aggressors and the victims of aggression, and where the military situation increasingly turns in favor of the heroic people of South Vietnam.

Our people believe that after the upcoming Presidential election in the United States—even if there is a change in President—the nature of the United States imperialists' aggressive policy will not change. The Presidential elections in the United States only determine the distribution of positions in the hierarchy among the leading personalities of the parties of the ruling capitalist class. The forthcoming elections will lead the American people to realize the errors and defeats the Johnson administration has made in the aggressive war in Vietnam; the struggle of the American people against this aggressive war will thus be strengthened.

The economic and military potential of the United States, although large, is not limitless. The realities of the war in Vietnam have shown that even with large numbers of troops, good guns, and a lot of money, the Americans cannot extricate themselves from failure and stalemate and they will therefore be defeated.

Great Victory, Great Task

Using our own forces, while seeking assistance from the socialist bloc and from the progressive peoples of the world, is an important part of our strategy. It is the concrete expression of the strongly held point of view of the masses, one of absolute confidence in our nation and in our people who are permeated with an unconquerable tradition and who have sufficient opportunity and ability to defeat an aggressive enemy, even the United States imperialists.

The Liberation Armed Forces' method of attacking cities is being used on the southern battlefields. Small LAF units, supported by the people's political forces, have won huge victories and have destroyed a substantial portion of the enemy's mobility. Specifically, attacks launched by the LAF in the heart of Saigon, Hue, and other cities have aided the struggle of the urban compatriots, frightened the enemy, and filled the hearts of our compatriots with joy. The attacks on the cities have all shown the tremendous courage, skill, and flexibility of the LAF.

On the southern battlefield, LAF tactics in attacking military communications—especially important centers of communication—have proved very effective. The LAF has disrupted and crippled the enemy's logistical supply movement and has enfeebled his mobility on the battlefield. In order to protect and clear their communications, the United States and puppet troops have been forced to move a large part of their troops. But even now, the enemy's military communications are far from being free of difficulties and their main strategic routes are attacked and threatened constantly and forcefully.

The Upcoming Plots of the Imperialists

From Johnson and McNamara to Westmoreland, the imperialists have all realized that their situation in Vietnam is at an impasse. But they have not been able to come up with a solution. They have finally resorted to troop reinforcements, but they are running into great problems. If they send in small reinforcements, they cannot improve their situation because their troops are threatened on every battlefield. If they send in large numbers of reinforcements, this will greatly affect both the political and economic life of the American people and the global strategy of the United States, and will still not save the United States imperialists from defeat.

On the political front, the pacification efforts have met with increasing failure and have had no positive results. The puppet troops are weaker and weaker and have lost more and more of their effectiveness. After their fraudulent elections,* the puppet administration is still incapable of overcoming its conflicts, its disorder, and its hopeless situation. The conflicts among the American lackeys, the puppet generals, and between the military and the civilian cliques, have become increasingly severe. The United States imperialists attempted to use the fraudulent farce of an election to apply a fresh layer of paint to the Thieu-Ky clique, but the Thieu-Ky clique was only exposed more clearly than ever as traitors to Vietnam and lackeys of the United States. Public opinion in the United States also reflects the increasing isolation of the Saigon administration as it is faced with the widespread and vigorous development of the struggle of the heroic southern army and people.

The American imperialists are also faced with new problems in the international arena. Since they have been committed to an aggressive war in Vietnam and yet have failed repeatedly, they have exposed their flaws and weaknesses over and over again. Revolutionary people the world over have learned that the United States imperialists are rich but weak and that their economic and military potential, although great, has its limits. The American imperialists are being beaten by a small but heroic people. The longer they continue their aggressive war in Vietnam, the more they are isolated in international politics.

The United States imperialists must deal with a new front in the

---

* Elections were held on September 3, 1967; they resulted in the questionable victory of the Thieu-Ky ticket.

Middle and Near East. The temporary military victories of the American lackeys—the Israeli mercenaries—have not ended the seething national liberation movements in the Arab countries; rather they have simply been a signal for a new stage in these movements. The people in the Arab countries are carrying on their struggle and will continue until they win their liberation. The temporary victories won by the American imperialists and the Israeli mercenaries have turned into strategic mistakes and are causing them greater and greater difficulties in every area.

In Latin America—which the United States imperialists have always regarded as their own backyard—revolutionary movements have been growing rapidly, and the Latin American people have defended themselves against the aggressive interventionist policy of the United States imperialists and the lackey reactionary governments in the area.

In the United States itself, the Johnson administration is faced with a conflict between the ruling clique and the growing protests of the American people. The widespread rebellion of the American Negro is a fierce aggressive blow at the Johnson clique's domestic and foreign policies. Never before has Johnson been at such an impasse as he is now. *U.S. News & World Report* of August 14, 1967, admitted that the Vietnam war, racial conflict, a growing budget deficit, and trouble with Congress, the allies, and the dollar are all bad news, and are putting pressure on the administration from all sides. The White House is suddenly like a building whose roof is about to fall in.

What plans do the American imperialists have?

1. They will continue to expand the limited war by increasing the number of troops in the South and by fiercely attacking the North. After making involved calculations, Johnson has decided to send another 50,000 men to South Vietnam, bringing the total United States forces to over 500,000 by July 1968.

2. The United States imperialists may expand their limited war over all our country. We are prepared for this possibility. If the

American imperialists expand the limited war into the North, it is certain that they will be rapidly and totally defeated. Even with over one million men at their disposal, they have failed in the South. If they send infantry troops into the North, how many more would be needed? Attacking the North would mean opening another front. Their forces would be even further dispersed and would be more easily destroyed.

Our armed forces and people must deal out fitting punishment for each new step in the escalation of the war. We must vigorously increase the moral, material, political, and military strength of the socialist North, and at the same time effectively use the aid from the socialist countries to defeat American aggression. We must be increasingly watchful and firmly face the continuous, prolonged, and determined nature of our task of fighting against the destructive war of the United States imperialists. We have never had any illusions about the American imperialists' desire for peace. Strong and continued attacks on their air force, navy, and artillery are the most realistic and effective means to guarantee coordination with the heroic southern armed forces and people and are also encouraging for the armed forces and people throughout the entire country.

We must work to increase the fighting power of our armed forces and the different branches of the people's army and to make our fire nets more effective against U.S. aircraft, warships, and artillery units, to destroy as much American force as possible and to protect the socialist North more effectively.

Now that we are confronted with new plots and acts of sabotage by the American imperialists, it is all the more necessary for us to invent more courageous and resourceful tactics to surprise the enemy constantly and to inflict heavy defeats on him. We must also concentrate on perfecting and inventing fighting methods to use against the U.S. naval forces and artillery units. With stalwart, militant, determination, with heroism, courage, and intelligence, we can work to make those weapons we have superior and to invent highly effective tactics in order to punish American naval and artillery units as they deserve.

Under President Ho's banner, which calls for "Determination to defeat the United States aggressors," let our entire army and people take advantage of victories to move ahead. The Vietnamese people are determined to defeat the over one million United States, puppet, and satellite troops. The American imperialists' neo-colonialist war of aggression will certainly be defeated. The people's war of the heroic Vietnamese people will certainly win total victory.

The Final Phase of Battle

The Vietnamese people are waging the greatest war of resistance in the nation's history and are writing new, extremely glorious pages of history. We are defeating the United States imperialists in their biggest local war of aggression since World War II, which is also their biggest neo-colonialist war of aggression against the national liberation movement which is surging forward like a tidal wave. We have defeated the United States imperialists' war of destruction carried out by air and naval forces against North Vietnam, an important strategic policy in their scheme to intensify their war of aggression against our country. Blinded by their aggressive nature, the United States imperialists have recklessly attacked an indomitable and heroic people with a centuries-old record of glorious struggle to build and defend their country.

As a result of their foolish calculation, the United States aggressors have run into the indomitable strength of our thirty-one million compatriots from the South to the North united to fight a great people's war and have invited upon themselves ignominious setbacks.

Directly confronting the United States aggressors on the great front of their country, the heroic South Vietnamese people and armed forces, under the banner of the South Vietnam National Liberation Front, have braved all hardships and sacrifices and fought valiantly and persistently against the foreign aggressors. Though the United States imperialists have taken their local war to a high level, raising the strength of the United States puppet and satellite armies to 1,200,000 men, our compatriots and Liberation Armed Forces, maintaining and developing their offensive position, have smashed one

---

This is an abridged text of a speech delivered at an Army Day Rally in Hanoi on December 21, 1968. It is an official translation made available to us by the London representatives of *Cuu Quoc*.

The Final Phase of Battle 309

after another all the counteroffensives of the enemy. Especially since early spring this year, compatriots and fighters in the South, stirred by a vigorous offensive mettle and a burning revolutionary spirit, have launched repeated general offensives and widespread uprisings and have recorded unprecedentedly big and all-around victories. Within a short period of time, the revolution in the South made a leaping bound, ushering in a new situation to our great advantage and to the great disadvantage of the enemy. Our strength, military and political, has grown unceasingly while that of the United States puppets has suffered heavy losses, in live forces as well as in war means. We have vigorously developed our position of attack and encirclement toward the enemy. On the contrary, the enemy battle order has been upset, and they are sinking ever deeper into passive defense and into a strategic position of being attacked and encircled on all battlefields. Our ardor and determination are rising while the United States aggressive will has shaken visibly.

After four years of conducting a local war with more than half a million United States troops as the hard core, the United States imperialists have had to think of "de-Americanizing" the war. Thus, they have admitted the error and failure of their decision to bring United States troops into South Vietnam to save the puppet army and administration from collapse.

That is a vicious circle, an impasse for the United States imperialists. They have been compelled to fall back onto the path of failure which they had trodden and which had led the Ngo Dinh Diem clique to downfall and their "special war" strategy to complete bankruptcy.

We are confident that the armed forces and people of South Vietnam, by developing the big victories already recorded, will certainly march forward and defeat completely every new scheme and maneuver of the United States aggressors and their henchmen and score still bigger victories in their advance to final victory.

In the North, under the clear-sighted leadership of our Party, our armed forces and people have won a very big victory over the United

States aggressors, smashing their war of destruction, foiling all their foolish ambitions and all their strategic objectives.

The United States aggressors have attempted to shake our people's fighting will through the massive use of bombs and shells. However, our people's determination to defeat them is now higher and firmer than ever before. They have attempted to sever the blood-sealed relations between North and South Vietnam by means of destruction and massacre, but our thirty-one million compatriots are now united more closely and are standing shoulder to shoulder to carry on the fight.

By attacking North Vietnam, the United States imperialists hoped to weaken our economic and national defense potential. But through the test of war our national defense strength has grown by leaps and bounds, and our socialist economy has fully demonstrated its superiority and has ceaselessly grown in wartime. Communications and transport have remained open in all circumstances; our people's life has been stabilized; culture, education, and public health have continued to develop. After four years of extremely valiant fighting against the enemy's war of destruction, socialist North Vietnam today has become stronger than ever before in all fields and has constantly served as the solid revolutionary base for the whole country.

The army and people in North Vietnam have shot down more than thirty-two hundred of the most up-to-date aircraft of the United States, killing or capturing a sizable number of top American pilots, and have sunk or set fire to hundreds of enemy vessels. The so-called air superiority of the United States imperialists—the chieftain of imperialism which used to boast of its wealth and weapons and which is notorious for its cruelty—has received a staggering blow at the hands of the Vietnamese people. They had to stop unconditionally the bombardment of the Democratic Republic of Vietnam. They have been forced not only to admit openly the error and failure of their policy of bombing North Vietnam but also to re-examine their over-all policy of aggression against our country. This constitutes a very big victory on our part and a very bitter defeat for

The Final Phase of Battle 311

the United States imperialists. This almost unbelievable thing for many persons has now become an evident reality of our times. Our people and army can be proud of the fact that under the talented leadership of our Party headed by esteemed President Ho Chi Minh, undaunted socialist North Vietnam has really become a steel rampart and our heroic Vietnamese land, a real fortress. Any enemy of the Vietnamese people who refuses to realize this truth and still nurtures the illusion of invading our country will surely meet with ignominious failure.

The reality of our victory and of the United States failure on the Vietnam battlefield proves that in the present era a nation which has resolutely stood up in arms to wage a war of resistance for independence and freedom along a correct line, which is determined to fight and knows how to fight, can certainly defeat any aggressor, even United States imperialism.

The fiasco of the United States is an extremely grave one in all fields—military, political, strategic, and tactical; a fiasco of neo-colonialism in all its forms; a fiasco of the "local war" which has reached a high level; and a common fiasco of the capitalist monopolies that have replaced one another at the helm of the United States. It is the biggest fiasco of the United States imperialists throughout the history of their aggressive wars.

That failure has thrown the United States into enormous difficulties in the political, military, economic, financial, and social fields and has had a grave impact on the global strategy of United States imperialism.

The victory of our people is a very big and all-around revolutionary line, a victory of justice, a victory of a heroic people resisting a brutal and unjust war imposed on them by the chieftain of the imperialist camp, a victory of the blood-sealed solidarity between North and South Vietnam, a victory of the strategy and tactic of people's war developed to a high level against the neo-colonialist schemes and maneuvers and the obsolete military outlook of the bourgeoisie. Our people's victory is also one of the socialist camp, of the brotherly

Indochinese peoples, of the national liberation movements, and of the revolutionary peoples throughout the world. This victory is greatly inspiring our brothers and friends in the five continents, frightening the enemy and strengthening the confidence of the armed forces and people throughout our country and their determination to fight till final victory.

On this occasion, we sincerely thank the fraternal socialist countries for their very valuable and great support and assistance; we sincerely thank the peoples of Laos and Cambodia, the progressive people all over the world including the progressive people in the United States, for their sympathy with, and vigorous support of, the Vietnamese people's sacred war of resistance against United States aggression, for national salvation.

The history of our nation is one of resistance against foreign aggression to build our country into an independent country, an independent nation. The struggle to overcome the danger of annihilation has given birth to extremely powerful national sentiments —to a strong spirit of independence and self-reliance and to an eager will for national unity.

For independence and freedom our forefathers have fearlessly risen up, those in the rear taking the place of those in the front who have fallen, the whole country united as one man, and have defeated many aggressor armies many times bigger than themselves.

Today, under the leadership of the Party, and also for independence and freedom, our thirty-one million compatriots have closed their ranks and risen up in two wars of resistance, fighting with all their moral and physical strength, with their lives and property, in the spirit of sacrificing everything rather than reconciling themselves to losing their country and accepting slavery, determined to smash all aggressive designs of imperialism to save their country and their families.

Our strength is the strength of a heroic nation, the strength of the tradition of determination to fight and to win, the invincible strength of thousands of years of history, the strength of today and also of tomorrow.

The great victory of our people also stems from the fully correct and very creative revolutionary and military line of our Party. This line is actually the Marxist-Leninist theory ingeniously applied to the realities of Vietnam. It reflects the thoroughgoing revolutionary spirit of the Vietnamese working class, the Vietnamese people's tradition of resistance to foreign aggression, the valor and wisdom of the patriotic Vietnamese. At the same time, it crystallizes the finest revolutionary spirit of progressive mankind. Our Party has applied Marxism-Leninism to the specific conditions of Vietnam and the realities of our times. It has made clear the character of our people's war of resistance against United States aggression, for national salvation, as a revolutionary war, a national liberation war against the neo-colonialist war of aggression waged by United States imperialism. That war is a fight for the independence, freedom, and unity of the Vietnamese fatherland and at the same time a fight to defeat part of the counter-revolutionary global strategy of United States imperialism contributing to the defense of the socialist camp and the safeguarding of peace in Asia and the world. It is a people's war led by the working class, which has been taken to a high level, a protracted war conducted by the entire people and in all respects relying mainly on the people's own forces; it will surely be crowned with victory.

Our Party has deeply analyzed the character of our era and made an important contribution to working out the offensive strategy of the world revolution aimed at repelling imperialism and old and new colonialism, step by step, and overthrowing it part by part and ultimately wiping it out wholly and completely.

Proceeding from this strategy, in the conditions of a country not very large and with a population not very large, our Party has made it clear that the strategy of our people's revolutionary war is an offensive strategy, using revolutionary violence, combining armed struggle with political struggle to launch active, resolute, continual, and all-around offensives in all forms, turning to account our absolute moral and political superiority in order to defeat a cruel enemy with a very big economic and military potential.

Upholding the heroic tradition and the powerful national sentiments of the Vietnamese people, our Party has enriched the genuinely patriotic and nationalist sentiments of our people with Marxism-Leninism and proletarian internationalism, raised it to a high level, and made it into Vietnamese revolutionary heroism, the great source of strength of the present fight for national and class liberation.

On that political and ideological basis, our people have created the Vietnamese military science and art and have worked out the directive to fight the enemy and the guideline for leading the fight, have promoted the collective wisdom of the revolutionary masses, and have realized the watchword that the entire people fight against the aggressors. All thirty-one million of our people are valiant fighters, using a small force to fight a bigger one, defeating a stronger force with a smaller one, combining big, medium-sized, and small battles, stepping up big-unit fighting and at the same time carrying out widespread guerrilla warfare, constantly striking the enemy from a strong position and achieving very high combat efficiency, becoming ever stronger and winning ever bigger victories as they fight.

Since the United States imperialists started their war of destruction against the North, our Party has creatively applied people's war to cope with a very new kind of war of aggression. It has organized the entire people to take part in the fight with the armed forces as the hard core, fighting the enemy in all fields, combining the fight against the enemy with strengthening civilian air defense, carrying out the war of resistance while building socialism, fighting the enemy while boosting production, ensuring communications and transport, maintaining public order and security, fostering and developing our forces, firmly defending the socialist North, fulfilling our duty toward the big front. This has led to glorious victories.

The Final Phase of Battle

Our Party has organized the heroic armed forces of the Vietnamese people composed of the regular army, the regional armed forces, and the militia and guerrillas. These are a wonderful army of our nation which, within only a score of years, has grown from small guerrilla bands into a mighty army and thus, together with the entire people, defeated Japanese fascism and French imperialism and is today defeating United States imperialism.

What a glory and pride for the Vietnamese people's armed forces to be the sons of the working people of Vietnam, of the heroic Vietnamese people!

What a glory and pride for our entire people and army fighting under the ever victorious banner of the glorious Vietnam Workers Party and esteemed President Ho Chi Minh!

Born of the people, led by the Party of the working class, carrying in them the blood of heroic people, and built along Marxist-Leninist lines, the Vietnamese people's armed forces pledge to fulfill meritoriously the glorious task assigned by history and the people, which is to unite with the entire people completely to defeat the United States aggressors, liberate the South, defend the North, and advance toward the peaceful reunification of the country.

With the brilliant successes recorded in both zones of the country since early this spring, the war of resistance of our entire people against United States aggression, for national salvation, has entered a new stage. The United States failure has become apparent, and it is certain that it will sustain ever heavier setbacks. Our people have won big victories and are advancing toward complete victory. However, the United States imperialists remain very stubborn and have not yet given up their aggressive designs against our country.

Though they have lost all hope of defeating us militarily, they still cling to the illusion of maintaining their neo-colonialist rule in South Vietnam. Like a mortally wounded beast, the United States aggressors are striking wildly. They have stopped at no barbarous maneuvers, using B-52 bombers, bombs, shells, and noxious chemicals to ravage towns and countryside, launched the so-called accelerated-pacification program, and stepped up repression and terror against all those in the areas under their control who yearn for national independence and peace.

With regard to North Vietnam, they obstinately carry on their spying and provocative activities, committing more crimes and encroaching upon the sovereignty and security of the Democratic Republic of Vietnam.

The military and political schemes and maneuvers of the United States imperialists are clear indicators of their present dark scheme of continuing to exert pressure on the battlefield, seeking a solution to the war favorable to them. On the other hand, these schemes and maneuvers, which are full of contradictions, spell the weakening and losing position of the aggressors as well as their confusion in their blind alley. Certainly, the more the United States and its henchmen prolong the war, the heavier will be their defeats.

At present, our compatriots and fighters throughout the country are facing a military and political situation more favorable than ever. New, great possibilities are being opened for them. The great successes in both zones of our fatherland are enhancing the mettle of revolutionary offensive of our people, giving us marvelous strength and speeding up the process of decline and disintegration of the United States and its puppets.

In their high tide of resistance to United States aggression, for national salvation, the thirty-one million Vietnamese people are valiantly marching forward, resolved to win complete victory while standing ready at all times to defeat the enemy should they prolong or widen the war. Millions as one, the people throughout our country are endeavoring to put into effect the sacred appeal of President Ho Chi Minh on November 3, 1968: "At present, it is the most sacred duty of our entire people to heighten their determination to fight and to win, liberate the South, defend the North, in order to advance toward the peaceful reunification of the fatherland."

So long as an aggressor remains in our land, we must continue to fight to sweep him away.

The Final Phase of Battle 317

Under the glorious banner of the Party, let our armed forces and people in the North give full scope to their revolutionary ardor and their deep feelings for the blood-sealed South, enthusiastically march forward, heighten their vigilance, work and fight with self-determination, redouble their efforts on all fronts—production, fighting, communications, and transport—actively build socialist North Vietnam and remain determined to smash every act of war of the United States aggressors and to materialize the slogan "All for victory over the United States aggressors, all for the blood-sealed South."

Let our compatriots and fighters in the South realize the tremendous significance of the fight in the current stage. Bring into full play the spirit of revolutionary offensive and strive to carry out the immediate tasks laid down by the conference of the Presidium of the Central Committee of the South Vietnam National Liberation Front on December 4, 1968, namely: "To make all-out efforts and dash forward to win yet bigger successes on the road to complete victory, thus attaining the goal of building an independent, democratic, peaceful, neutral, and prosperous South Vietnam, and of achieving the ultimate reunification of the fatherland."

As the shock force of the entire people in the war of resistance to the United States aggression and for national salvation, our people's armed forces pledge to fulfill thoroughly their glorious responsibility to continually sharpen their vigilance and heighten their combat capacity and be determined to join the rest of the people in defeating the United States aggressors completely and seize final victory.

With all the moral and material strength of a nation on the road to victory, our people and armed forces throughout the country serve the United States imperialists the following warning: the beautiful land of Vietnam belongs to the Vietnamese people; *there is decidedly no place for the United States aggressors here.* By recklessly sending troops to invade Vietnam, the United States has incurred bitter defeats. Now, if it persists in its recklessness and obstinacy, it will certainly meet with yet heavier defeats.

So long as South Vietnam is not liberated and our country is not reunified in real independence and freedom, our people and armed forces will continue to uphold the steel-like will: so long as an aggressor remains in our country, we must carry on the fight to sweep him away.

No matter how stubborn and perfidious the United States aggressors may be and whatever maneuver and trick they may resort to, they cannot reverse the law of history: the United States imperialists will certainly be defeated; the Vietnamese people will certainly win.

Our generation is having the honor to wage the greatest patriotic war in the history of our nation's resistance to foreign invasion.

Our nation is having the honor to stand at the forefront of the revolutionary struggle of the world's people against United States imperialism, the number one enemy of progressive mankind.

In our advance to complete victory, we still have to overcome many hardships and endure many sacrifices. For the independence and freedom of our fatherland in view of their noble internationalist duty, our people are resolved to strengthen solidarity, uphold the determination to fight and to win, fight and smash the aggressive will of the United States imperialists, and attain complete victory.

The sacred war of resistance against the United States aggressors and for national salvation of our Vietnamese nation is bound to win complete victory!

Long live a peaceful, unified, independent, democratic, and prosperous Vietnam!

Long live the Vietnam Workers Party!

Long live President Ho Chi Minh!

The United States Has Lost the War: An Interview

QUESTION: While visiting Vietnam for more than a month I have often heard quoted, not just on Radio Hanoi, but in my conversations with people in the street, this phrase from President Ho Chi Minh's December 25, 1967, message: "It is now clear that the Americans have lost the war. . . ."

ANSWER: In fact, our president correctly stated in his message to the nation: "It is now clear that the United States has lost the war." These words now take on their full meaning not only for us Vietnamese but also for world opinion. They reflect the great reality of our struggle against American aggression.

From the first days of this aggression, our people, under the leadership of our Party, with Ho Chi Minh at its head, rose up to fight resolutely. And from that day forward we had an unshakable conviction that the victory would be ours—that in spite of all its material, economic, and military power, the United States of America would lose the war in the end. We never doubted this.

You yourself have traveled a great deal in the rear, at the front, in the North and South of our country. You have seen what unalterable faith there is in victory and what resolution to fight for the country's independence. You have seen, too, how unshakable is the determination to fight for the cause of socialism and peace.

When we rose up against United States aggression, this unalterable faith of our entire people was shared by our brother peoples and countries, the socialist countries. They also believed in our victory. But some in the progressive world were worried. They supported

---

This interview was granted by General Giap to Madeleine Riffaud in May 1968 and was published in *l'Humanité* on June 4, 1968. Mme Riffaud has authorized its publication here.

our just cause; they admired our resolute and heroic people. But they were unnerved by the terrible material power, the enormous war machine of the United States, that was thrown against us. This sector of progressive public opinion, however, has come a long way over the months and years. In the face of reality, it no longer doubts: the United States is losing the war; the final victory will go to the Vietnamese people.

In America itself an ever larger part of the people thinks that America has lost the war, and this is recognized by the leading circles themselves. At the outset of the aggression, they thought in the White House and the Pentagon that the United States' formidable military power could turn the situation around overnight. Those were the bright days of official optimism. It was premature.

Around 1967, after two years of large-scale aggression against the South of our country and against the North, the United States leaders began to doubt their ability to solve the Vietnamese problem by force. They began to see that they could not win militarily. But they still believed that, in any case, they could not lose the war. The view of these circles also had to be brought along by the force of events. The problem has now become how to get out of this war, how to lose the war. That is what they call "without loss of honor" —the honor of the imperialists, of course, which means preserving the interests of the aggressor.

Our people are fighting for our national cause but also for socialism and for the other peoples in the world struggling for their liberation. The myth of the invincibility of the United States, this colossus supporting itself impotently on the H-bomb, is collapsing irretrievably. No matter how enormous its military and economic potential, it will never succeed in crushing the will of a people fighting for its independence. This is a reality which is now recognized throughout the entire world.

Why did the United States think that it would be victorious? It deployed an enormous war machine in our country. Westmoreland

The United States Has Lost the War: An Interview   321

is a general who found a way to boost the United States expeditionary force from twenty thousand men to more than five hundred thousand without offering Washington anything in return but a light at the end of a tunnel. The Americans based their confidence that they would win the war on their superior numbers, their overwhelming armament, their riches in dollars, and in the tons of bombs they are dropping.

Finding themselves in a more and more difficult situation, they are now accusing their generals of trying to settle things arithmetically—for example, in the matter of the balance of forces—while the Vietnamese have a "trigonometric" strategy. That is not correct. Our strategy is neither arithmetic nor trigonometric. It is quite simply the strategy of a just war, of a people's war. They will never be able to understand that.

Even before the Tet offensive, the United States had increased its forces to a level higher than that foreseen for a local war. Moreover, they had already had to raise this level several times. For America, the battleground in the South is a sinkhole for its soldiers. In spite of that, none of the five goals the Pentagon set in the South has been attained. Quite the contrary. These objectives were to exterminate the Liberation Army units (it is the American units which have been exterminated), to pacify the countryside, to blockade the South, to destroy the economic and military potential of the North, and to consolidate the puppet government.

It was a vital task for American imperialism, which is conducting a neo-colonialist war of aggression in our country, to reinforce the puppet army and prop up the puppet government.

Since the Saigon "government" is drowning, the United States intervention is a rescue operation. The more the Pentagon increases its forces in South Vietnam, the more the drowning government founders and sinks, dragging its rescuers with it into the disaster.

This is the most tragic defeat for the Americans. The Tet offensive marked a turning point in this war, as our president said. It burst like a soap bubble the artificial optimism built up by the Pentagon. The United States leaders wanted to make 1968, an election year, a year of successes in Vietnam—which Lyndon Johnson thought could serve his domestic political ambitions.

However, the spring 1968 offensive revealed abruptly to the Americans that the Vietnamese people do not give up easily and that their military strength has not been in any way impaired by United States aggression, no matter what its forms and its cruelty. Gone, and gone for good, is the hope of annihilating the Liberation forces. Gone are the "pacification" projects. They would have to start all over again from scratch. The United States troops had to entrench themselves on the defensive, blocked in their positions. The "McNamara line" proved its total ineffectiveness.

Gone also is the hope of refloating the drowned government. The Saigon government showed itself more and more to be a puppet government without any social base whatever. The purported United States commitment to support this "ally" has been unmasked more clearly than ever as a fraud, intended only as a cover-up for aggression.

In three years of escalating the air war in North Vietnam the United States has not been able to achieve a single one of its military, economic, or political aims. In these three years, America has lost an important part of its modern air force and the cream of its pilots. You see, no matter how modern it may be, you can take it for granted that air power will never decide the outcome of a war. Our people are more determined than ever to fight against the aggressor. And during this time we have continued to build socialism. The cars and trains are moving, as you have seen. The communication routes remain open, as the American press has recognized.

After these American experiences and these hard-to-make-good losses, it was inevitable that the United States would contemplate dropping the extension of the air war to North Vietnam. Several of its leaders understood that it was time to stop the bombing, which was a military and political error and brought them no advantage.

It was in these circumstances that President Johnson made his March 31 speech. This speech exploited for political purposes the military need to concentrate the bombing on the southern part of our country, of North Vietnam. We never believed in the good will of the American imperialists.

After the Tet offensive the Pentagon circles realized that they no longer had a chance of winning the war militarily. Furthermore, they saw that they were losing militarily.

It was in this situation that the problem of "peace with honor" was posed for them. This expression was used previously by the French colonialists before Dien Bien Phu. That the world's greatest imperialist power has been driven to seek such an outcome to a war of aggression is a very bitter thing for the imperialists and a very heartening one for us, for progressive humanity. This said, however, we know that our enemies have not yet, in spite of their failures, given up their aggressive aims.

If our people have succeeded in inflicting these defeats on them, it is because our struggle is just. We are fighting for our independence, for freedom, for the reunification of our country, which is a sacred task for the Vietnamese—the sacred duty of all our people.

QUESTION: "Of all our people," you said—let me interrupt you. The name General Giap is bound up with the idea of people's war. This concept seems like something new to a large part of European opinion.

ANSWER: In fact, it is all our people who are waging this war. But the idea of people's war is not entirely new. It has existed since peoples have emerged and taken form, since they have become aware of their fundamental rights and risen up against the invader.

Already in our most remote history our ancestors said, "Our whole country is rising up against the invader." In our literary tradition, the poet Nguyen Dinh Chieu, for example, the blind poet and singer of South Vietnam, celebrated the struggle of "simple villagers who volunteered for the army out of love of their country" and the delicate, fragile women who because the enemy was upon us "mounted horses, brandished banners, rowed boats, loaded guns, demolished citadels, and scaled ramparts."

Since the October revolution a new era has opened up and, with the higher consciousness of the peoples under the aegis of the proletariat, people's wars have developed, have acquired new content and thereby a new power, an invincible power.

The people's war in Vietnam is mobilizing all the patriotic classes: the peasants, the workers, the intellectuals, the national bourgeoisie —all classes in every region—into a very broad front. In the South recently the creation of the Alliance of National and Democratic Forces under the aegis of the NLF proved once again that all the people of Vietnam, including the intellectuals and the well-to-do strata in the cities, are against the Americans. The United States is warring not only against the Liberation Army in the South and the forces of the People's Army in the North. They are warring against an entire heroic people which is fighting under a firm and seasoned leadership in the South under the leadership of the National Liberation Front. And this is the reason for the American defeats.

Our generation has had the mission, and for us it is a conspicuous honor, of struggling for some decades against Japanese fascism, French colonialism, and now against United States imperialism. It has always been a just war that we have waged, a war of a whole people, a war of liberation.

But this war is a war of our entire people against United States neo-colonialism and against the aggression of the most powerful imperialist state in the capitalist world. This is why the present people's war has acquired all its power, exalting the heroism of all the patriotic classes to its highest peak. Never in our history have we had such a heroic national war.

Recently, this war has brought into play new forms of struggle: combined political and armed struggle, struggle in the mountainous regions, in the countryside, in the cities. These forms of struggle are mobilizing ever more broadly the masses of our people against the aggressor.

In the South, our compatriots and the Liberation Army are fighting under new conditions nationally and internationally. Our people is the people that made the August revolution. It has known people's power and has waged a long, hard war against imperialism. South Vietnam is half of a liberated country. The independent, socialist North is an always-existing source of encouragement and support for our compatriots in the South. In the North, we all feel that we are the rear of a great front. And the North intends to fulfill to the utmost its duty as the backup of the front.

If in the North we have succeeded in defeating the United States air attacks of the most modern, the most powerful air force in the world, it is also because after ten years of socialism our people's determination to be independent is firmer than ever. We are struggling to safeguard the conquests of socialism. Despite all his technical means and all his barbarism, the enemy has not been able to paralyze our economy. On the contrary, at the rear of the front, as you have seen, the North is stronger than ever from the military, economic, and naturally from the political point of view.

From the international standpoint, we are struggling in a world where the socialist system and the national liberation movements are stronger than ever. We have the firm support of our brother socialist countries and that of progressive opinion, even in the United States.

Does the American government want to get out of this war? Well, it has five hundred thousand troops in our country, which are invading our country, sowing death and ruin everywhere. If America wants peace, let it end its aggression, withdraw its troops. Nothing could be simpler. In Vietnam we also love peace, after twenty years of war. Our people is, I think, one of the world's most peace-loving peoples. But let it be understood, we are talking about real peace, not peace the American way, under the boot of the aggressor.

QUESTION: I have returned from the Fourth Zone,* from regions bombed day and night. It seemed to me in fact that the bombing there was more concentrated than at the time of my last trip. Am I right?

ANSWER: Exactly. The Americans are continuing the restricted bombing to which they were reduced by their defeats over a very important part of the Democratic Republic of Vietnam. They have concentrated this bombing on the Fourth Zone and have stepped it up. South of the twentieth parallel, they have redoubled their barbarism since Johnson's last speech, as if to prove what must be understood in the United States by "peaceful intentions."

Moreover, the Americans have publicly acknowledged—with what cynicism!—that they were intensifying their attacks over this large area of our territory. Every day they commit more crimes against the civilian population of those regions. Every day, furthermore, they are bringing new troops into the South. They are launching new military operations. They are bombing the population of Saigon-Cholon (Saigon, their last refuge . . .) with B-52's. They are trying to improve the armaments of the puppet troops. They are pressuring the governments of Thailand and South Korea to get new contingents of mercenaries. Is all this new evidence of the peaceful intentions of the United States?

Prospective defeats for them are looming up dramatically. They are still trying to turn South Vietnam into a neo-colony. Well! The people of the South want none of it. That is why they continue to struggle, and that is why the NLF is calling on the people in repeated declarations to continue the fight until victory.

As President Ho wrote in his recent letter to Nguyen Huu Tho and to the members of the NLF Central Committee: "While it talks about peace negotiations, the United States is intensifying the war, and that is why our compatriots, our fighters, must firmly join

---

* That part of North Vietnam nearest the Demilitarized Zone (including Thanh Hoa and Nghe An provinces).

hands, redouble their vigilance, and strengthen their resolve to fight and win."

We want peace and independence—without the Americans. If they think they can make South Vietnam into a neo-colony by talking about peace while they pursue their aggression, it will cost them dearly. They have already experienced defeat after defeat. They will suffer still more bitter ones. The Vietnamese people are determined more than ever to struggle on until the day the United States abandons its imperialist designs on our country. No peace can be achieved except on the basis of respect for our people's fundamental rights. For us, only one kind of peace is possible, real peace with independence and freedom, a peace which will recognize Vietnam's right to determine its own destiny.

Our people are going from victory to victory. We firmly believe that after the Japanese fascists and the French imperialists, our people will also get the better of United States aggression. Already in both the near and distant past Vietnam has withered the laurels of many foreign generals hungry for conquest and buried many hopes of the invaders' military strategy. This was the case with the Japanese and the French imperialists. And today it is American imperialism's turn.

We intend to carry on the struggle until victory, for the independence and unity of our country and for future generations. We are proud in so doing to make a contribution to the cause of socialism, of the national freedom of the peoples, and to the cause of peace in the world.

The final victory will be ours. And it will also be the victory of our brother socialist countries, the victory of all peoples throughout the world who cherish peace and freedom, the victory of all progressive humanity.

Their Dien Bien Phu Will Come: An Interview

LIBERATION NEWS SERVICE: General Giap, in many of your writings, you ask this question: who will be the definitive winner of the war in Vietnam? I'd like to ask you, right now, in this early part of 1969, can you say that the Americans have lost the war, that they've suffered a military defeat?

GIAP: They've recognized that themselves. To prove their military defeat, I'll go back to their political defeat, which is the basis of the whole thing.

The Americans made a big mistake in choosing South Vietnam for a battlefield. The Saigon reactionaries are too weak. Taylor and McNamara and Westmoreland all knew that. What they didn't know was that, in their weakness, the Saigon leaders wouldn't be able to take advantage of American aid. Because what was the purpose of the American aggression in Vietnam? To build up a new-style colony with a puppet government. But to build up such a colony you need a government that's stable, and the Saigon government is unstable in the extreme. It has no influence on the population; people don't believe in it.

So look what sort of jam the Americans have got themselves into. They can't withdraw from Vietnam even if they want to, because in order to withdraw they'd have to leave a stable political situation behind them. That is, a bunch of lackeys to take their place. But lackeys that are solid and strong. And the puppet government of Saigon isn't strong and it isn't solid. It's not even a good lackey. It can't be kept going even with tanks to hold it up. So how can the

---

This interview was granted by General Giap to the Liberation News Service in the spring of 1969.

Americans withdraw? And yet they have to get out. They can't keep six hundred thousand men in Vietnam for another ten or fifteen years. That's their political defeat: they can't win politically in spite of all their military apparatus.

In Washington, Westmoreland was greeted like a hero, but he couldn't help knowing that the war was getting to be too expensive, something that Taylor had known all along. Korea cost the Americans $20 billion, and Vietnam has cost them $100 billion. Fifty-four thousand Americans died in Korea, and there are even more deaths in Vietnam. . . .

LNS: Thirty-four thousand, the Americans say, General.

GIAP: I'd say twice that many. The Americans always say less than the truth. At their most honest they say three for five. They can't have just thirty-four thousand dead. We've brought down over 3,200 planes! They admit one plane out of every five. In these five years of war, I'd say they lost at least 60,000 men, maybe more.

We haven't yet won, and the Americans can't be called defeated. They're still numerically strong; nobody can deny that. It will take a lot of effort on our part to give them a definitive military beating. The military problem—now I'm speaking as a soldier—they have plenty of arms, but arms don't do them any good, because the Vietnam war isn't just a military matter. Military strength and military strategy can't help to win, or even to understand it.

The United States has a strategy based on arithmetic. They question the computers, add and subtract, extract square roots, and then go into action. But arithmetical strategy doesn't work here. If it did, they'd already have exterminated us. With their planes, for example. Of course they thought they could bring us to heel by dumping billions [of tons] of explosives on us. Because, as I told you, they figure everything in billions, billions of dollars. They don't reckon on the spirit of a people fighting for what they know is right, to save their country from invaders.

They can't get it into their heads that the Vietnam war has to be understood in terms of the strategy of a people's war, that it's not a question of men and matériel, that these things are irrelevant to the problem.

Victory calls for something more, and that's the spirit of the people.

When a whole people rises up, nothing can be done. No money can beat them.

That's the basis of our strategy and our tactics, that the Americans fail to understand.

LNS: If you're so sure, General, that they'll be definitively beaten, can you give us any idea of when?

GIAP: Oh, this isn't a war that can be won in a few years. War against the United States takes time. They'll be beaten with time, worn out. And to wear them out we have to go on, to endure. That's what we've always done. We're a small country, only thirty million people. We were only a million at the beginning of the Christian era, when the Mongols descended upon us. But the million of us beat them. Three times they came, and three times we beat them. We didn't have weapons like theirs. But we held fast and lasted out. The whole people, we said even then, has to get into the fight. And what was true in the year 1200 is still true today. The problem is the same. We're good soldiers because we're Vietnamese.

LNS: But, General, the South Vietnamese who are fighting alongside the Americans are Vietnamese, too. What do you think of them as soldiers?

GIAP: They can't be good soldiers, and they aren't good soldiers. They don't believe in what they're doing, and so they have no fighting spirit. The Americans know this (and, incidentally, they're better fighters). If they hadn't known that these puppets couldn't fight, they wouldn't have brought over many of their own troops.

LNS: General, let's talk about the Paris Conference. Do you think that peace will come from Paris, or from a military victory such as you won at Dien Bien Phu?

Their Dien Bien Phu Will Come: An Interview

GIAP: Dien Bien Phu . . . Dien Bien Phu . . . the fact that we've gone to Paris shows that we have good intentions. And nobody can say that Paris isn't useful, since the Liberation Front is there, too. In Paris they've got to transfer what's happening here in Vietnam to a diplomatic level. Paris, madame, is for the diplomats.

LNS: You mean, then, that the war won't be settled in Paris, General, is that it? That it calls for a military, rather than a diplomatic, solution? That the American Dien Bien Phu is yet to come and will come some day?

GIAP: Dien Bien Phu, madame . . . Dien Bien Phu . . . history doesn't always repeat itself. But this time it will. We won a military victory over the French, and we'll win it over the Americans, too. Yes, madame, their Dien Bien Phu is still to come. And it will come. The Americans will lose the war on the day when their military might is at its maximum and the great machine they've put together can't move any more. That is, we'll beat them at the moment when they have the most men, the most arms, and the greatest hope of winning. Because all that money and strength will be a stone around their neck. It's inevitable.

If they didn't feel beaten, the White House wouldn't talk of peace with honor. But let's go back to the days of Geneva and the Eisenhower government. How did the Americans start out in Vietnam? In their usual way—with economic and military aid to a puppet government. In short, with dollars. Because they think that with dollars they can settle anything. They thought they could set up a free and independent government with dollars and an army of puppets paid in dollars, with thirty thousand "military advisers" paid in the same, and dollar-built "strategic hamlets." But the people stepped into the picture, and the Americans' plan collapsed. The "strategic hamlets," the "military advisers," and the puppet army all fell to pieces, and the Americans were forced into the military intervention which Ambassador Taylor had already recommended.

Then came the second phase of the aggression, the "special war." With a hundred and fifty thousand men and $18 billion they thought they could finish it by the end of 1965, or 1966 at the latest. But in 1966 the war wasn't finished at all: they had sent over two hundred thousand more men and were talking of a third phase, that of "limited war," Westmoreland's pincer program: winning over the people on the one hand and wiping out the liberation movement on the other. But the pincers didn't hold their grip, and Westmoreland lost his war. He lost it as a general in 1967 when he asked for more men and Washington gave out a rosy report that 1968 would be a good year for the war in Vietnam, so good that Johnson would be re-elected.

MONTHLY REVIEW

an independent socialist magazine
edited by Paul M. Sweezy and Harry Magdoff

Business Week: ". . . a brand of socialism that is thorough-going and tough-minded, drastic enough to provide the sharp break with the past that many left-wingers in the underdeveloped countries see as essential. At the same time they maintain a sturdy independence of both Moscow and Peking that appeals to neutralists. And their skill in manipulating the abstruse concepts of modern economics impresses would-be intellectuals. . . . Their analysis of the troubles of capitalism is just plausible enough to be disturbing."

Bertrand Russell: "Your journal has been of the greatest interest to me over a period of time. I am not a Marxist by any means as I have sought to show in critiques published in several books, but I recognize the power of much of your own analysis and where I disagree I find your journal valuable and of stimulating importance. I want to thank you for your work and to tell you of my appreciation of it."

The Wellesley Department of Economics: ". . . the leading Marxist intellectual (not Communist) economic journal published anywhere in the world, and is on our subscription list at the College library for good reasons."

Albert Einstein: "Clarity about the aims and problems of socialism is of greatest significance in our age of transition. . . . I consider the founding of this magazine to be an important public service." (In his article, "Why Socialism" in Vol. I, No. 1.)

DOMESTIC: $11 for one year, $20 for two years, $9 for one-year student subscription.
FOREIGN: $13 for one year, $23 for two years, $10 for one-year student subscription. (Subscription rates subject to change.)

62 West 14th Street, New York, New York 10011

Modern Reader Paperbacks

The Accumulation of Capital by Rosa Luxemburg	$ 6.95
The Age of Imperialism by Harry Magdoff	3.45
The Alienation of Modern Man by Fritz Pappenheim	3.45
American Radicals, edited by Harvey Goldberg	3.45
The American Revolution: Pages from a Negro Worker's Notebook by James Boggs	1.65
Anarchism: From Theory to Practice by Daniel Guérin	3.45
The Arab World and Israel by Ahmad El Kodsy & Eli Lobel	2.25
Armed Struggle in Africa: With the Guerrillas in "Portuguese" Guinea by Gérard Chaliand	1.95
Art and Society: Essays in Marxist Aesthetics by Adolfo Sanchez Vazquez	4.50
Away With All Pests: An English Surgeon in People's China, 1954-1969 by Dr. Joshua S. Horn	3.75
The Black Man's Burden: The White Man in Africa from the Fifteenth Century to World War I by E. D. Morel	1.95
Capitalism and Underdevelopment in Latin America by Andre Gunder Frank	5.50
Caste, Class, and Race by Oliver C. Cox	7.95
China Shakes the World by Jack Belden	5.95
The Chinese Road to Socialism: Economics of the Cultural Revolution by E. L. Wheelwright & Bruce McFarlane	3.95
The Communist Manifesto by Karl Marx & Friedrich Engels, including Engels' "Principles of Communism," and an essay, "The Communist Manifesto After 100 Years," by Paul M. Sweezy & Leo Huberman	2.25
Consciencism by Kwame Nkrumah	2.65
Corporations and the Cold War, edited by David Horowitz	3.95
Cuba: Anatomy of a Revolution by Leo Huberman & Paul M. Sweezy	3.95
Cultural Revolution and Industrial Organization in China by Charles Bettelheim	2.95
The Debt Trap: The International Monetary Fund and the Third World by Cheryl Payer	4.50
Dependence and Transformation: The Economics of the Transition to Socialism by Clive Y. Thomas	5.95
The Economic Transformation of Cuba by Edward Boorstein	5.50
The Education of Black People by W. E. B. DuBois	3.75
The End of White World Supremacy: Four Speeches by Malcolm X, edited by Benjamin Goodman	2.45
The Energy Crisis by Michael Tanzer	3.75
Essays on the Political Economy of Africa by Giovanni Arrighi and John Saul	6.50
The Formation of the Economic Thought of Karl Marx by Ernest Mandel	3.95

Ghana: End of an Illusion by Bob Fitch & Mary Oppenheimer	2.95
The Great Tradition in English Literature by Annette Rubinstein (2 vols.)	7.95
The Growth of the Modern West Indies by Gordon K. Lewis	4.50
Guatemala: Occupied Country by Eduardo Galeano	2.25
The Hidden History of the Korean War by I. F. Stone	5.95
Huan-Ying: Workers' China by Janet Goldwasser and Stuart Dowty	5.95
Imperialism and Revolution in South Asia, edited by Kathleen Gough and Hari P. Sharma	6.95
Imperialism and Underdevelopment: A reader, edited by Robert I. Rhodes	5.95
Introduction to Socialism by Leo Huberman & Paul M. Sweezy	2.65
Labor and Monopoly Capital by Harry Braverman	5.95
Latin America: Underdevelopment or Revolution by Andre Gunder Frank	6.50
Lenin and Philosophy and Other Essays by Louis Althusser	4.50
Long March, Short Spring by Barbara & John Ehrenreich	1.95
Man's Worldly Goods by Leo Huberman	4.95
Marx and Modern Economics, edited by David Horowitz	5.95
Marx, Freud, and the Critique of Everyday Life by Bruce Brown	3.95
Marxism and Philosophy by Karl Korsch	3.45
Marxist Economic Theory by Ernest Mandel (2 vols.)	11.90
Mau Mau from Within by Donald L. Barnett & Karari Njama	4.50
Middle East Oil and the Energy Crisis by Joe Stork	5.95
The Military Art of People's War: Selected Political Writings of General Vo Nguyen Giap, edited by Russell Stetler	3.95
Monopoly Capital by Paul A. Baran & Paul M. Sweezy	4.95
The Myth of Black Capitalism by Earl Ofari	3.25
The Myth of Population Control by Mahmood Mamdani	3.95
Notes on the Puerto Rican Revolution by Gordon K. Lewis	4.50
On the Transition to Socialism by Paul M. Sweezy & Charles Bettelheim	2.95
Open Veins of Latin America by Eduardo Galeano	4.95
Pan-Americanism from Monroe to the Present by Alonso Aguilar	2.95
The Pillage of the Third World by Pierre Jalée	2.95
The Political Economy of Growth by Paul A. Baran	5.50
Politics and Social Structure in Latin America by James Petras	5.95
Régis Debray and the Latin American Revolution, edited by Leo Huberman & Paul M. Sweezy	1.95
Return to the Source: Selected Speeches by Amilcar Cabral	2.95
Selected Political Writings of Rosa Luxemburg, edited by Dick Howard	6.95
Socialism in Cuba by Leo Huberman & Paul M. Sweezy	3.95
Strategy for Revolution: Essays on Latin America by Régis Debray	2.95

The Theory of Capitalist Development by Paul M. Sweezy	5.50
The Third World in World Economy by Pierre Jalée	3.95
Toward an Anthropology of Women, edited by Rayna Reiter	5.95
The Trial of Elizabeth Gurley Flynn by the American Civil Liberties Union, edited by Corliss Lamont	2.45
Unequal Exchange: A Study of the Imperialism of Trade by Arghiri Emmanuel	6.95
The United States and Chile: Imperialism and the Overthrow of the Allende Government by James Petras and Morris Morley	4.50
Vietnam: The Endless War by Paul M. Sweezy, Leo Huberman, and Harry Magdoff	2.25
Vietnam Songbook by Barbara Dane & Irwin Silber	3.95
The Watchdogs: Philosophers and the Established Order by Paul Nizan	2.95
We, the People by Leo Huberman	5.50
White Niggers of America: The Precocious Autobiography of a Quebec "Terrorist" by Pierre Vallières	2.95
Who Rules the Universities? An Essay in Class Analysis by David N. Smith	4.50